ROYAL HISTORICAL SOCIETY

STUDIES IN HISTORY

New Series

HAROLD WILSON'S COLD WAR

THE LABOUR GOVERNMENT AND EAST-WEST POLITICS, 1964–1970

HAROLD WILSON'S COLD WAR

THE LABOUR GOVERNMENT AND EAST-WEST POLITICS, 1964–1970

Geraint Hughes

THE ROYAL HISTORICAL SOCIETY
THE BOYDELL PRESS

First published 2009
Paperback edition 2015

A Royal Historical Society publication
Published by The Boydell Press
an imprint of Boydell & Brewer Ltd
PO Box 9, Woodbridge, Suffolk IP12 3DF, UK
and of Boydell & Brewer Inc.
668 Mt Hope Avenue, Rochester, NY 14620–2731, USA
website: www.boydellandbrewer.com

ISBN 978 0 86193 298 6 hardback
ISBN 978 0 86193 332 7 paperback

ISSN 0269–2244

A CIP catalogue record for this book is available
from the British Library

This publication is printed on acid-free paper

TO MY MOTHER AND BROTHER, ELUNED AND DAVID HUGHES,
AND TO PROFESSOR SAKI DOCKRILL

Contents

Map 1. Central and Eastern Europe during the Cold War.

Acknowledgements

This book could not have been written without the assistance of a large number of institutions and individuals. I am indebted to the staffs at the National Archives in Kew, the Liddell Hart Centre for Military Archives in King's College London, the British Library for Political and Economic Sciences, the British Library Newspaper Depository, Churchill College Archives in Cambridge and the Bodleian Library in Oxford, all of whom helped me with my queries and assisted my research. I would also like to thank Mr Iain Goode and the Ministry of Defence Records Organisation, who attended to my requests for the declassification of government documents under the terms of the Freedom of Information Act.

During my visit to the United States in the autumn of 2000, the archivists of the National Archives and Records Administration at College Park, Maryland, and at the Lyndon B. Johnson Presidential Library in Austin, Texas, assisted my burrowing into contemporary US government documents. I also received valuable co-operation from the staffs at the National Security Archives at George Washington University and at the Cold War International History Project at the Woodrow Wilson Center, both in Washington DC. Permission to use the image on the front cover was kindly granted by Philip Grimwood-Jones of Getty Images™, and I would like to thank the Perry-Castaneda Library at the University of Texas for allowing me to use the map of Eastern Europe.

I am also grateful to my fellow doctoral students and tutors at the War Studies Department at King's College London for their professional assistance and their friendly support over the past decade, particularly during the early phases of my academic career. Eden Cole, Dr Anastasia Filippidou, Dr Shawn Grimes, Anthony Hampshire, Dr Malcolm Llewellyn Jones and Maria Vlahou shared the trials and tribulations of the doctoral student – not to mention more than a few cups of coffee and a couple of glasses of the stronger stuff. Dr William Rosenau and his wife Annie offered me their warm hospitality during my stay in Washington DC, and Tammi Onaka likewise gave me a roof over my head at the tail end of my American trip. Professors Lawrence Freedman, Saki Dockrill and Brian Holden Reid gave me the opportunity to teach at KCL at a time when I wondered if I would ever be employed as an academic, and helped me to step onto the first rung of the higher education ladder. I also owe a debt of thanks to Professor Peter Hennessy and Professor John Young; to Dr Peter Catterall, Dr Simon Moores, Dr James Ellison, and other scholars from the International History Group in the Institute of Historical Research; and to Professor Howell Harris of the Department of History at the University of Durham.

A particularly crucial role was played by Saki Dockrill and my editor,

Dr Neil Gregor of the University of Southampton. Saki was not just my doctoral supervisor, but has been my mentor, a much-valued friend and, above all, an example to me as a scholar, which is why she is one of the three people I have dedicated this book to. Neil's guidance has been hugely important in the shaping of this book; I am grateful to him not only for the advice and constructive criticism he has offered me over the past two years, but for recommending this book for publication as part of the Royal Historical Society's *Studies in History* series. I would also like to thank Professor J. S. Morrill, Sue Carr and Christine Linehan for their assistance in the final stages of this book's preparation. Frankie Kennedy also provided invaluable help in both proof-reading the final draft and compiling the index. It should be noted here that any factual errors in the text that may have escaped my attention are my own responsibility.

My work on this book was delayed in 2004 due to my mobilisation for active service with the British Army during that year. I am particularly grateful for the understanding that Colonel Jeremy Mooney, former Commanding Officer of the London Regiment (TA), showed in helping me to meet my teaching commitments to KCL prior to call-up in March 2004. I also owe a great deal to Lieutenant Christopher Panton, Sergeant-Major Robert Denman and my comrades in 4 Platoon, Messines Company, all of whom watched my back during a stressful six months spent in Iraq. It is no exaggeration to say that without them this book might not have been written.

Since July 2005 I have taught in KCL's Defence Studies Department, based at the Joint Services Command and Staff College in Shrivenham. I remain grateful for the collegiality and friendship shown to me by all my colleagues. In particular, Professor Matt Uttley, Dr Stuart Griffin and Dr Andrew Dorman did much to maximise the time available to me to concentrate on this book. I would also like to acknowledge the support offered by Professor Greg Kennedy, Drs Tim Bird, Tim Benbow, Huw Davies, Robert Dover, Guy Finch, Tracey German, Jonathan Hill, Ashley Jackson, Anne Lane, Alex Marshall, Helen McCartney, Patrick Porter, Srinath Raghavan, Christian Tripodi and Ms Rachael Vincent. My good friend Khanh Harris also deserves credit for offering her encouragement to this project during tough times.

Finally, I owe more than I can say to three people I dearly love. My father, Dr John Hughes, who passed away in May 1991 and who is still sorely missed; my mother, Eluned Hughes; and my brother, David Hughes. In the same spirit that I dedicated my thesis to the first Dr Hughes, I therefore humbly dedicate this book to my mother and brother for all their love and support over the years, during my studies and the many months of research that led to this book. I hope that this book goes some way to saying 'diolch yn fawr' to both of them.

Geraint Hughes,
30 September 2008

Abbreviations

ABM	Anti-Ballistic Missile system
AIR	Air Ministry (TNA)
ANF	Atlantic Nuclear Force
BAOR	British Army of the Rhine
BoT	Board of Trade
BRIXMIS	British Commanders'-in-Chief Mission to the Soviet forces in Germany, stationed in East Berlin
CAB	Cabinet Office (TNA)
CENTO	Central Treaty Organisation, founded in 1955 (UK, Turkey, Iran, Pakistan)
CDS	Chief of Defence Staff (COS)
CDU	Christlich Demokratische Union Deutschlands (Christian Democratic Party)
CMEA	Council for Mutual Economic Assistance (*Comecon*)
COCOM	Co-ordinating Committee on strategic trade with Communist states
COS	Chiefs of Staff
CPCS	Communist Party of Czechoslovakia
CPGB	Communist Party of Great Britain
CPSU	Communist Party of the Soviet Union
CRO	Commonwealth Relations Office
CSCE	Conference on Security and Cooperation in Europe
CSU	Christlich-Soziale Union in Bayern (Christian Social Union)
CTBT	Comprehensive Test Ban Treaty
DEA	Department of Economic Affairs
DEFE	Ministry of Defence (TNA)
DIS	Defence Intelligence Staff (MoD)
DOHP	Diplomatic Oral History Programme (Churchill College, Cambridge)
DRV	Democratic Republic of Vietnam
EESD	East European and Soviet Department (name given to the former Northern Department when the FCO was established in October 1968)
ESC(O)	Strategic Exports (Official) Committee, established to oversee trade with Communist and other potentially hostile powers
FCO	Foreign and Commonwealth Office, established after the amalgamation of the Foreign Office and CRO on 14 October 1968

FO	Foreign Office (TNA)
FRG	Federal Republic of Germany
GCHQ	Government Communications Headquarters. The British SIGINT (signals intelligence) service
GDR	German Democratic Republic
GRU	Glavnoe Razvedyvatelnoi Upravlenie ('Main Intelligence Directorate'). The Soviet military intelligence service
GSFG	Group of Soviet Forces in Germany
ICC	International Control Commission. Set up to oversee implementation of the 1954 Geneva Accords on Indochina, consisting of Canada, India and Poland
INR	State Department Bureau of Intelligence and Research (USA)
IRD	Information Research Department
JCS	Joint Chiefs of Staff (USA)
JIC	Joint Intelligence Committee
KGB	Komityet Gosudarstvennoi Bezopasnosti ('Committee for State Security'). The USSR's foreign intelligence and internal secret police force
LBJLIB	Lyndon B. Johnson Presidential Library, Austin, Texas
LTBT	Limited Test Ban Treaty
MBFR	NATO-Warsaw Pact Mutual and Balanced Force Reduction negotiations
MfS	Ministerium für Staatssicherheit ('Ministry for State Security')
Mintech	Ministry of Technology
MI5	British domestic security service
MLF	Multilateral Force
MoD	Ministry of Defence
MRBM	Medium Range Ballistic Missile (600–1,500 nautical miles range)
NAC	North Atlantic Council (NATO)
NARAII	National Archives and Records Administration, College Park, Maryland
NATO	North Atlantic Treaty Organisation
NBC	Nuclear, Biological and Chemical weapons
ND	Northern Department (FO)
NLF	National Liberation Front of South Vietnam (Viet Cong)
NPG	NATO Nuclear Planning Group
NPT	Non-Proliferation Treaty
NSA	National Security Agency (USA)
NSC	National Security Council
OPD	Overseas Policy and Defence (Ministerial) Committee
OPD(O)	Overseas Policy and Defence (Official) Committee
PAVN	People's Army of Vietnam. The official name of the DRV's

	armed forces
PN	Cabinet Nuclear Policy Committee
PRC	People's Republic of China
PREM	Prime Minister's Office (TNA)
PUSD	Permanent Under-Secretary's Department (FO)
RVN	Republic of Vietnam
SEAD	South-East Asia Department (FO)
SEATO	South-East Asia Treaty Organisation, founded in 1954 (USA, UK, France, Pakistan, Thailand, the Philippines, Australia, New Zealand)
SIGINT	Signals Intelligence
SIS	Secret Intelligence Service. The British foreign intelligence service
SPD	Sozialdemokratische Partei Deutschlands (Social Democratic Party). The principal democratic left party in the FRG
StB	*Statni Bezpecnost* (Czech for 'State Security', or *Statna Bezpecnost* in Slovak). The Czechoslovak foreign intelligence / secret police force
TNA	The National Archives, Kew
WO	War Office (TNA)

Journals and Serials

CBH	*Contemporary British History*
CEH	*Contemporary European History*
CWH	*Cold War History*
CWIHP	*Cold War International History Project*
DBPO	*Documents on British policy overseas, series 3 (1968–1975)*, London 1997–
DDF	*Documents diplomatiques français, 1964*, Paris–Brussels 1964–
DS	*Diplomacy and Statecraft*
FA	*Foreign Affairs*
FRUS	*Foreign Relations of the United States*, Washington, DC 1992–
IA	*International Affairs*
IHR	*International History Review*
IS	*International Security*
JCWS	*Journal of Cold War Studies*
JSS	*Journal of Strategic Studies*
RIS	*Review of International History*

Glossary

Bundestag	Lower house of West German parliament
Bundeswehr	West German armed forces
Lao Dong	Vietnamese Workers Party
Nomenklatura	Generic name given to the ruling elite in the USSR and other Communist countries
Ostpolitik	The name given to the West German government's efforts to improve relations with the Warsaw Pact powers from the mid-1960s onwards
Politburo	CPSU leadership. Known as the *Presidium* before 1966

Politicians, Officials and Personalities

BELGIUM
Harmel, Pierre   Foreign Minister (from Feb. 1966)

CAMBODIA
Sihanouk, Prince Norodom   Sovereign

CUBA
Castro, Fidel   President (from Jan. 1959)

CZECHOSLOVAKIA
Cernik, Oldrich   Premier (Jan.1968–Jan. 1970)
Dubcek, Alexander   First Secretary, CPCS (Jan.1968–Apr. 1969)
Husak, Gustav   First Secretary, CPCS (from Apr. 1969)
Novotny, Antonin   First Secretary, CPCS; President (until Jan. 1968)

DEMOCRATIC REPUBLIC OF VIETNAM
Ho Chi Minh   President
Nguyen Duy Trinh   Foreign Minister
Pham Van Dong   Prime Minister

EGYPT
Nasser, Gamal Abdul   President

FEDERAL REPUBLIC OF GERMANY
Brandt, Willy   Foreign Minister (Nov. 1966–Oct. 1969);
                             Chancellor (from Oct. 1969)
Erhard, Ludwig   Chancellor (until Nov. 1966)
Kiesinger, Kurt   Chancellor (Nov. 1966–Oct. 1969)
Strauss, Franz-Josef   Leading CSU politician; former Defence Minister

FRANCE
Debre, Michel   Foreign Minister (May 1968–Apr.1969)
de Gaulle, Charles   President (until Apr. 1969)
Pompidou, Georges   President (from Apr. 1969)

GERMAN DEMOCRATIC REPUBLIC
Ulbricht, Walter   First Secretary, East German Socialist Unity
                             party

HUNGARY
Kadar, Janos   First Secretary, Hungarian Communist party

INDONESIA
Sukarno, Ahmed   President (until Mar. 1967)

PEOPLE'S REPUBLIC OF CHINA

Yi, Chen	Foreign Minister (until Aug. 1967)
Zedong, Mao	Chairman, Chinese Communist party

POLAND

Gomulka, Wladyslaw	First Secretary, Polish Communist party
Lewandowski, Janusz	Representative, ICC
Rapacki, Adam	Foreign Minister (until Apr. 1968)

ROMANIA

Ceausescu, Nicolae	Secretary, Romanian Communist party (from Mar. 1965)

UK

Benn, Tony	Minister of Technology (June 1966–June 1970)
Barker, William	HM ambassador to Prague (from Dec. 1966)
Brimelow, Thomas	Minister, Moscow embassy (until Sept. 1966); HM ambassador to Warsaw (until Feb.1968); Deputy Permanent Under-Secretary at the Foreign Office
Brooke, Gerald	British lecturer imprisoned in the USSR, July 1965–Oct. 1969
Brown, George	First Secretary, DEA (Oct. 1964–Aug. 1966); Foreign Secretary (Aug. 1966–Mar.1968)
Callaghan, James	Chancellor of the Exchequer (Oct. 1964–Nov. 1967); Home Secretary (Nov. 1967–June 1970)
Castle, Barbara	Cabinet minister and close colleague of Harold Wilson
Clutton, George	HM ambassador to Warsaw (until Sept. 1966)
Courtney, Commander Anthony	Backbench Conservative MP; critic of government policy towards Eastern bloc diplomatic missions in UK
Crosland, Anthony	President of the Board of Trade (Aug. 1967–Oct. 1969)
Crossman, Richard	Cabinet minister; close colleague of Harold Wilson
Dean, Patrick Dean	HM ambassador to Washington (from Apr. 1965)
Douglas-Home, Alec	Prime Minister (Oct. 1963–Oct. 1964); Leader of the Conservative Party (Oct. 1964–July 1965); Shadow Foreign Secretary (July 1965–June 1970); Foreign Secretary
Gordon-Walker, Patrick	Foreign Secretary (Oct. 1964–Jan. 1965)
Gore-Booth, Paul	Permanent Under-Secretary, FO (Jan.1965–Feb. 1969)
Greenhill, Denis	Deputy Undersecretary, FO (Jan 1965–Feb.1969); Permanent Under-Secretary, FO (Feb. 1969–)
Hackett, General Sir John	Commander in Chief of NORTHAG (1966–8)
Harrison, Geoffrey	HM ambassador to Moscow (Aug. 1965–Aug. 1968)

Healey, Denis	Secretary for Defence (Oct. 1964–June 1970)
Heath, Edward	Leader of the Opposition (July 1965–June 1970); Prime Minister (June 1970–Mar. 1974)
Jay, Douglas	President of the Board of Trade (Oct. 1964–Aug. 1967)
Jenkins, Roy	Chancellor of the Exchequer (Nov. 1967–June 1970)
Mountbatten, Admiral Lord	Chief of Defence Staff (until July 1965)
Owen, David	Parliamentary Under-Secretary of State for Defence, Royal Navy (July 1968–June 1970)
Palliser, Michael	Foreign Office official and Private Secretary to the PM (Apr. 1966–)
Roberts, Goronwy	Minister of State at FO/ FCO (Aug. 1967–Aug. 1969)
Smith, Howard	Head of Northern Department, FO (until Jan. 1969); HM ambassador to Prague
Stewart, Michael	Foreign Secretary (Jan.1965–Aug.1966; Mar.1968–June 1970)
Trend, Burke	Cabinet Secretary
Trevelyan, Humphrey	HM ambassador to Moscow (until July 1965)
Wilson, Duncan	HM ambassador to Belgrade (Sept. 1964–Oct.1968); HM ambassador to Moscow
Wilson, Harold	Prime Minister (Oct. 1964–June 1970)
Wright, Oliver	FO official; Private Secretary to PM (until Apr. 1966)
Zuckerman, Solly	Chief Scientific Advisor to the Prime Minister

USA

Ball, George	Under-Secretary of State (until Sept. 1966)
Bruce, David	Ambassador to London (until Mar.1969)
Bundy, McGeorge	National security advisor to President Johnson (until Feb. 1966)
Cleveland, Harlan	Head of US delegation to NATO (from Sept. 1965)
Cooper, Chester	NSC official
Goldwater, Barry	Senator for Arizona; Republican presidential candidate, November 1964
Gronouski, John	Ambassador to Warsaw (until Jan. 1969)
Johnson, Lyndon	President (until Jan. 1969)
Lodge, Henry Cabot	Ambassador to Saigon (Aug. 1963–June 1964; July 1965–Apr.1967)
McCone, John	Director, CIA (until Apr. 1965)
McNamara, Robert	Secretary of Defense (until Feb. 1968)
Nixon, Richard	President (from Jan. 1969)
Rostow, Walt	National security advisor to President Johnson (from Apr. 1966)
Rusk, Dean	Secretary of State
Thompson, Llewellyn	Ambassador to Moscow (from Dec. 1966)

USSR

Andropov, Yuri	Chairman, KGB (from Apr. 1967)
Brezhnev, Leonid	First Secretary, CPSU (from Oct. 1964)
Dobrynin, Anatolii	Ambassador to Washington
Gorshkov, Admiral Sergei	Commander-in-Chief, Soviet Navy
Grechko, Marshal Andrei	Defence Minister (from Apr. 1967)
Gromyko, Andrei	Foreign Minister
Khrushchev, Nikita	First Secretary, CPSU; Soviet Premier (until Oct. 1964)
Kosygin, Alexei	Premier (from Oct. 1964)
Podgorny, Nikolai	President (from Dec. 1965)
Polyanskii, Dmitrii	Deputy Premier (from Oct. 1964)
Shelepin, Alexander	*Politburo* member; former KGB chairman
Shelest, Pyotr (Petro)	Secretary, Ukrainian branch of CPSU
Smirnovsky, Mikhail	Ambassador to London (from Jan. 1966)
Soldatov, Aleksandr	Ambassador to London (until Jan. 1966)
Suslov, Mikhail	*Politburo* member and principal CPSU ideologist

YUGOSLAVIA

Broz, Josip (Marshal Tito)	President

Introduction

In October 1964 the Labour party won the British general election after more than a decade in the political wilderness. Labour regained power under a young, technocratic and charismatic leader, whose personality and political beliefs seemed more in tune with contemporary society than those of his uninspiring Conservative rival. The new prime minister claimed that his government would harness the 'white heat' of the technological revolution to transform the UK's economy and society, halting the process of decline that the country had suffered in comparison with its European competitors. Labour portrayed itself to the electorate as the party of progressive, evolutionary change, in contrast with a Conservative party hobbled by class prejudice, economic incompetence and the taint of scandal and corruption. The successful implementation of Labour's domestic agenda would have external implications, as international policies progressed beyond the worst years of Cold War hostilities towards East-West *détente*. Britain's claim to a major role on the world stage would no longer rest solely on the outdated basis of an imperial legacy – rendered obsolete by the process of decolonisation – but through the transformative effect of applying modern technology and managerial procedures to British industry and commerce.

Four years later, the Labour government was widely condemned for having broken its election pledges. Britain's economic performance had worsened, the balance of payments deficit remained unbridgeable and a prime minister who prided himself on his fiscal expertise devalued the pound in November 1967.[1] Far from epitomising the ideals and hopes of the 'baby boomers', the Labour government was assailed by the younger generation to which it had tried to appeal. One of the latter's many grievances was America's military intervention in a small Third World country, and the bloody, escalating insurgency which had ensued. What was particularly galling, and what caused unease within Labour's ranks, was the apparent subservience of a British prime minister to a Texan president with a tin-ear for diplomacy, and a penchant for using force in defiance of international opinion.[2]

The traditionally poor press that Harold Wilson has received reflects the contrast between promise and performance during his first term as prime minister; not to mention an undistinguished second term from 1974 to 1976 which ended with his controversial retirement from politics. Furthermore,

---

1   G. O'Hara and H. Parr, 'Introduction: the fall and rise of a reputation', CBH xx/3 (2006), 295–7. Devaluation reduced the value of the pound from £1:$2.80 to £1:$2.40.
2   For the political, social and cultural aspects of the Wilson era see D. Sandbrook, *White heat: a history of Britain in the swinging sixties*, Boston, MA 2006.

Wilson was regarded by both left- and right-wing critics as a charlatan, focusing more on style than on the substance of policy, and exaggerating his attributes as an international statesman.[3] In his diaries Cecil King, the proprietor of the *Daily Mirror*, condemned Wilson's 'façade of buoyant optimism' in the face of economic crisis at home and foreign policy failures over Rhodesia, Vietnam and Europe. King wrote that '[Wilson's] vanity is quite astounding – each failure is hailed as a brilliant breakthrough; realism never shows up.' King was a hostile observer, but the image of Wilson as a shallow opportunist with a penchant for deceit and self-delusion, a 'Yorkshire Walter Mitty', has proved to be pervasive, hence the contemporary quip that had he been Captain of the *Titanic* 'he would have informed the passengers [that] the ship had stopped to take on a supply of ice cubes'.[4]

During the 1990s Wilson's political career received a more balanced treatment. Ben Pimlott and Philip Ziegler both wrote substantial biographies, while the collection of essays in *The Wilson governments, 1964–1970*, edited by Richard Coopey, Steven Fielding and Nick Tiratsoo, has contributed many valuable insights into this period of British political history.[5] However, these works concentrate principally on domestic policy, with foreign affairs issues such as Vietnam being discussed (if at all) exclusively in terms of the so-called 'special relationship' between a declining Britain and its superpower ally. This reflects the fact that studies of Britain's foreign policy since 1945 focus on the topics of decolonisation and Anglo-American relations. It is certainly true that successive prime ministers from Clement Attlee to Gordon Brown have had to manage the complexities of the 'special relationship' and the consequences of the 'end of empire'. Yet from 1945 to 1991 British foreign policy was profoundly influenced by the dynamics of the Cold War, and during the 1960s the Wilson government had to address the challenges and problems posed by two interrelated external issues. The first was how to manage the UK's adversarial relations with the USSR, China and other Communist states. The second concerned diplomatic and strategic issues which arose from the UK's membership of NATO, and its alliance ties with the USA and other Western countries.

Approaches to British foreign policy in the 1960s therefore remain incomplete if they overlook the Cold War. For example, the Wilson government deserves condemnation for its callous decision to turn the Indian Ocean island of Diego Garcia into a military base and to evict its Ilois inhabit-

---

[3] P. Foot, *The politics of Harold Wilson*, London 1968; Andrew Roth, *Harold Wilson: Yorkshire Walter Mitty*, London 1977; C. Ponting, *Breach of promise: Labour in power, 1964–1970*, London 1989; A. Morgan, *Harold Wilson*, London 1992.

[4] C. King, *The Cecil King diary, 1965–1970*, London 1972, 114, entry for 15 Feb. 1967; S. Loory and D. Kraslow, *The diplomacy of chaos*, London 1968, 188.

[5] B. Pimlott, *Harold Wilson*, London 1993; P. Ziegler, *Wilson*, London 1993; C. Wrigley, 'Now you see it, now you don't: Harold Wilson and Labour's foreign policy, 1964–1970', in R. Coopey, S. Fielding and N. Tiratsoo (eds), *The Wilson governments, 1964–1970*, London 1993.

ants to Mauritius. Yet the militarisation of Diego Garcia was not a mere act of wanton colonialism, but was a response to geopolitical developments in the mid-1960s. As Cold War relations in Europe stabilised, British officials concluded that the focus of East-West rivalries had shifted eastwards, particularly as a consequence of the Vietnam War, the low-level conflict (or 'confrontation') fought between British Commonwealth and Indonesian forces in Borneo, and the radical direction China took during the 'Cultural Revolution' inspired by Mao Zedong. Critics of the Diego Garcia decision risk oversimplifying a complex issue if they do not take account of the wider aspects of contemporary power-politics, including the efforts by regional adversaries of the Western powers (notably China and, before 1966, Indonesia) to extend their diplomatic and military influence beyond their own boundaries.[6]

The past two decades have experienced a growth in studies covering the effect of the Cold War on British foreign and defence policies, from the aftermath of the Second World War to the Cuban missile crisis of October 1962. This book extends this area of research to cover the Wilson government's approach to East-West relations, with particular reference to policy towards the USSR, in the three key areas of British external policy: diplomatic interaction with foreign powers (the traditional definition of 'foreign policy'); the requirements of defence; and international trade.[7] It also augments other works on Labour's conduct of external policy, including recent studies of Wilson's attempt to take Britain into the EEC, and the withdrawal of British forces from 'East of Suez'.[8] Due to the 'Thirty Year Rule' governing the declas-

6 This failing is evident in M. Curtis's *Web of deceit: Britain's real role in the world*, London 2003, 414–31; DP43/64 (Final), 'The nature of military operations, 1968–1980', 27 Mar. 1964, TNA, DEFE 4/173.

7 'Britain and the Cold War: the forgotten war', *The Economist*, 13 Nov. 1999, 46. For studies of Britain's Cold War policies see M. Kitchen, *British policy towards the Soviet Union during the Second World War*, London 1998; M. Folly, *Churchill, Whitehall and the Soviet Union, 1940–45*, Basingstoke 2000; A. Bullock, *Ernest Bevin: Foreign Secretary, 1945–1951*, Oxford 1985; R. J. Aldrich, *The hidden hand: Britain, America and Cold War secret intelligence*, London 2001; J. Young, *Winston Churchill's last campaign*, Oxford 1996; Saki Dockrill, *Britain's policy for West German rearmament, 1951–1955*, Cambridge 1991; J. Gearson, *Harold Macmillan and the Berlin Wall crisis, 1958–1962*, London 1998; K. Newman, *Macmillan, Khrushchev and the Berlin crisis, 1958–1960*, Abingdon 2007; L. V. Scott, *Macmillan, Kennedy and the Cuban Missile crisis*, London 1999; and S. Greenwood, *Britain and the Cold War, 1945–1991*, London 2000. See also *DBPO III*, i–iii.

8 John Young provides a comprehensive overview in *The Labour governments, 1964–1970, II: International policy*, Manchester 2003. See also J. Callaghan, *The Labour party and foreign policy: a history*, Abingdon 2007; H. Parr and M. Pine, 'Policy towards the European Economic Community', and R. Vickers, 'Foreign policy beyond Europe', in P. Dorey (ed.), *The Labour governments, 1964–1970*, Abingdon 2006, 108–46; O. Daddow (ed.), *Harold Wilson and European integration: Britain's second application to join the EEC*, Basingstoke 2003; S. Dockrill, *Britain's retreat from East of Suez*, Basingstoke 2002; S. Ellis, *Britain, America, and the Vietnam War*, Westport, CT 2004; A. May (ed.), *Britain, the Commonwealth, and Europe*, Basingstoke 2000; and H. Parr, 'Britain, America, East of

sification of official documents, it is only since 1995 that archival material from Wilson's first term has been made available to researchers. As a consequence, historians are therefore aware of Charles de Gaulle's emphasis on improved Franco-Soviet relations, and the development of West Germany's policy of Ostpolitik during the late 1960s and early 1970s.[9] In contrast, British policy towards East-West détente has generally been overlooked.

An understanding of the evolution of East-West relations is central to the wider study of British external policy in the post-war era. This is especially so in the case of the Wilson government, whose conduct of foreign affairs cannot be treated in isolation from the general course of East-West relations during the 1960s and 1970s and the key developments of that period: the wars in the former French colonies of Indochina; political turbulence in Eastern Europe; superpower arms talks; 'proxy' conflicts in the Middle East; and the origins of the Conference on Security and Co-operation in Europe. The rise of détente – the collective effort to reduce tensions between the superpowers and their respective allies – constituted an important period in post-1945 politics. Détente involved an attempt by the USA and USSR to manage their mutual rivalry and to avert crises which could end in a third world war. Although tentative efforts at improved superpower relations had been made after Joseph Stalin's death in March 1953, and with Nikita Khrushchev's visit to the USA six years later, significant progress was only made after the Cuban crisis of 1962. Even then superpower détente developed unevenly. The progress made by Richard Nixon and Leonid Brezhnev from 1969 to 1974 was followed by a slump in US-Soviet relations, which reached their nadir between 1979 and 1984. The Washington-Moscow relationship subsequently revived under Mikhail Gorbachev, culminating in the terminal decline of both the Cold War and the Soviet bloc in 1989–91. Behind these dramatic developments lay a less obtrusive, but by no means insignificant, process of European détente, as the USA's West European allies used commercial and cultural contacts to stabilise political relations with the USSR and the East European client states.

There were therefore two versions of détente practised by the Western powers, which sometimes operated in parallel but on other occasions conflicted with each other. Looking beyond Wilson's premierships to the early 1980s, while US contacts with the Soviet bloc were frozen as a consequence of the Afghan war and the Solidarity crisis in Poland, West European countries (including Britain) defied the Reagan administration by maintaining

---

Suez and the EEC: finding a role in British foreign policy, 1964–1967', CBH xx/3 (2006), 403–21. See also the special edition of CBH xx/3 (2006), edited by O'Hara and Parr, passim.
[9]   R. Crockatt, The fifty years war: the United States and the Soviet Union in world politics, 1941–1991, Abingdon 2000, 209–10; R. Garthoff, Détente and confrontation: American-Soviet relations from Nixon to Reagan, Washington, DC 1994, 123–45.

trading relations with the Warsaw Pact powers.[10] The principal issue was a differing emphasis on the part of American and of West European statesmen and decision-makers as to what *détente* was supposed to achieve. Proponents of power-politics concentrated on what social scientists now call the 'hard' aspects of military security, and saw *détente* as a means of managing and moderating East-West rivalry and averting increased tensions and a global thermonuclear holocaust. The alternative view emphasised 'soft' security issues such as trade, economic assistance, tourism, cultural exchanges and human rights, and envisaged *détente* as the only feasible way of overcoming ideological divisions and of ending the Cold War peacefully. During the late 1970s and early 1980s both schools of thought were assailed by critics, predominantly but not exclusively American in nationality, who saw *détente* as misconceived, and concluded that the Western world had underestimated the aggressive designs of the Soviet state and its ideologically-inspired plans for expansion. This attitude was reflected in the rise of neo-conservatism, and found an echo in the early policies of Ronald Reagan's presidency.[11]

In his analysis of US *détente* policy Raymond Garthoff identified three schools of thought amongst senior American politicians and officials from the late 1960s onwards. The 'essentialists' (notably the neo-conservative opponents of *détente*) regarded the USSR as not only 'inherently expansionist but evil', and as intent as had been Nazi Germany on world domination. Western policies of *détente* were therefore as misconceived as appeasement had been in the 1930s. 'Mechanists' adopted a less visceral and more hard-headed approach to dealings with the USSR. While officials adhering to 'mechanism' had no faith in the benevolent intentions of their Soviet counterparts, they regarded them as pragmatic and cautious opportunists, who would seek momentary advantage in their rivalry with NATO powers (whether seeking favourable terms in arms control negotiations or backing anti-Western 'liberation' movements in the Third World) while avoiding a potentially catastrophic confrontation with the USA and its allies. Proponents of 'mechanism' concluded that while negotiations on specific issues were feasible, the prospects for a lasting accommodation with the USSR were slim. In contrast, the third school of thought – 'interactionists', as Garthoff describes them – 'tended to find greater diversity in internal Soviet politics and therefore greater potential for the evolution of the Soviet system'. 'Interactionists' were more optimistic about the potential benefits of diplomatic contacts with the USSR and other Warsaw Pact governments as a means of easing East-West tensions. Garthoff's definitions are a reminder that ideology – defined by the anthropologist Clifford Geertz as providing

---

10 H. Sjursen, *The United States, Western Europe and the Polish crisis*, London 2003.
11 R. Pipes, '*Détente*: Moscow's view', in R. Pipes (ed.), *Soviet strategy in Europe*, London 1976, 3–44. For a contemporary British critique of *détente* policy see R. Conquest, *Present danger: towards a foreign policy*, London 1979; R. Garthoff, *The great transition: Soviet-American relations and the end of the Cold War*, Washington 1994.

5

both a conceptual model of reality (shaping a perception of political and social interaction) and a model for action (influencing political decisions) – had an important influence not only on Soviet external policy during the Cold War, but on that of the USA and of its Western adversaries.[12] Just as Soviet policy-makers analysed international politics within the Marxist-Leninist framework of rivalry and confrontation between 'socialist' and 'imperialist' powers, so their opposite numbers in Washington, London and other Western capitals debated whether the USSR's hostility towards their countries was an inevitable feature of international relations, or whether this animosity towards the West could be tempered or even overcome by long-term diplomatic engagement with the Communist states.

As far as the UK's role in the Cold War was concerned, Brian White has argued that the moderation of East-West tensions was 'a recurring theme in post-war British foreign policy', and that while co-operating with the USA and other Western allies to 'contain' the perceived Communist threat, British policy-makers also sought to normalise relations with the USSR and other Communist states. According to White, Britain showed a traditional preference for mediation as a means of addressing international disputes, for maintaining diplomatic and commercial contacts with other states irrespective of ideological differences and for preserving the *status quo*.[13] British interest in *détente* also derived from more fundamental considerations of national survival. The UK had a vested interest in European security and in averting a major East-West conflict. The implications of an all-out clash between the Communist world and the Western powers would have been cataclysmic, particularly for a small archipelago off the north-west European coast well within range of attack by Soviet bombers and ballistic missiles. While the French, the West Germans and other Europeans were comparative latecomers to *détente*, British policy towards the Cold War combined the more confrontational characteristics inherent in 'containment' with a less adversarial approach focused on coexistence. Although Clement Attlee, Winston Churchill, Anthony Eden and Harold Macmillan all regarded NATO, the US commitment to Europe and the development of a nuclear deterrent as vital British security interests, they also saw the UK as a mediator between East and West, concluding that transnational contacts in commercial and other fields could be used gradually to overcome Cold War hostilities.

The Labour government entered office at a time when East-West tensions had eased considerably, and Wilson and his ministers did not have to face a crisis as severe as that of 1962. None the less, the Cold War was still the principal factor influencing contemporary international politics. The new prime minister had shown a consistent interest in Anglo-Soviet relations,

[12] Garthoff, *Détente and confrontation*, 176–7; C. Geertz, *The interpretation of cultures*, New York 1973, 93–5, 221.
[13] B. White, *Britain, détente and changing East-West relations*, Abingdon 1992, 1–7, 36–49.

particularly in bilateral trade, since serving as a junior Minister at the Board of Trade in 1947. One of Wilson's declared aims upon entering 10 Downing Street in October 1964 was to develop more amicable relations with the Soviets, but this proved to be a difficult task. Bilateral relations between London and Moscow were affected by the intensification of Sino-Soviet rivalry, Vietnam, the development of US-Soviet contacts on arms control, discord between the USA and its European allies (especially France) and the pressures for internal reform in Eastern Europe which culminated in the 'Prague Spring' of 1968.

An additional challenge for the Labour government was the development of separate policies towards the Eastern bloc by NATO powers, the most notable being de Gaulle's overtures to the USSR from 1964 onwards and the evolution of *Ostpolitik*. The latter was largely welcomed by politicians and senior diplomats who had criticised the West German policy-making establishment's hitherto inflexible attitude towards national reunification, East German sovereignty and relations with the Eastern bloc states, notably those (Czechoslovakia, Poland and the USSR) which held territory that had hitherto belonged to a unified Germany. None the less there was still an undercurrent of suspicion and uncertainty within both Whitehall and the Labour party as to the future direction of the Federal Republic of Germany's foreign policy, and the possible revival of German xenophobic nationalism. De Gaulle's version of *détente* presented its own problems because it complemented the French president's hostility to NATO integration and to the American military presence in Europe. France's unilateral approach to East-West diplomacy threatened to inspire other West European countries to develop their own strategies of *détente* irrespective of common NATO interests, thereby weakening an alliance which blocked further Soviet expansion in Europe. The paradox here was that while improved diplomatic and transnational contacts with Warsaw Pact powers could ease East-West tensions, 'competitive *détente*' between NATO countries could also undermine the basis of Western security.

The key issues in this book therefore concern how the Labour government responded to developments within the Communist world – in particular the Sino-Soviet split and the emergence of 'polycentrism' within Eastern Europe – and to the gradual development of European *détente*. Britain's attempt to seek a less adversarial relationship with the Soviet bloc states was inevitably affected by the course of superpower rivalry and general trends in East-West relations. It is for this reason, as well as the importance of the UK's alliance ties with the USA, that this study refers to contemporary American attitudes towards the Cold War. Despite Lyndon Johnson's declared intention to 'build bridges' between the USA and the Eastern bloc states, American military intervention in Vietnam delayed superpower *détente*, and it also had an adverse impact on Anglo-Soviet relations. At the same time, it should also be noted that since the late 1940s the USSR had been considered by British politicians and officials to be a strategic threat, and this study will also discuss what impact the growth of Soviet military power during the 1960s and the invasion of Czechoslovakia in August 1968 had on Britain's defence policy.

The principal sources for this book are the declassified papers available at the National Archives in Kew, the published memoirs of leading politicians and officials, secondary source monographs and articles, private papers, oral history interviews and contemporary newspaper reports. Due to the nature of the Anglo-American 'special relationship', and its significance for British external policies, this study also relies on declassified US government material available in archives on both sides of the Atlantic. Although I make use of recent research into the policies of the Soviet, Chinese and East European Communist regimes, this work is not strictly speaking a study of Anglo-Soviet relations, as its main emphasis is on British, rather than Soviet, foreign and defence policies. In addition, despite the Thirty Year Rule (for which historians have the Wilson government to thank), a considerable amount of documentary material relating to intelligence matters and nuclear policy remains classified.[14] For example, researchers can read a wide range of Joint Intelligence Committee papers from this period, as well as the sanitised files of the Cabinet Nuclear Policy Committee established by Wilson. Yet certain areas, such as the material intercepted and decrypted by GCHQ (the British signals intelligence service), remain inaccessible. By the mid-1960s GCHQ claimed the lion's share of the British intelligence budget, and its product shaped Whitehall's assessment of Soviet policy intentions and military capabilities. The fact that SIGINT-related material is closed to scholars imposes significant limitations on studies of post-war British external policy, given the importance of espionage and nuclear matters not only to the Cold War but also Anglo-American co-operation in the fields of defence and intelligence-gathering.[15]

This is a study of official, rather than popular, attitudes and opinions, although at certain points reference will be made to public and media perceptions of the USSR. The imprisonment of Gerald Brooke and the Soviet regime's treatment of dissidents were heavily criticised by the British press, but on the other hand the Soviet premier, Alexei Kosygin, received a warm welcome from the public when he visited the UK in February 1967. The following year Foreign Office officials were concerned that popular opinion overlooked both the unsavoury aspects of the USSR's internal system and the Soviet government's foreign policy objective of 'driving wedges' between the Western powers. Civil servants concluded that the British public needed to be reminded that the USSR was still a powerful potential foe.

[14] On the Thirty Year Rule see R. Crossman, *The diaries of a Cabinet minister*, I: *Minister of Housing, 1964–1966*, London 1975, 303–4, entry for 5 Aug. 1965.
[15] R. J. Aldrich, 'British intelligence and the Anglo-American "special relationship" during the Cold War', *RIS* xxiv/3 (1998), 334; G. Wigg to H. Wilson, 17 Aug. 1966, TNA, PREM 13/202.

Scholars of international history run the risk, as one of its practitioners noted, of depicting 'the policies and reactions of states as if they emerged from monolithic units, each with a single interpretation of the national interest and a single voice with which to proclaim and pursue it'.[16] While by 1964 there was a broad consensus incorporating both the Labour front-bench and government departments in Whitehall on the need to promote *détente*, there were often disputes between the Wilson Cabinet and civil service subordinates (and amongst the latter) over the practical aspects of policy towards the USSR and the Eastern bloc. Two of the examples discussed subsequently include Foreign Office scepticism over the prime minister's efforts to engage the Soviet leadership in his Vietnam peace initiatives, and the inter-departmental debate over Britain's trade policy towards the Eastern bloc. Both Wilson and Foreign Office officials had differing expectations as far as Anglo-Soviet relations were concerned. The prime minister's were more ambitious in scope, and presumed that both he and the country he represented in the international arena could become valued interlocutors promoting dialogue and compromise between East and West, and the super-powers in particular. Departmental opinion within the Foreign Office also emphasised the potential benefits of *détente*, with officials concluding that East-West *rapprochement* could be used to promote gradual and incremental political and economic reform within the Communist states. The origins and developments of both Wilson's and Foreign Office thinking on East-West relations are examined in chapter 2, which also analyses the collective responses of the Labour party, British officialdom and allied governments towards contemporary Cold War challenges and *détente*. This chapter also describes the first efforts made by the Wilson government to establish contacts with its Soviet opposite numbers, an effort which stalled largely as a consequence of the diametrically opposed positions that both governments adopted over the Vietnam War. The impact of Vietnam on Anglo-Soviet relations – and Wilson's attempts to alleviate it through his involvement in abortive peace initiatives – are discussed in the third chapter.

US military intervention in South-East Asia affected not only British diplomacy but also the UK's defence policy, particularly as the Wilson government inherited its Conservative predecessor's commitment to retain Britain's global role and its military presence 'East of Suez' (to employ contemporary parlance). Chapter 4 examines how Wilson and his Cabinet sought to balance the 'world role' with the strategic and financial burdens entailed by the NATO commitment and the UK's nuclear deterrent, as well as the key defence decisions the Labour government made between 1964 and 1968 in the context of existing perceptions within the British and allied policy-making establishments concerning the Soviet 'threat'.

16 C. Thorne, *Allies of a kind: the United States, Britain and the war against Japan*, Oxford 1978, 91.

The fifth and six chapters concentrate specifically on the Labour government's approach to East-West *détente*. British officials agreed with the central premise of the 'Harmel review' of NATO's collective security policy in 1967, arguing that the Atlantic Alliance could maintain a posture of mutual defence against the Warsaw Pact, while concurrently forging diplomatic ties with the USSR and Eastern European states to alleviate Cold War tensions and to achieve compromise solutions on the key issues affecting continental security. These included arms control, the division of Germany and the military build-up in Central Europe. While the resolution of these issues was impossible without a fundamental reversal of policy by either of the bilateral alliances involved (which eventually took place within the Kremlin during the late 1980s), Western governments responded to public interest in *détente* by developing closer political and commercial ties with Eastern bloc states.

However, the British experience during the late 1960s demonstrated that engagement was theoretically easy, but hard to achieve in practice. Wilson's attempts to conclude a 'friendship treaty' with the Soviet leadership were spurned, and British diplomats and intelligence officers grew increasingly alarmed at the expansion of KGB espionage operations in the UK during the late 1960s. The forcible suppression of internal reform in Czechoslovakia by the Warsaw Pact's military intervention in the summer of 1968 undermined the Foreign Office's hopes in the long-term liberalisation of Eastern Europe. It also provided an additional source of contention in Anglo-Soviet relations, as the USSR's leadership accused the British government of using the Czechoslovak crisis to incite anti-Soviet sentiment in Western Europe and sabotage *détente*. Having initially been at the forefront of Western efforts to promote East-West *rapprochement*, by 1970 the British government was widely perceived within NATO as the 'Cassandra of the Western Alliance', and of being the least receptive towards *détente* and the most suspicious of Soviet intentions amongst its members.[17] The reasons behind this decline in Anglo-Soviet relations, and the failure of the Labour government to overcome the USSR's ideological and diplomatic hostility towards the UK, are summarised in the concluding chapter.

In order to place the Wilson government's approach to *détente* in its proper historical context, the first chapter provides an overview of the UK's role in East-West relations during the first two decades of the Cold War. This focuses on most important aspects of British policy – the NATO commitment, the alliance with the USA, East-West trade and diplomatic contacts with the Soviet leadership – which became established under the Labour and Conservative governments of this period, and which had their own impact on the Wilson government's conduct of relations with the Communist

---

[17] K. Hamilton, 'The last Cold Warriors: Britain, *détente* and the CSCE, 1972–1975', unpublished paper, St Anthony's College, Oxford, European Interdependence Research Unit EIRU/991, July 1999.

powers following the commencement of its term in office in mid-October 1964. The initial policy decisions made by Wilson's Cabinet were affected not only by transformational changes within the international system, but by the precedents and established policy goals set by its predecessors.

1

The Evolution of British Cold War Policy, 1945–1964

The tangible spirit of optimism which accompanied Wilson's accession to power rested in part on the promise of improvement in East-West relations. Unlike Attlee, Churchill or Macmillan, Wilson faced a situation in which Cold War tensions had eased, and the risk of a major international crisis, let alone a global war, had diminished considerably. None the less the state of rivalry between the superpowers and their respective rivals had not vanished completely. In order to appreciate the impact of East-West politics on the Labour government which took office in October 1964, it is necessary to survey how the Cold War shaped the conduct of British external policy under Wilson's predecessors. The first two decades of the Cold War were characterised by intense East-West competition, punctuated by the crises over Berlin (1948–9, 1958–61), Korea (1950–3), Indochina (1954), Taiwan (1955, 1958) and Cuba (1962). These crises shaped Western adversarial perceptions of the Soviet bloc and China, and had a similar effect on how the Soviet and Chinese leaderships assessed the intentions of the 'imperialist' powers which confronted them. However, the confrontations over Berlin, the Cuba and East Asian 'flashpoints' were West-West as well as East-West in nature, and often involved disputes between the UK and its allies over how to respond to policy decisions initiated by Stalin, Khrushchev, Mao and other Communist leaders. This was particularly evident as far as relations between the USA and Britain were concerned.

The preservation of the Anglo-American 'special relationship' was an essential British interest, as Western Europe's security ultimately rested on US military and economic power. However, during the first two decades of the Cold War decision-makers in Washington and London often disagreed over their respective assessments of the Soviet threat, and of political developments within the Communist bloc. It is therefore important to examine American perceptions of East-West relations, and also those of France and the Federal Republic of Germany, the UK's two main allies in Western Europe. At certain stages in this period the four main Western powers were at odds over how to manage their relations with Communist powers. The principal controversy, which was a particular feature of Anglo-American relations, concerned the possibility of moderating East-West tensions through negotiation.

It is also necessary to examine the process of British policy-making not only during the crisis periods of the early Cold War, but also during the periodic lulls in East-West hostilities, when officials in the Foreign Office, Ministry of Defence and other government departments debated whether it was possible to alleviate, or even resolve, the intractable ideological, diplomatic and strategic conflicts between the West and the Communist 'bloc'.[1] These apparently arcane exchanges of correspondence and opinions within Whitehall may appear to conform to the cliché of 'diplomatic history' being 'the record of what one clerk said to another clerk',[2] but the conclusions reached by British officials about the nature of the Soviet system and on internal developments within the Communist world are essential to this particular study. Deliberations over how to manage tense relations with the USSR, China and the East European states – and on how to counterbalance the risks of confrontation and global war with the need to preserve British and Western security interests against the perceived threat of Communist expansion – helped to influence Britain's approach to the Cold War throughout Wilson's first term in office, and beyond.

From World War to Cold War, 1945–51

Prior to the Second World War the USSR had played a peripheral role in world politics, but by 1945 the Soviets dominated Eastern and Central Europe. Britain, though nominally one of the victorious allied powers, emerged from the war economically exhausted and militarily over-stretched. Before 1941 relations between the UK and USSR had been blighted by mutual suspicion and ideological hostility – the Soviet government remembered British military intervention on behalf of the anti-Communist 'Whites' during the Russian civil war (1918–21), while British policy-makers recalled the Nazi-Soviet Pact of 1939. The 'Grand Alliance' was characterised by frequent quarrels pitting the Soviets against with their American and British allies, with the conduct of the war against Nazi Germany and the nature of the post-war settlement as the principal sources of contention.[3] During the final stages of the war, the Foreign Office and the Chiefs of Staff clashed over their respective assessments of future Soviet policy; this interdepartmental debate over the respective merits of what would eventually be termed 'containment' or 'coexistence' was to be repeated in different contexts within and between

---

[1] From 1965 onwards the Foreign Office used the phrase 'Soviet bloc' (or 'Eastern bloc') to refer to the USSR and its Warsaw Pact allies. The latter (in addition to Yugoslavia and Albania) were referred to simply as 'East European countries': ND note, 11 June 1965, N1981/1, and E. Youde (ND) note, 16 June 1965, N1981/2, TNA, FO 371/182529. I have used these three phrases in a similar sense, and I also use the descriptions 'Communist bloc', 'Communist powers' or 'Communist world' when discussing East-West relations before the Sino-Soviet split.

[2] This quotation has been attributed to the historian G. M. Young (1882–1959).

[3] G. Roberts, *The Soviet Union in world politics*, Abingdon 1999, 2–3; Crockatt, *Fifty years war*, 51–4.

14

Western governments in subsequent decades. The COS were unabashed proponents of containment, pessimistically envisaging the need for Britain to align with other 'Western' powers to withstand Soviet expansionism. In contrast, Foreign Office officials, particularly those of the Northern Department (overseeing relations with the USSR and other East European states), concluded that the Kremlin would focus upon internal reconstruction and the containment of Germany, and that these objectives provided the basis for post-war Anglo-Soviet co-operation. Winston Churchill believed that he had established a strong personal relationship with Stalin, although on occasions he was worried by future Soviet intentions. During the spring of 1945 the prime minister envisaged the possibility of war between the USSR and the Western allies.[4] In the British general election that summer the Labour party proclaimed that 'Left understands Left', and after Clement Attlee's government took office in July, ministers assumed that Britain's new social-democratic government could establish friendly relations with the USSR. However, by early 1946 Ernest Bevin, the Foreign Secretary, publicly complained about Soviet hostility towards the UK.[5] In the months which followed the defeat of Nazi Germany – and despite expectations within the Foreign Office as well as the Labour Party – Anglo-Soviet relations deteriorated sharply.

This decline reflected the collapse of the wartime alliance, resulting from fundamental disagreement over Germany's future and Anglo-American concerns over Stalin's foreign policy objectives. In its analyses of Soviet policy the JIC frankly admitted that while assessing the USSR's military capabilities was comparatively easy, it had scant information on Soviet intentions because of the secretive nature of the decision-making process within the Kremlin. This was a problem which constantly affected Britain's assessments of the 'Soviet threat', and during the late 1940s this factor led officials to assume the worst.[6] British officials showed little concern at the imposition of Soviet client regimes on the East European states – as demonstrated by Churchill's 'percentages agreement' with Stalin on the respective British and Soviet spheres of influence in the Balkans (October 1944). However, the USSR's expressed interest in expanding its influence in the Eastern Mediterranean and Middle East posed a threat to Britain's overseas empire. During the autumn and winter of 1945 Stalin's inherent paranoia led him to reassess the USSR's foreign policy, and to mobilise the Soviet economy and populace for a resumption of rivalry with the capitalist

4 Kitchen, British policy, 244, 260–1; Aldrich, Hidden hand, 52–63
5 H. Thomas, Armed truce, London 1986, 296; M. Hopkins, 'Herbert Morrison, the Cold War and Anglo-American relations', in M. Hopkins, M. Kandiah and G. Staerck (eds), Cold War Britain, 1945–1964, Basingstoke 2003, 21.
6 JIC(47)7/1 (Final), 'Soviet interests, intentions and capabilities', 6 Aug. 1947, TNA, CAB 158/1; P. Hennessy, The secret state: Whitehall and the Cold War, London 2002, 3, 12–14.

world.[7] From the British perspective the USSR had changed from an alliance partner (albeit an obstreperous one) to a potential enemy. The Foreign Office had initially adopted a sanguine view of Soviet intentions in 1944, but the Northern Department's response to the three despatches sent by the *chargé* of the Moscow embassy, Frank Roberts, in March 1946 demonstrated how attitudes had changed.

In Roberts's opinion, the USSR considered that the UK's financial difficulties and diplomatic isolation presented opportunities to expand its influence in Europe and Asia. Soviet ideology stressed that tensions, or 'contradictions', between Western states (notably between the UK and USA) would lead to the disintegration of capitalism and the triumph of world Communism; this conclusion, that Stalin believed that capitalist states were preordained to clash with each other, has been confirmed by recent research.[8] Roberts emphasised the fundamental difference between pre-war Anglo-Soviet relations and the situation after 1945 by stating that all the other powers that had hitherto blocked the USSR's expansion had been devastated during World War Two. Although he qualified this assessment by commenting on the inherent inefficiency and backwardness of the Soviet system, Roberts's despatches had an effect in London similar to that which George Kennan's 'Long Telegram' (February 1946) had on officials in Washington.[9] One Northern Department official expressed the widely held opinion that the Soviets were 'practising the most vicious power politics in the political, economic, and propaganda spheres' against British interests, and that the USSR would 'stop at nothing short of war' to achieve its objective of a Communist world. In retrospect this rhetoric appears alarmist, but the extent of Soviet espionage in Britain – conducted by Donald Maclean, Kim Philby and other traitors in the Foreign Office and intelligence services – showed that official fears of a hostile USSR and of Communist subversion were not unjustified.[10]

Roberts's despatches had a clear influence on the Foreign Secretary, who in April 1946 told Attlee that the Soviets 'have decided upon an aggressive policy based upon militant Communism and Russian chauvinism'. Bevin and his subordinates were aware that Britain could not counter the Soviet 'threat' alone, but in the immediate aftermath of the war the administration of Harry S. Truman had shown complete disinterest in retaining alliance

---

[7] Bullock, *Bevin*, 124–37; V. Zubok and C. Pleshakov, *Inside the Kremlin's Cold War*, Cambridge, MA 1996 36–40.
[8] V. Mastny, 'NATO in the beholder's eye: Soviet perceptions and policies, 1949–56' (CWIHP working paper xxxv, 2002), 36–7; Zubok and Pleshakov, *Kremlin*, 52–3, 73–4.
[9] F. Roberts (Moscow) to E. Bevin, 14, 17, 18 Mar. 1946, N4065/97/38, N4156/97/38, N4157/97/38, FO 371/56763; interview with Frank Roberts, DOHP, Churchill College Archives, Cambridge, transcript, 13.
[10] C. Warner (ND), 'The Soviet campaign against this country', 2 Apr. 1946, in R. Aldrich (ed.), *Espionage, security and intelligence in Britain, 1945–1970*, Manchester 1998, 174–5; Hennessy, *Secret state*, 83.

ties with the UK. The Foreign Secretary and his officials toyed with the concept of a 'third force' bloc – incorporating the West European states and their African colonies – but concluded that this proposal was unrealistic. About the same time that the Attlee government came to regard the USSR as a hostile state, the Truman administration likewise gradually adopted a policy of restraining the expansion of Soviet influence. During 1946 the COS and British intelligence services established close ties with their American counterparts, and the following year the US and British governments began openly to collaborate with each other in a policy of 'containing' the USSR.[11]

Until the spring of 1948 British officials regarded East-West rivalries as being confined to the political, economic and diplomatic spheres, and did not perceive the USSR to be an overt military threat. The JIC concluded that due to the human and material losses the latter suffered during World War Two, the Soviet government would focus on reconstruction and the consolidation of its authority over Eastern Europe. The USSR and its satellites would be in no position to wage war until the mid-1950s at the earliest, but would continue to use diplomatic and subversive means to weaken the capitalist world. As far as British officials were concerned, this assessment was confirmed by Yugoslav, Albanian and Bulgarian support for the Greek Communist insurgents fighting the pro-Western regime in Athens (1944–9). In this respect, the Attlee government shared the American concern that Western Europe was vulnerable to internal collapse and Communist takeover, and Labour ministers therefore supported both the Marshall Plan for European economic recovery and integration (June 1947), and the foundation of the Federal Republic of Germany two years later. After the Communist *coup* in Czechoslovakia (February 1948) and the Berlin blockade (July 1948-June 1949) British officials were concerned not only that the French and Italian Communist Parties might emulate their Czechoslovak comrades, but by the apparent imbalance between Soviet and Western military power in Europe. By March 1948 the Foreign Secretary's tone was more strident, depicting the USSR as an existential threat to the Western political and social order. Bevin persuaded his Cabinet colleagues that Britain had to align with the USA, the Commonwealth states and other West European democracies to counter the Soviet threat. Events in Czechoslovakia and Berlin served to reinforce Bevin's arguments. Having backed American efforts to promote West European economic recovery with the Marshall plan, the British played the principal role in creating the Brussels defence pact with France and the Benelux states in March 1948 (subsequently named the Western European

---

11 Bullock, *Bevin*, 234; C. Bartlett, *'The special relationship': a political history of Anglo-American relations since 1945*, London 1991, 13, 23–5; J. Dickie, *'Special' no more: Anglo-American relations: rhetoric and reality*, London 1994, 33–68.

Union, WEU). The UK also made a significant contribution to the conclusion of the North Atlantic Treaty in April 1949.[12]

Attlee had embarked on an 'Atlanticist' policy of aligning with the USA and other Western powers to restrict Soviet expansion, but the British government was still determined to maintain a world role and refused to participate in the early stages of European economic integration. The Labour government's decision to develop an independent nuclear programme in January 1947 was intended to reaffirm the UK's great power status as well as to establish a deterrent to Soviet aggression. Moreover, the Labour government did not completely rule out using diplomatic contacts with the USSR as a means of resolving East-West differences, even though the prospects for such a dialogue while Stalin retained power appeared non-existent. Furthermore, following the first Soviet nuclear test (August 1949) both the British government and public opinion were also increasingly concerned with averting a third global conflict which was likely to result in the UK's annihilation.[13]

The Attlee government's policy towards Mao Zedong's China reflected British hopes of moderating East-West tensions, which became particularly evident following the outbreak of the Korean War (June 1950). Two months after the Communist victory in the Chinese civil war (October 1949), the UK recognised the People's Republic of China, in spite of the Truman administration's decision to treat the Guomindang regime in Taiwan as the legitimate government of China. Although the Labour government committed British forces to supplement the US-led war effort in Korea, after the PRC's intervention in November 1950 British officials feared that the Korean conflict would lead to all-out war. When Truman announced that the USA was considering the use of nuclear weapons in Korea, Attlee flew to Washington in December to urge restraint. For its part, the Truman administration opposed British attempts to negotiate with the Soviets and Chinese, believing that a conciliatory approach to the USSR or the PRC would be as disastrous as the appeasement of Adolf Hitler in the 1930s. Throughout the Korean war (1950–3), British anxiety concerning excessive American belligerence was met by accusations of 'appeasement' from Washington, and Anglo-American relations were characterised by similar differences in successive Cold War crises.[14]

While the Labour government was privately criticised by officials of the Truman administration for its supposedly irresolute attitude towards

---

[12] JIC(47)7/1(Final), 6 Aug. 1947, CAB 158/1; Aldrich, *Hidden hand*, 137–40; Bullock, *Bevin*, 368–71; CM(48)19th Cabinet conclusions, 5 Mar. 1948, CAB 128/12; J. Young, *Cold War Europe, 1945–1989: a political history*, London 1991, 6–7.

[13] P. Hennessy, *Muddling through: power, politics and the quality of government in postwar Britain*, London 1997, 103; C. Keeble, *Britain and the Soviet Union, 1917–89*, Basingstoke 1990, 207; Bartlett, 'Special relationship', 34–7.

[14] P. Lowe, *Containing the Cold War in East Asia: British policies toward Japan, China and Korea, 1948–53*, Manchester 1997, 109–11, 124–31, 195–7.

Communism, it was also accused by its own backbenchers of showing slavish obedience to the aggressive Americans. The split within the Labour party widened after the Cabinet agreed in January 1951 to raise defence expenditure from £3.6 to £4.7 billion over a three-year period. This was a response to the post-Korea rearmament effort on the part of the North Atlantic Treaty Organisation, but Labour's left wing showed scepticism over the extent of the Soviet threat, and believed that rearmament would destroy the welfare state. In April 1951 three ministers – Aneurin Bevan, John Freeman and Harold Wilson – resigned from the government on the grounds that the new defence programme would not only affect social spending, but would undermine the British economy and indirectly assist the Communist cause. Five months later a divided Labour party lost the 1951 general election. Although a consensus developed between the Conservatives and Labour's front-bench with respect to their policies on East-West relations, throughout Labour's thirteen years in opposition the party's right wing quarrelled furiously with 'Bevanite' MPs, who accused their opponents of following a confrontational and pro-American foreign policy agenda.[15] This left-right debate over the correct approach to East-West relations and dealings with the USSR manifested itself in different forms in subsequent decades throughout the duration of the Cold War.

Between 'Scylla' and 'Charybdis',[16] 1951–8

In October 1951 the Conservatives returned to office in Britain, and the following year Dwight D. Eisenhower won the US presidential election. Stalin died in March 1953 and was succeeded by a 'collective leadership' consisting of his former henchmen. During these three years, the American, Soviet and British governments reassessed their respective policies towards both national security and East-West relations. Churchill had reinforced his anti-Communist reputation with his 'Iron Curtain' speech at Fulton, Missouri, in March 1946, yet five years later he was an advocate of direct negotiations with Stalin aimed at relaxing, if not ending, the Cold War. Churchill distinguished between 'appeasement' (concessions made from weakness) and what he called 'easement', and he argued that the West could 'negotiate from strength' with the Soviets and settle seemingly intractable issues such

15 M. Dockrill, *British defence since 1945*, London 1988, 42–4; Pimlott, *Wilson*, 157–62; D. Keohane, 'Labour's international policy: a story of conflict and contention', in B. Brivati and R. Hefferman (eds), *The Labour party: a centenary history*, Basingstoke 2000, 363–82.
16 This section title is taken from a quotation by Pierson Dixon, a Russia Committee official: J. Young (ed.), 'The British Foreign Office and Cold War fighting in the early 1950s: PUSC(51)16 and the 1952 "sore spots" memorandum' (Leicester University discussion papers in politics, no.195/2 1995), 5.

as the future of Germany. Churchill's attitude was partly a product of his renowned egotism, but it was also motivated by a genuine intention to avert the horrors of a nuclear conflagration, hence his statement that 'to jaw-jaw is better than to war-war'. He was also convinced that increased East-West contacts through trade would undermine an already moribund Communist system.[17] The prime minister's opinions were criticised not only by the Americans but by the Foreign Office, notably the officials of the Permanent Under-Secretary's Department which had been established to co-ordinate the conduct of external policy. British diplomats saw summitry as potentially dangerous, as domestic pressure could lead Western governments to conclude superficially attractive agreements with the Soviets, with adverse long-term repercussions. Churchill's intention to hold a summit with Stalin led the PUSD to review Britain's Cold War policy, the conclusions being produced in PUSC(51)16, 'Future policy towards Soviet Russia', in mid-January 1952. The assessments outlined in this document deserve attention, as they influenced subsequent British official assessments on both internal developments within the Communist world and on the course of the Cold War.

The PUSD paper started with the assertion that 'the present Soviet leadership is inspired not only by traditional Russian ambitions' – manifested by its hegemony over Eastern Europe and its ambitions in the Middle East – but 'also by a fanatical and dynamic revolutionary spirit which utterly rejects the very idea of a lasting settlement with the non-Communist part of the world'. Its authors summarised British (and, by implication, Western) objectives as being, first, to achieve 'equilibrium' between the USSR and NATO powers; second, to establish a *modus vivendi* as a basis for 'co-existence' with the Soviets; and finally, to pursue negotiations towards a 'more stable settlement' of East-West disputes. Unlike Churchill, PUSD officials considered that the Western powers still had to rearm and consolidate their alliance ties before proceeding to the second stage of 'co-existence'. Rearmament would impose economic strains on the UK and its allies, but the Foreign Office was confident that the Western states could withstand the 'long haul' of Cold War rivalry. The success of any negotiations aimed at a general settlement of East-West problems depended on a gradual change (or 'evolution') in Soviet ideology, and an end to the intransigent hostility that Stalin had showed towards the West.

The PUSD's conclusions underpinned the British approach to East-West relations over the following decade. This paper regarded Britain's economic recovery as a priority, and concluded that while the attainment of 'equilibrium' involved a Western military build-up, the UK was not prepared to 'lightly embark on courses involving serious risk of war'. This statement reflected the significant concern within Whitehall, reflected also amongst Churchill's ministers, that the USA might launch a preventive war while it

---

[17] Young, *Churchill's last campaign*, 27–31, 159–60, 269.

retained nuclear supremacy over the USSR. PUSD officials had American efforts to 'roll back' Communist power in Europe in mind when they asserted that there were 'sore spots' in Soviet foreign policy which, if pressed, could provoke a violent response from Moscow. The main 'sore spot' was Eastern Europe, and Foreign Office officials believed that their American counterparts were too sanguine in believing that the 'satellites' could be detached from Soviet domination. Following the Czechoslovak *coup* senior British diplomats and military officers had initially supported Anglo-American covert operations to assist anti-Communist guerrillas in Albania, the Baltic States and Ukraine. Yet by 1951–2 policy-makers in Whitehall concluded that East European resistance movements would fail without Western military assistance, and that Britain should restrain any provocative American action in the USSR's sphere of influence. Their opposite numbers in Washington responded to these conclusions with scorn, and the chairman of the US Joint Chiefs of Staff commented that their ally's criticisms of covert action had 'an appeasement ring' to them. This divergence of opinions concerning 'roll back' reflected a wider dispute between the USA and UK over the prospects for a *modus vivendi* with the Communist world.[18]

The differences between Churchill and the Foreign Office concerned methods rather than objectives. 'Future policy towards Soviet Russia' concluded that negotiations with the USSR were unlikely to succeed because of Stalin's attitude, and inadvisable until the Western world had achieved 'equilibrium' with the Communist states. Even then PUSD officials thought that any agreements reached would be limited in scope. In this respect, Churchill's intention to re-establish a 'working relationship' with Stalin was unrealistic, given the extreme paranoia the latter displayed during his final two years. Stalin's successors were also suspicious of the prime minister's motives, and doubted whether his policy of 'easement' had any influence on American policy-making. Significantly, both Churchill and the Foreign Office placed their hopes on the long-term liberalisation of Communist doctrine. The prime minister argued that East-West contacts would eventually erode the ideological basis of the Soviet bloc, while Foreign Office thinking emphasised the long-term adoption of less dogmatic domestic and external policies by the USSR. The Foreign Secretary, Anthony Eden, shared his officials' opinion that in the meantime the Western powers should focus on building up their economic and military strength. This involved addressing, in particular, the controversy surrounding West German rearmament.[19] The COS's 'Global strategy' paper of 1952 likewise emphasised the

18 PUSC(51)16, 'Future policy towards Soviet Russia', 17 Jan. 1952, is in Young, '"Sore spots"'. See also Aldrich, *Hidden hand*, 142–9, 160–79, 327–33, and CC(54)52nd Cabinet conclusions, 23 July 1954, CAB 128/27.
19 U. Bar-Noi, 'The Soviet Union and Churchill's appeals for high-level talks, 1953–54: new evidence from the Russian archives', *DS* ix/3 (1998), 110–33; Young, *Foreign Office*, 6; R. Service, *A history of twentieth-century Russia*, London 1998, 324–8.

need for Western states to concentrate on economic and military consolidation. While recommending the creation of a British nuclear force, and (like 'Future policy towards Soviet Russia') advocating 'psychological operations' to play on Sino-Soviet tensions and other weaknesses in the Communist world, the COS were initially wary of the consequences of rearming West Germany, another potential 'sore spot' in East-West relations. By 1952 there was therefore a general consensus in Whitehall that Britain was obliged – to use the classical metaphor employed by one senior Foreign Office official – to 'steer between the Scylla of another war and the Charybdis of an appeasement policy which might forfeit us United States sympathy', thereby undermining the alliance ties upon which the UK's security ultimately depended.[20]

Following Stalin's death, Churchill's interest in 'easement' was revived when one member of the 'collective leadership', Georgi Malenkov, declared on 15 March 1953 that 'there is no disputed or unresolved question that cannot be settled peacefully by mutual agreement among the interested countries'. The prime minister responded to these comments in his House of Commons speech on 11 May, in which he proposed a summit meeting with the Soviets. Malenkov shared Churchill's concerns over the escalation of the superpower arms race and the development of thermonuclear weapons, and concluded that a world war would destroy both Communism and capitalism. Although Malenkov was later expelled from the leadership by his rivals, Nikita Khrushchev subsequently used similar arguments in his public pronouncements.[21] Malenkov's statement was treated with scepticism in the Foreign Office, where the consensus was that the new leadership was 'adopting a much cleverer policy for dividing and weakening the West than Stalin ever did'.[22] In Washington, the Republican administration undertook its own reappraisal of the perceived Soviet menace, and its 'New Look' strategy envisaged a 'long haul' of East-West rivalry, in which economic prosperity would be as crucial to Western security as military strength. While the Conservatives scrapped the Attlee government's rearmament programme, Eisenhower likewise rejected the conventional military build-up which his predecessor had initiated, relying on the expansion of US nuclear forces. Yet if American opinions on the military means needed to deter the USSR had changed, neither the president nor his senior advisors believed that Soviet

[20] D(52)26, 'Defence policy and global strategy', 17 June 1952, CAB 131/12; J. Baylis, *Ambiguity and deterrence: British nuclear strategy, 1945–1964*, Oxford 1995, 396–9, 403–4; Young, '"Sore spots"', 5.

[21] R. C. Nation, *Black earth, red star*, Ithaca, NY 1992, 204–5; *Parliamentary debates, Hansard*, 5th series (515 HC.Deb5s), dxv, London 1953, cols 863–98; Zubok and Pleshakov, *Kremlin*, 167–9.

[22] R. Bevins and G. Quinn, 'Blowing hot and cold: Anglo-Soviet relations, 1955–1964', in W. Kaiser and G. Staerck (eds), *British foreign policy, 1955–1964: contracting opinions*, Basingstoke 2000, 211–12. The quotation is taken from E. Shuckburgh, *Descent into Suez: diaries, 1951–1956*, London 1986, 82–3, entry for 24–30 Mar. 1953.

objectives had been altered by Stalin's death. Eisenhower expressed this view in coarse terms in a conversation with Churchill and the French premier, Georges Bidault, during the Bermuda Conference in December 1953, stating that 'Russia was a woman of the streets and whether her dress was new, or just the old one patched, it was certainly the same whore underneath'.[23]

Regarding West German rearmament, in the last resort Britain was less concerned with upsetting Soviet or East European sensibilities than with achieving 'equilibrium' with the Eastern bloc. This was to have been facilitated by the creation of a European Defence Community, based around a pan-European army. Not surprisingly, the prospect of rearming Germans so soon after World War Two aroused controversy amongst NATO powers, and was the cause of a bitter Franco-American row. After months of convoluted inter-allied wrangling, Eden brokered a settlement at the London conference (28 September–3 October 1954). The FRG was permitted to establish its own armed forces (the *Bundeswehr*), which were fully integrated into NATO's military structure, but had to pledge not to acquire nuclear, biological or chemical weapons. In return, NATO members recognised the FRG as the only legitimate German state, and the UK committed itself to maintain the British Army of the Rhine to help defend its NATO and WEU partners. One result of the London agreement was that the USSR and its East European 'satellites' founded the Warsaw Treaty Organisation (or 'Warsaw Pact') in May 1955. British officials calculated that the Soviet response to the FRG's admission to NATO would not go beyond propaganda invective and, with the establishment of the Warsaw Pact, the formalisation of the USSR's dominance over Eastern Europe. However, the financial costs of maintaining BAOR contributed to frequent quarrels between the American, West German and British governments, as the latter sought to reduce the scale of their commitment to European defence.[24]

British officialdom's unwillingness to exacerbate East-West tensions by placing pressure on 'sore spots' was particularly evident in East Asia, notably during the crises concerning Indochina and Taiwan. In the first instance, Churchill blocked American intervention to save French forces from defeat at Dien Bien Phu, favouring a negotiated settlement to end the Franco-Viet Minh war. Eisenhower's Secretary of State, John Foster Dulles, quarrelled with Eden at the Geneva conference on Indochina, and the latter's private secretary noted that the British delegation had a better working relationship with the Soviets than with the Americans, who refused to ratify the accords

23 S. Dockrill, *Eisenhower's new look national security policy, 1953–61*, Basingstoke 1991, 42–7; J. Colville, *The fringes of power: Downing Street diaries*, II: *October 1941–April 1955*, London 1987, 347–8, entry for 4 Dec. 1953.

24 S. Dockrill, *Rearmament*, 12–15, 56–8, 153–5; Mastny, *NATO*, 64–5; H. Zimmerman, 'The sour fruits of victory: sterling and security in Anglo-German relations during the 1950s and 1960s', *CEH* ix/2 (2000), 225–34.

reached at the end of the conference (22 July 1954).[25] The Conservative government did publicly endorse the Eisenhower administration's support for Taiwan when the PRC shelled the two offshore islands of Jinmen and Mazu (which were both held by *Guomindang* troops) in February 1955 and September 1958. However, in private there were profound differences between the two allies regarding China and the Taiwan question. While US officials concluded that their British counterparts lacked the resolve to deal with the Chinese threat to Western interests in Asia, the latter concluded that the Americans had an excessively alarmist attitude towards the PRC, and were convinced that Taiwan's occupation of Jinmen and Mazu was a source of regional instability.[26]

Churchill's efforts to seek a ground-breaking summit with Malenkov in April 1954 provoked a Cabinet revolt. Ministers were angered both by the prime minister's failure to consult them, and by Churchill's readiness to accept Soviet protestations of goodwill at face value.[27] There were indications suggesting that compromise agreements could be reached with Communist powers, notably the armistice agreement in Korea (July 1953) and the conclusion of the Austrian State Treaty (May 1955). However, the Geneva summit meeting between the American, British, Soviet and French leaders in July 1955 produced little but ephemeral goodwill. As Foreign Secretary and (after April 1955) as Churchill's successor, Eden was associated with a series of proposals to reunify Germany and to reduce military forces in Central Europe, but the German problem proved to be an intractable one, afflicted by the competing and incompatible demands of the USSR and the FRG over reunification.[28] The following year Eden received the Soviet Premier, Nikolai Bulganin, and the First Secretary of the CPSU, Nikita Khrushchev, on a state visit to Britain. The most significant feature of this visit was the botched attempt by the British external intelligence service to place a Soviet cruiser, the *Ordzhonikidze*, under surveillance while it was moored in Portsmouth. Khrushchev and Bulganin had sailed to Britain on the *Ordzhonikidze*, and Eden was both furious and embarrassed when the SIS's abortive operation was exposed by the press.[29] This would not be the last occasion when bilateral diplomatic relations would be adversely affected

---

[25] *The Macmillan diaries: the Cabinet years, 1950–1957*, ed. P. Catterall, Basingstoke 2003, 309–10, entry for 25 Apr. 1954; Shuckburgh, *Descent into Suez*, 180–5, entries for 28, 30 Apr. 1954.

[26] M. Dockrill, 'Britain and the first Chinese offshore islands crisis', in M. Dockrill and J. Young (eds), *British foreign policy, 1945–56*, Basingstoke 1989, 173–96; CC(58)72nd conclusions, 25 Sept. 1958, CAB 128/32.

[27] Young, *Churchill's last campaign*, 272–9; Keeble, *Britain and Soviet Union*, 139, 248.

[28] FO to missions, no.97 Intel, 24.5.57, W1072/1, FO 371/137078; S. Dockrill and G. Bischof (eds), *Cold War respite: the Geneva Summit of 1955*, Baton Rouge, LA 2000.

[29] K. Morgan, *The people's peace: British history, 1945–1990*, Oxford 1992, 146–7; A. Eden to E. Bridges (Treasury), 9 May 1956, in Aldrich, *Espionage*, 33–4.

by an espionage scandal involving either the British or Soviet intelligence services.

The diplomatic fall-out from this failed operation was overshadowed not only by the Suez crisis, but by two serious outbreaks of popular unrest in Eastern Europe, the Poznan riots in Poland and the anti-Communist rising in Hungary (October–November 1956). British officials were convinced that efforts to inspire revolts behind the Iron Curtain were futile unless backed by Western support. Yet no NATO power was prepared to provide overt assistance to any East European rebellion, and the Hungarian revolution was therefore doomed to failure. The Soviet army's brutal suppression of the Hungarians demonstrated both the USSR's determination to preserve its hegemony over Eastern Europe, and the hollowness of the Eisenhower administration's 'roll back' rhetoric. Khrushchev had, however, shown considerable pragmatism in October 1956 in accepting the emergence of Wladyslaw Gomulka's 'national Communist' regime in Warsaw.[30] Traditionally, British governments had never shown much interest in events in Eastern Europe unless they had implications closer to home, as was thought to be the case with Czechoslovakia in 1948. The Eden government's attention was focused on Suez, and Cabinet ministers therefore paid little if any regard to events in either Hungary or Poland.[31] In the aftermath of the Hungarian and Polish crises, the JIC concluded that the Soviets were 'prepared to go to any lengths to keep the Soviet bloc intact', but that Gomulka's rise to power showed that Moscow would tolerate 'limited concessions … as the price of subduing popular discontent' in order to preserve Communism in Poland.[32] The aftermath of the 1956 upheavals, in particular the reforms of Gomulka's comparatively liberal regime in the late 1950s, subsequently shaped official assessments within Whitehall on the prospects of non-violent, evolutionary change in Eastern Europe.

Harold Macmillan became prime minister after Eden's resignation in January 1957. His immediate priority was to restore the damage done to the 'special relationship' by the Suez débâcle.[33] Macmillan also hoped to promote East-West détente, and was concerned by the escalating superpower strategic arms race, although his support for an international ban on nuclear

---

30 R. Crampton, *Eastern Europe in the twentieth century*, Abingdon 1994, 283–303; B. Heuser, *Western 'containment' policies in the Cold War: the Yugoslav case, 1948–53*, Basingstoke 1989, 137–40; C. Bekes, 'The 1956 Hungarian revolution and world politics '(CWIHP working paper xvi, 1996).
31 See CM(56)68th-85th conclusions, 3 Oct.-20 Nov. 1956, CAB 128/30. The only file on Hungary, in PREM 11/1388, contains an appeal for assistance by Hungarian *émigrés* to Eden, dated 21 October 1956. See A., '"A different 1956": British responses to the Polish events, June–November 1956', *CWH* vi/4 (2006), 455–76.
32 JIC(56)123(Final)(Revise), 'Soviet policy in the light of the situation in the Middle East and the satellites', 6 Dec. 1956, CAB 158/26; JIC(56)97th, 101st meetings, 25 Oct., 9 Nov. 1956, CAB 159/25.
33 Bartlett, *'Special relationship'*, 86–7; K. Kyle, *Suez*, London 1991.

tests conflicted with the development of the RAF's V-bomber force. The 1957 defence review committed the UK to develop its own deterrent, but cut defence expenditure from 10 to 7 per cent of gross national product. However, Britain still had to support not only BAOR, but defence obligations arising from both colonial commitments and membership of the Central Treaty Organisation and the South-East Asia Treaty Organisation.[34] The defence review provided part of the rationale behind Britain's intention to reduce BAOR, but Macmillan also presumed that the UK could fulfil its NATO commitment with fewer forces. After months of bargaining within the WEU – and a protracted dispute between the US, British and West German governments – BAOR was reduced from 77,000 to 55,000 troops by December 1959. Officials in Washington and Bonn were also annoyed by the equivocal British response to the proposal by the Polish Foreign Minister, Adam Rapacki, for a nuclear-free zone in Central Europe. NATO rejected the Rapacki plan because its implementation would not address the Warsaw Pact's superiority in troop numbers, but Selwyn Lloyd (the Foreign Secretary) advised his West German counterpart that 'we should avoid giving the impression that new proposals and initiatives [from East European countries] ... are automatically rejected by the West'.[35]

The West German Chancellor, Konrad Adenauer, suspected that the British government was using military disengagement in Central Europe as an excuse for further reductions in BAOR and for reneging on the UK's commitment to the WEU. There were similar suspicions in Washington, even though the Eisenhower administration had also intended to reduce the US military presence in Europe.[36] Ironically, Khrushchev had ordered the reduction of Soviet conventional forces, partly because he favoured an increased emphasis on nuclear power, but also because of the economic burden of maintaining existing troop levels. Khrushchev's thinking was similar to that which had influenced the 'New Look' and the 1957 British defence review, but any intention by policy-makers in Washington, Moscow or London of reducing force levels further was rendered impossible by the outbreak of the Berlin crisis.[37]

[34] I. Clark, *Nuclear diplomacy and the special relationship: Britain's deterrent and America, 1957–1962*, Oxford 1994, 222–3; M. Dockrill, *British defence*, 65–71.

[35] S. Dockrill, 'Britain's motives for troop reductions in Western Germany, 1955–1958', *JSS* xx/3 (1997), 45–65; S. Lloyd to C. Steel (Bonn), 4 Jan. 1958, W1072/6, FO 371/137078.

[36] Gearson, *Berlin crisis*, 25–30; W. Loth, *Overcoming the Cold War: a history of détente, 1950–1991*, Basingstoke 2002, 44–7; Lloyd to H. Macmillan, 26 Apr. 1958, PREM 11/2347.

[37] M. Evangelista, 'Why keep such an army?' Khrushchev's troop reductions' (CWIHP paper xix, 1997); M. O'Neill, 'The Cold War on the ground, 1945–1981', in R. Higham and F. W. Kagan (eds), *The military history of the Soviet Union*, Basingstoke 2002, 231.

Berlin, Cuba and 'cold détente', 1958–64[38]

Soon after Khrushchev emerged victorious from the power struggle between Stalin's successors, East-West rivalries took a sharp turn for the worse. This was partly a consequence of the effect of Suez and the Hungarian revolution on international relations, but was also due to the Soviet leader's mercurial conduct. Through a combination of crude bluster and intimidation he alienated Western governments and alarmed his own compatriots. Khrushchev was confident that the economic and technological prowess of the Soviet system would surpass that of the capitalist world, but by expressing this belief with the phrase '[we] will bury you', he contributed to Western fears of a more aggressive Soviet foreign policy.[39] These concerns were intensified by Khrushchev's threat in November 1958 to hand over responsibility for Berlin and its access routes to the German Democratic Republic, unless the three other powers occupying the city (the USA, UK and France) agreed to a formal peace treaty resolving the German question.

This ultimatum was prompted by the East German leader, Walter Ulbricht, who was frustrated by the flight of refugees from his country, but because the Western powers did not recognise the GDR, Khrushchev's actions provoked a major crisis. The Berlin issue also exposed intra-Western divisions over the German question, particularly regarding the GDR's sovereignty and the legal status of Germany's post-1945 borders. The USA, Britain and France officially supported reunification, although because a unified Germany within NATO would be as unacceptable to the Soviets as a Communist equivalent would be to the West, the three powers tacitly upheld the *status quo*. The satirical contemporary quip 'we love Germany so much that we are glad there are two of them' accurately reflected the private concerns of the FRG's allies over the potential resurgence of hyper-nationalism in a united Germany, which was particularly evident within policy-making circles in Whitehall. British politicians and officials also considered Soviet and East European pronouncements on West German 'revanchism' to be motivated in part by genuine fear of a historical aggressor's revival, and to a lesser degree shared the concerns of the UK's Warsaw Pact adversaries over the potential implications of a unified Germany. As far as Germany's post-1945 borders were concerned, Foreign Office officials privately conceded that these could not be revised – irrespective of public pronouncements from the FRG – and even secretly assured the Poles in 1962 that they informally recognised the *de facto* Polish-German border (the 'Oder-Neisse line') as legitimate.[40]

---

38 This phrase is used in D. C. Watt (ed.), *Survey of international affairs, 1963*, Oxford 1979, 3–4.
39 Zubok and Pleshakov, *Kremlin*, 174–5. See also W. Taubman, *Khrushchev: the man and his era*, London 2003.
40 R. G. Hughes, *Britain, Germany and the Cold War: the search for a European détente, 1949–1967*, Abingdon 2007, 106–10; COS140/27/1/58, 27 Jan. 1958, FO 371/135627;

This attitude directly contrasted with that of the Adenauer government, which was not prepared to give up its declared intention to reunify Germany, although in practice the Chancellor's main concerns lay with the diplomatic, military and economic integration of his country with other Western powers. The FRG also refused to recognise any state other than the USSR which had diplomatic relations with the GDR (this was the essence of the 'Hallstein doctrine') or to accept the Oder-Neisse line and the border with Czechoslovakia.[41] Before Khrushchev's ultimatum, the British ambassador to Moscow warned London that NATO powers had to preserve their solidarity in order to resist 'further blackmail or splitting tactics' by the Soviet leader. Yet during the Berlin crisis, the British were suspected by the French and West Germans of being prepared to recognise the GDR, and thereby sacrificing the allied position in West Berlin, in order to avert conflict with the USSR. Officials of the Eisenhower administration also privately wondered whether Macmillan was preparing to appease Khrushchev in the same way as Neville Chamberlain gave way to Hitler at Munich.[42]

Throughout the crisis, Britain's main differences lay mainly with the two other principal West European powers, rather than with the USA. Macmillan was worried that the dispute with the Soviets over Berlin would provoke a war, and he was determined to find a diplomatic solution to the crisis. However the French President de Gaulle thought that Khrushchev was bluffing and sought to develop Franco-German *rapprochement* and to concurrently weaken 'Anglo-Saxon' influence in Western Europe. Macmillan's trip to Moscow (February 1959) – the first peace-time visit by a British prime minister to the USSR – went ahead despite the open opposition of de Gaulle and Adenauer, and some unease on Eisenhower's part. The prime minister was harshly received by Khrushchev, who tried to bully and humiliate his guest. The Soviet leader made a gesture by lifting the deadline on a German peace treaty which he had imposed the previous November, but Macmillan's hopes for a negotiated settlement were subsequently dashed by the collapse of the four-power summit in Paris in May 1960. John F. Kennedy's election victory six months later did lead to a convergence of US and British views. The new president saw Berlin as militarily untenable, and did not want it to be the focus of a showdown with the USSR. It was also significant that Kennedy publicly emphasised his readiness to uphold allied rights in *West* Berlin, but not in the city as a whole. The US and British governments

Newman, *Berlin crisis*, 46. The 'Germany' quotation originated with the French writer Francois Mauriac. See T. Garton Ash, *In Europe's name: Germany and the divided continent*, London 1994, 29.

[41] Gearson, *Berlin Wall crisis*, 54–5; Newman, *Berlin crisis*, 52–3, 167–78; Zubok and Pleshakov, *Kremlin*, 196–8; W. Hanrieder, *Germany, America, Europe: forty years of German foreign policy*, New Haven, CT 1989, 160–3.

[42] P. Reilly (Moscow) to Lloyd, 12 Feb. 1958, PREM 11/2347; Lloyd to Macmillan, 15 Feb. 1960, PREM 11/2998; F. Bozo, *Two strategies for Europe: De Gaulle, the United States and the Atlantic alliance*, Lanham, MD 2000, 29–34.

therefore acquiesced in Ulbricht's decision to sever East from West Berlin in August 1961, concluding that the construction of the Berlin Wall provided a resolution – albeit a ruthless and inhumane one – to an intractable and potentially destabilising Cold War confrontation.[43]

The Berlin crisis was one factor behind the Kennedy administration's revision of US strategy. Eisenhower's successor oversaw the expansion of American military power in order to maintain nuclear superiority over the USSR, and to give the USA greater strategic flexibility than considered possible within the bounds of the 'New Look'. 'Flexible response' challenged the NATO strategic concept agreed in 1957 (MC70), which concluded that any response to Soviet aggression would involve the immediate use of nuclear weapons. Kennedy's Secretary of Defense, Robert McNamara, intended to increase the Alliance's conventional military forces to give NATO a non-nuclear capability to resist a Warsaw Pact attack. In practice, however, the Kennedy administration did little to reinforce US troop levels in Europe. The president felt that the European NATO powers were not bearing their share of the Alliance's defence burden, and Washington wanted its allies to undertake the conventional force build-up which would make 'flexible response' a practical option.[44] The Kennedy administration's approach to European defence persisted and contributed to NATO's internal crisis in the third year of Johnson's term in office.

British officials agreed with McNamara's view that MC70 was out of date, but opposed his intention to build up NATO's conventional power. In the summer of 1961, the MoD reviewed NATO strategy on the basis of British assessments of the Soviet threat. The JIC took the view that the USSR would not deliberately risk a global war which would lead to mutual destruction, as Soviet military doctrine stated that even a 'limited' East-West conflict in Europe would inevitably escalate into thermonuclear war. On the basis of this assessment the MoD study, known as the Mottershead report, concluded that there was a slight risk of war by 'accident' (caused by a border clash in Central Europe) or by 'miscalculation' (involving a Warsaw Pact probing attack to test NATO's resolve). It nevertheless concluded that NATO did not need to increase its force levels in order to meet either contingency. While McNamara was 'thinking the unthinkable' by envisaging the possibility of a non-nuclear war in Central Europe, British thinking was focused on deterrence. This attitude subsequently provided the basis for both the

---

43 Gearson, *Berlin Wall crisis*, 156, 202–3; L. Freedman, *Kennedy's wars: Berlin, Cuba, Laos and Vietnam*, New York 2000, 60–1, 71, 74–5; K. Larres, 'Britain, East Germany and *détente*: British policy towards the GDR and West Germany's "policy of movement", 1955–65', in W. Loth (ed.), *Europe, Cold War and coexistence, 1953–1965*, London 2004, 117.
44 J. S. Duffield, *Power rules: the evolution of NATO's conventional force posture*, Stanford, CA 1995, 157–65; F. Gavin, 'The myth of flexible response: United States strategy in Europe during the 1960s', *IHR* xxvii/4 (2001), 849–50, 858–60.

UK's perceptions of Soviet military power, and also the NATO strategic review during the 1960s.[45]

The Mottershead report did not anticipate the possibility that the USSR could encroach on Western interests outside NATO, as was the case in Cuba in 1962. In April, Khrushchev decided to deploy a substantial, nuclear-armed Soviet force to support Fidel Castro's regime. Six months later, the discovery of Soviet medium-range ballistic missiles on Cuban soil sparked off a superpower crisis which nearly ended with a global war. Britain's role in the Cuban crisis was peripheral, and before the MRBMs were discovered British intelligence analysts regarded American concerns of a Soviet missile build-up in Cuba as far-fetched.[46] Two months after the crisis was resolved, the JIC confidently concluded that Khrushchev's miscalculation 'in no way invalidated [our] earlier assessment' that the Soviets 'would be more cautious in the pursuit of their foreign policy'. Post-Cuba, the superpowers made a conscious effort to manage and moderate their rivalry, and the tentative US-Soviet *rapprochement* led to the Limited Test Ban Treaty between the USA, USSR and UK in August 1963. Macmillan encouraged Kennedy's efforts to negotiate the LTBT with Moscow, although in this respect the prime minister was pushing at an open door; the US president had demonstrated his personal commitment to *détente* with his American University speech on 10 June.[47] Following Kennedy's assassination in November 1963, Lyndon Johnson inherited his predecessor's policy on East-West relations, and officials like Roswell Gilpatric (the assistant Secretary of Defense) considered it 'possible, though not assured, that we shall at last find a more than temporary easing' of Cold War tensions.[48] As an expression of official thinking in Washington, this statement was strikingly similar to the prevailing opinion as expressed in Whitehall or Westminster.

Paul Gore-Booth, the Permanent Under-Secretary of the Foreign Office from January 1965 to February 1969, retrospectively observed that by early 1964 there were 'no serious irritants' affecting Anglo-Soviet relations, and that British officials were more concerned with crises concerning the emergence of newly-independent Third World states than with East-West relations. The old bipolar order that Frank Roberts had described in 1946 appeared to be disintegrating. The post-war economic revival of Western Europe was symbolised by the founding of the European Economic Commu-

---

[45] Annex to JP(61)86(Final), 18 July 1961, DEFE 4/137; B. Heuser, *NATO, Britain, France and the FRG: nuclear strategy and forces for Europe, 1949–2000*, Basingstoke 1997, 39, 48–50.

[46] Taubman, *Khrushchev*, 529–77; G. D. Rawnsley, 'How special is special? The Anglo-American alliance during the Cuban Missile crisis', *Contemporary Record* ix/3 (1995), 586–601; Aldrich, *Hidden hand*, 621.

[47] JIC(62)63rd meeting, 6 Dec. 1962, CAB 159/38; J. See, 'An uneasy truce: John F. Kennedy and Soviet-American *détente*, 1963', *CWH* ii/2 (2002), 161–94.

[48] Loth, *Détente*, 76–80; R. Gilpatric, 'Our defense needs: the long term view', *FA* xlii/3 (1964), 369.

nity in 1957, Macmillan's belated application for British membership in 1961, and the Franco-German Elysée Treaty of January 1963, signed in the same month that de Gaulle vetoed Britain's bid to join the EEC.[49] Western Europe's increased self-confidence was mirrored by 'polycentrism' in Eastern Europe and, after 1961, by the emergence of China as a rival to both the USSR's authority over the Communist world and Soviet efforts to enhance their influence globally, particularly in the decolonised Third World.[50] The consequences of these developments for British policy were left for Labour to manage once it returned to power in the autumn of 1964.

A British approach to East-West relations?

For all the efforts made by successive British governments during this period, during the first two decades of the Cold War *détente* was often conspicuous by its absence. Britain's attempts to maintain diplomatic lines of contact with the Communist world while supporting the US-led policy of 'containment' contributed to the disputes which arose with allies during successive East-West crises, when British advocacy of restraint and negotiation was often associated with appeasement. This was not only a feature of Anglo-American relations during the early Cold War era – during the Berlin crisis of 1958–61, Macmillan's attempts to mediate with Khrushchev aroused contempt and hostility from de Gaulle and Adenauer. Irrespective of whether the Conservative or Labour parties were in power, there was a certain consistency in British policy towards East-West relations from the late 1940s to the early 1960s. Moreover, despite the collapse of the British empire senior politicians and decision-makers rejected the argument that their country 'had lost an empire and not yet found a role' (as the former US Secretary of State, Dean Acheson, put it), and still assumed that Britain was an important actor both in global politics and in East-West relations.[51] The challenges the Wilson government faced in balancing the 'world role' with European interests and NATO responsibilities were inherited from predecessors who still perceived that Britain had international responsibilities despite its decline as an imperial power.

The evolution of a distinct approach to Britain's Cold War policy can be seen in three areas: security, diplomacy and 'transnational' contacts in trade and other fields with the Eastern bloc. Since 1948 two basic objectives of British national security policy had been the preservation of the Anglo-

---

49 P. Gore-Booth, *With great truth and respect*, London 1974, 330–2; W. Hitchcock, *The struggle for Europe: the turbulent history of a divided continent*, London 2003, 147–55; J. Lacouture (trans. A. Sheridan), *De Gaulle: the ruler*, London 1991, 355–9.
50 O. A. Westad, *The global Cold War: third world interventions and the making of our times*, Cambridge 2005, 160–5.
51 Morgan, *People's peace*, 216.

American alliance and the collective defence of Western Europe, reinforced by a US troop presence on the continent and by the USA's nuclear arsenal. Senior British civilian and military officials were generally confident that as long as these two factors existed, the USSR would not risk the consequences of deliberate aggression. Yet successive British governments were also anxious not to provoke a world war, particularly following the first Soviet nuclear test in 1949. During Cold War crises American officials fretted about the possibility of the British 'doing a Munich', while their counterparts in London were equally concerned that American recklessness would result in another Sarajevo, and the quarrels which pitted 'sabre-rattling' Americans against 'appeasement-minded' allies occurred frequently throughout the Cold War.[52]

Scholars of ideology have noted the contrast between the moralist language of American political discourse and the more pragmatic and power-political European equivalent. During the early Cold War US officials showed a tendency to regard diplomatic contacts with the Communist powers as almost unethical: this attitude was evident in Dulles's demeanour at the Geneva conferences of 1954 and 1955.[53] Soviet-American contacts were institutionalised by Eisenhower and Kennedy's summit meetings with Khrushchev at Camp David (1959) and Vienna (1961), and by the installation of the Washington-Moscow telephone 'hotline' in 1963, but the USA still refused to recognise the PRC or Castro's government. In contrast, British policy-makers were capable of accepting diplomatic concessions towards Communist powers (manifested for example by the UK's readiness to admit China to the UN, and unofficial contacts with the Polish Foreign Ministry regarding the Oder-Neisse line) in the interests of *détente*. As White observes, Britain had a tradition of disregarding ideology as an influence on diplomacy. Paul Gore-Booth wrote in March 1967 that '[our] need to oppose Communism cannot be based simply on our strong distaste for it as a system', as Britain was 'compelled to live with and even sometimes co-operate with other distasteful regimes'. What was unacceptable was the Soviet and Chinese objective of spreading their ideology worldwide, and while Britain was determined to maintain diplomatic relations and to negotiate with Communist states whenever possible, the policy of containment remained unchanged. In addition, the UK government's reluctance to support anti-Communist rebellions did not extend to covert efforts to discredit the ideological foundations of the Soviet and Chinese regimes through the unattributable propaganda disseminated by the Foreign Office's

---

[52] White, *Britain, détente*, 10, 42. COS(52)28, appendix (n.d.1952), DEFE 13/352; HDC(55)3, 'The defence implications of fall-out from a hydrogen bomb', 11 Mar. 1955, CAB 134/940.

[53] L. Nuti and V. Zubok, 'Ideology', in S. Dockrill and G. Hughes (eds), *Advances in Cold War history*, Basingstoke 2006, 76–82; J. L. Gaddis, *Strategies of containment: a critical appraisal of post-war American national security policy*, New York 1982, 189.

euphemistically-named Information Research Department.[54] This approach reflected Britain's reduced influence worldwide. For example, the British could not act as though Mao's regime did not exist as long as their interests in Hong Kong were at stake. It was also significant that British politicians – both Labour and Conservative – avoided the strident and vitriolic anti-Communist rhetoric which characterised American political discourse, and that there was no equivalent of 'McCarthyism' in London.[55]

As far as commercial, cultural and scientific contacts were concerned, both Eden and Macmillan stated that Anglo-Soviet co-operation in these areas would have mutually beneficial results: the latter's visit to Moscow led to the conclusion of a five-year bilateral trade agreement. The Soviets had an interest in acquiring Western consumer goods and sophisticated technology, while from the UK's perspective commercial contacts were a means of encouraging internal change in the Eastern bloc.[56] The British therefore sought to develop trading links with the USSR, and frequently clashed with the Americans over the extent of the strategic trade embargo imposed on the Communist powers, regulated since 1950 by the Co-ordinating Commission.[57] The idea that the influence of Communist ideology on the policies of the Soviet bloc states would gradually diminish, and that closer transnational contacts in trade and cultural relations could encourage this process, had been expressed by Churchill and the PUSD in the early 1950s. A decade later, the presumption that the Communist states would slowly liberalise their Stalinist political and economic systems helped to influence Foreign Office thinking on the long-term future of the Soviet bloc.

54 White, Britain, détente, 37–40; SC(67)17, 'Communist policies and propaganda: our response', 6 Mar. 1967, TNA, FCO 49/58.
55 Hennessy, Secret state, 86–97.
56 D. Wilson, 'Anglo-Soviet relations: the effect of ideas upon reality', IIA i/3 (1974), 386–7; SC(67)17, FCO 49/58.
57 I. Jackson, The economic Cold War: America, Britain and East-West trade, 1948–63, Basingstoke 2001, 7, 66–72, 109–11, 125–7; Macmillan diaries, 133, 289–90, entries for 17 Jan. 1952 and 18 Jan. 1954.

2

The UK and East-West Relations, 1964–1965

Labour won the 1964 general election with a bare majority of only three parliamentary seats. Moreover, soon after Wilson occupied 10 Downing Street on 16 October he had to address several pressing issues with a direct effect on Britain's economic and foreign policies:

> The Chinese had, the previous day, exploded their first nuclear weapon ... There was a telegram appraising the situation in the Soviet Union following the overthrow, less than twenty-four hours earlier, of Mr Khrushchev and the appointment of Mr Kosygin ... There was anxious news of the 'confrontation', the war between Indonesia and Malaysia, ... [and], grimmest of all, there was the economic news.[1]

Throughout the election campaign Labour assailed the government of Sir Alec Douglas-Home for its mismanagement of the economy, but Wilson and his ministers later professed to be shocked by the scale of Britain's economic difficulties. Labour inherited a balance of payments deficit of £800 million which contributed to a prolonged struggle to prevent devaluation. The threat of devaluation not only dominated much of the government's term in office, but it also had important implications for the UK's defence policy and, indirectly, its Cold War strategy.[2]

East-West relations were rarely mentioned during Labour's election campaign, aside from a few statements by Wilson and other senior shadow ministers which reflected the general impression that tensions between the USSR and other Western powers had eased perceptibly, and that the prospects for *détente* were promising. The foreign affairs section of Labour's 1964 manifesto placed a greater emphasis on political and commercial ties with the Commonwealth, and on the provision of aid to newly-independent former colonies, notably in Africa, than on issues more germane to the Cold War such as arms control and Germany.[3] This reflected Labour's ideology on international affairs, which emphasised the importance of international co-operation (particularly through the UN) at the expense of policies calcu-

---

[1] Pimlott, *Wilson*, 282–3; H. Wilson, *The Labour government, 1964–1970: a personal record*, London 1971, 2–3.
[2] The effect of economic underperformance on Labour's defence policy is discussed in greater detail in chapter 4 below.
[3] I. Dale (ed.), *Labour Party general election manifestos, 1900–1997*, Abingdon 2000, 119–22; P. Alexander, 'A tale of two Smiths: the transformation of Commonwealth policy', *CBH* xx/3 (2006), 303–6.

lated on the basis of national self-interest, and many of its MPs believed that the focus of British external policy should be on the development of the post-colonial world, rather than the Cold War confrontation with the Communist powers.[4] The contrast between the idealism of the Labour core and the pragmatic calculations ministers had to make once in office had been demonstrated by the dispute over rearmament policy in 1951, and contributed to the dispute between the Wilson government and the core of the party over Vietnam from 1965 onwards.

To a certain extent Wilson shared these ideals, and he assumed office with a pronounced pro-Commonwealth bias as far as external affairs were concerned. However, he rejected the left's ideas on post-imperialism, and expressed his government's determination to maintain Britain's military presence East of Suez. The new prime minister believed that even after decolonisation the British armed forces could be employed as a stabilising, peacekeeping force within Britain's former imperial spheres of influence. The economic and strategic burdens of balancing East of Suez with NATO commitments created a dilemma for the government which was gradually resolved in late 1967–early 1968, when Labour opted for a more Eurocentric approach to external affairs. None the less, it is important to recognise that the Wilson government initially viewed all aspects of foreign policy – including relations with the USSR – through the prism of Britain's 'world role', and throughout its term in office Labour had to address foreign policy problems which were of peripheral relevance to East-West politics – notably the 'confrontation' between Indonesia and Malaysia caused by the former's territorial claims on Northern Borneo, the unilateral declaration of independence by the white separatist regime in Rhodesia (November 1965), and the Nigerian civil war (July 1967–January 1970) – which competed for time and attention with policy issues more pertinent to the Cold War.[5]

Looking retrospectively at the first months of the Wilson government it is easy to forget that the Cold War was still being waged, albeit at a lower intensity than at the beginning of the 1960s, and that the USSR, the East European 'satellites' and China still constituted significant problems for British foreign and defence policies. Wilson entered office with his own views on Anglo-Soviet relations, based on his previous experiences in the USSR both as a visiting minister and as an opposition MP, and he was keen to improve commercial ties with the Soviet bloc states. However, throughout its term in office the Wilson government's approach to East-West relations was shaped by three factors. The first was Labour's own internal debates on Cold War-related foreign and defence policy issues, which originated with the disputes between the party's left and right wings during its thirteen years in opposition. The second was the policy precedents established under

---

4   Callaghan, *Foreign policy*, passim; Keohane, 'Labour's international policy', passim.
5   Interview with Oliver Wright, DOHP, transcript, 12; D. Easter, *Britain and the confrontation with Indonesia, 1960–66*, London 2004.

previous governments, and the deliberations within the Foreign Office, MoD and other Whitehall departments over internal developments within the Eastern bloc and the effect that these would have on East-West relations as a whole. The third factor related to wider trends in international politics, notably superpower relations, developments within the Communist world (in particular the Sino-Soviet split), and the dynamics of intra-Western relationships, especially the evolution of alliance ties between the USA and Western European states.

The policy-making structure in Whitehall

Before examining the foreign policy aspect of what the Wilson government (in a conscious echo of Kennedy's rhetoric) called its first 'hundred days', it is worth summarising the characteristics of, and influences upon, the decision-making process in Whitehall as it existed in late 1964. At its apex were the prime minister and the Cabinet, supported by the Cabinet Office and its network of committees, such as Overseas Policy and Defence, which, like all other ministerial committees, had its own counterpart comprised of officials, OPD(O). During his premiership, Wilson limited the Cabinet's role in foreign and defence policy issues, most notably regarding British nuclear policy, preferring to devolve decision-making to either *ad hoc* committees, such as PN or to the OPD.[6] Aside from the OPD and OPD(O), the JIC played an important role in co-ordinating the analysis of Britain's foreign intelligence-gathering efforts. The Foreign Office provided the chairman, and consensus was thrashed out between the external affairs ministries (the Foreign Office, the Colonial Office (until its merger with the Commonwealth Relations Office in 1967) and the CRO), the MoD, COS and the intelligence services (SIS, the MoD's Defence Intelligence Service (DIS), GCHQ, and the internal security service, MI5) before assessments were passed on to ministers.[7] The JIC also had four subcommittees overseeing regions crucial to the UK's overseas interests – in Germany, Cyprus, the Middle East and in Singapore. In April 1968 the JIC was subdivided into two committees, with JIC(A) focusing on political and military intelligence, and JIC(B) focusing on economic assessments. Critics argue that the attempts by the JIC to impose consensus and to iron out inter-departmental and inter-service controversies meant that its assessments represented a 'bureaucratic lowest common denominator, devoid of any imagination'. The British intelligence community's failure to anticipate the Soviet invasion of Czechoslo-

[6] S. James, *British Cabinet government*, Abingdon 1992, 126–7, 146–7; P. Hennessy, *The prime minister*, London 2000, 289.
[7] M. Herman, *Intelligence power in peace and war*, Cambridge 1996, 29–35.

vakia in August 1968 showed that the JIC's analysis and assessment structure had evident flaws.[8]

Richard Crossman, one of Wilson's closest political allies, was convinced that ministers were in thrall to Whitehall's officials, and were unable to challenge established agendas within their respective departments. However, the prime minister and members of Cabinet retained considerable influence on policy-making.[9] Following Kosygin's visit in February 1967 Wilson cajoled a reluctant Foreign Office into negotiating a 'treaty of friendship' with the USSR. Michael Stewart's career as Foreign Secretary (January 1965–August 1966; March 1968–June 1970) shows that a minister who shares the departmental view on a particular policy issue is not necessarily under the excessive influence of his subordinates. The fact that Stewart accepted Foreign Office recommendations to adopt a tougher line towards the Soviets in the spring of 1968 derived mainly from of his own views on the course of contemporary East-West relations.

Critics of the Foreign Office tended to claim that its officials were either inflexible Russophobes, or were 'soft' on the Soviets.[10] During the period of the first Wilson government, prevailing opinion within the Foreign Office, notably within the PUSD, supported *détente* in principle. However, the opinions of individual officials differed as far as the practical conduct of East-West relations was concerned. Two of the ambassadors to Moscow during this period, Geoffrey Harrison and Duncan Wilson, frequently stressed the importance of Anglo-Soviet contacts as a means of improving East-West relations. On the other hand, there were individuals who were more sceptical about the prospects of improved bilateral relations, and were more suspicious of Soviet intentions. Thomas Brimelow, who subsequently became Deputy Under-Secretary, witnessed Stalin's annexation of Latvia in 1939 and the mass deportation of civilians by the NKVD, and these experiences shaped his own impressions of the fundamental nature of the Soviet system. According to Denis Greenhill, the Deputy Undersecretary responsible for defence and intelligence-related issues, there were also some initial concerns within the Foreign Office regarding how Labour ministers would deal with 'the high priests of socialism' in the Kremlin. Greenhill noted in his memoirs that 'senior members of the Labour Party often felt ill at ease meeting Soviet leaders. It was as if they were non-conformists meeting the Pope'. Greenhill and other officials did not consider Labour politicians to be disloyal to their country's interests, but wondered whether they would be fooled by Soviet protestations of goodwill. These concerns became particularly prevalent in

---

8   Young, *Labour governments*, 16; M. Urban, *UK eyes alpha: the inside story of British intelligence*, London 1997, 8–9.

9   *Crossman diaries*, i. 616, entry for 24 Aug. 1966; M. Williams, *Inside Number 10*, London 1972, 123, 148–9; James, *Cabinet government*, 37–8.

10 R. Armstrong (PM's office) to B. Trend (Cabinet Office), 3 Aug. 1970, PREM 15/174; Gore-Booth, *With great truth*, 419.

the late 1960s, when the Warsaw Pact states proved adept at exploiting pro-détente sentiment in the West in order to undermine NATO unity.[11]

The MoD and the COS naturally played a significant role in the security aspects of East-West relations, particularly regarding the military dimensions of the Soviet 'threat'. The service chiefs were exasperated with the Wilson government's defence reviews, arguing that the British armed forces were stretched to their limit in meeting their NATO and East of Suez commitments. However the Treasury applied constant pressure to cut defence expenditure, particularly as the pressure on the pound intensified and Britain's balance of payments deficit worsened. Denis Healey's sour comment that the MoD was caught between the Treasury (which knew 'the price of everything and the value of nothing') and the Foreign Office (treating 'every commitment as an invaluable pearl without price') reflected the bureaucratic wrangling between the three departments involved, which contributed in particular to the controversy over BAOR's foreign exchange costs in 1966–7.[12]

As far as Britain's trading relations with the Soviet bloc were concerned, the Foreign Office had to consult other Whitehall departments, notably the Board of Trade and the Ministry of Technology, the latter established by Wilson in October 1964. While BoT officials generally doubted that trade with the Eastern bloc would yield any substantial commercial or political benefits, Mintech was more willing to explore areas of technological co-operation with the Warsaw Pact states. According to Stephen Dorril and Robin Ramsay, this made Mintech the 'focus of hostility from the UK-USA military and intelligence [services]'.[13] COCOM rules did restrict the scope of East-West technological exchanges, but a closer examination of British commercial policy shows that hostility towards increased trade and civilian scientific co-operation with Eastern bloc countries was far less widespread within Whitehall than Dorril and Ramsay suggest.

A final factor shaping British policy towards East-West relations concerns the complex alliance ties linking the UK with other Western powers. The 'special relationship' with the USA counted because of Western Europe's dependence on American military power, and because of the close co-operation between the Americans and British on defence, nuclear and intelligence issues.[14] Britain was also obliged to consider the interests of its European allies not only on diplomatic and military matters (within NATO and the WEU) but also on the economic aspects of East-West relations

[11] D. Greenhill, More by accident, York 1993, 120; G. Walden, Lucky George: memoirs of an anti-politician, London 1999, 141–6.

[12] COS(65)1st meeting, 5 Jan. 1965, DEFE 4/179; P. Catterall (ed.), 'Witness seminar: the East of Suez decision', Contemporary Record vii/3 (1993), 634; Crossman diaries, i. 615–16, entry for 24 Aug. 1966; D. Healey, The time of my life, London 1990, 256.

[13] I. Gray (BoT) to G. Scullard (FO), 16 June 1965, N1905/2, FO 371/182525; S. Dorril and R. Ramsay, Smear! Wilson and the secret state, London 1992, 194.

[14] US embassy, London, to State Dept, A-3692, 1 June 1968, NSF, LBJLIB, UK country file 212.

(through COCOM and, after 1967, due to Britain's attempt to join the EEC). For example, the Wilson government's attempt to gain membership of the EEC, and its interest in encouraging West Germany to seek *rapprochement* with the Eastern bloc states, led the UK to focus more on its relationship with the FRG, which had been damaged by the Berlin crisis and Macmillan's animosity towards Adenauer. Fortunately for Wilson, Adenauer retired in October 1963, and was succeeded as chancellor by the less assertive and more conciliatory Ludwig Erhard. None the less, the Erhard government was apprehensive about Wilson's election victory because of Labour party pronouncements on disengagement and its ill-disguised misgivings over German reunification.[15] Given the essential importance of the German question to the Cold War in Europe, the Anglo-German relationship was of direct relevance to British policy towards the Soviet bloc.

British assessments of the USSR and the Communist world in 1964

The point of departure for official analyses of Soviet foreign policy was, unsurprisingly, the fact that the USSR was a military power second only to the USA. The MoD and JIC had concluded in 1961 that Soviet military doctrine had no concept of 'limited war', and that the USSR was unlikely to risk the consequences of a third global conflict. The COS were confident that the only contingencies that NATO needed to prepare for, other than a nuclear response to a general Warsaw Pact offensive, were 'accidental' border clashes or probing attacks initiated by the Soviets to test the Alliance's resolve. If NATO could not deal with either of these contingencies by conventional means, tactical nuclear weapons would be used against the aggressors. At the same time, the Alliance would employ diplomatic channels to '[convince] the Soviets of NATO's resolve to defend itself and of the dangers of escalation, possibly uncontrolled, to the strategic nuclear exchange'. The service chiefs were none the less convinced that, in the words of the Chief of the Defence Staff, Lord Mountbatten, 'there is no Soviet objective in Europe which they consider worth the devastating price they would pay in their attempt to achieve it'.[16] There was more than a degree of complacency in Mountbatten's predictions. Recent research confirms that Warsaw Pact contingency plans involved the instant use of nuclear weapons in any war against NATO, and that senior Soviet military officers were confident that the USSR and its allies would inevitably prevail even in this scenario. The

---

[15] R. G. Hughes, '"We are not seeking strength for its own sake": the British Labour party, West Germany and the Cold War, 1951–64', *CWH* iii/1 (2002), 67–94.
[16] JIC(64)18(Final), CAB 158/52; DP33/64(Final), 26 Apr. 1964, DEFE 4/168; COS 245/64, 26 Aug. 1964, DEFE 5/153; COS 63rd/64 meeting, 27 Oct. 1964, DEFE 4/176.

COS's assessment that that the escalation in any East-West conflict could be controlled was therefore entirely unrealistic.[17]

The consensus within American and British officialdom was that after the setbacks over Berlin and Cuba the USSR had an interest in easing East-West tensions. This conclusion derived from State Department and Foreign Office analyses of internal developments within the USSR and its sphere of influence during the late 1950s and early 1960s. The period immediately preceding Labour's election victory had been marked by considerable changes in Soviet politics and society. Khrushchev began the process of de-Stalinisation with his 'secret speech' at the twentieth congress of the CPSU in February 1956. The Soviet leader was constrained both by the need to preserve the Communist party's authority and by his close association with Stalin's brutal regime, and although he curbed the powers of the KGB, freed thousands of political prisoners and granted limited cultural freedoms (as symbolised by the publication in 1962 of Alexander Solzhenitsyn's *One day in the life of Ivan Denisovich*), the USSR remained a totalitarian state. De-Stalinisation also affected the Soviet sphere of influence in Eastern Europe. Stalin had broken off inter-party relations with Yugoslavia in 1948 because of Marshal Tito's independent policies, and the East European Communist parties were subsequently purged of 'Titoite' members (namely, those who were less than subservient to Moscow's leadership). Khrushchev's visit to Belgrade in 1955 not only demonstrated Soviet acceptance of Yugoslavia's right to follow its 'own road' to socialism, but it also undermined those East European leaders who had risen to power in the late 1940s (the so-called 'little Stalins'). The following year Khrushchev acquiesced in Gomulka's rise to power in order to preserve Communism in Poland, but his response to the Hungarian rising showed that the USSR would use force to prevent any challenge to its dominance over Eastern Europe.[18]

Having assumed complete control over the party and government by 1957, Khrushchev initiated ambitious economic and agrarian programmes, notably the 'Virgin Lands' scheme which opened large tracts of Siberia and Kazakhstan to agricultural cultivation. At the twenty-second CPSU Congress (November 1961), he boasted that by 1980 the USSR would have a truly 'Communist' economic system which would be more productive than that of the USA. However, the Soviet economy suffered not only from the arms race with the Americans, but from the failure of the Virgin Lands plan, and poor harvests fuelled outbursts of public unrest and an uprising in the South Russian city of Novocherkassk (June 1962). In 1963 the USSR had to import grain from the West, which was costly in terms of both foreign exchange

---

[17] P. Lunak, 'Planning for nuclear war: the Czechoslovak war plan of 1964', *CWIHP Bulletin* xii/xiii (2001), 289–8.

[18] Taubman, *Khrushchev*, 270–99; Crampton, *Eastern Europe*, 283–303. Khrushchev's speech was translated and reprinted in the *Guardian* on 28 April 2007.

expenditure and in prestige.[19] Due to the scale of internal economic problems – agricultural failures, slow economic growth and hard currency shortages – the Soviets had an ostensible interest not only in easing the burden of military expenditure, but also in developing trading links with the West and in securing foreign credits.[20]

However, there were two significant constraints on the USSR's ability to seek *rapprochement* with the West, the first of which involved the ideology of the CPSU's elite and the delicate balance of power within the *Politburo*. British officials were aware that Khrushchev, who had thwarted one effort to overthrow him in 1957, could face future challenges to his leadership. The key question here was whether he could both pursue reform and maintain his personal authority over his peers, many of whom adopted a more conservative stance emphasising ideological purity and the preservation of the political *status quo*. The JIC optimistically concluded that as a consequence of the USSR's economic plight, the Soviet leadership was obliged to 'adapt its policies to the realities of life'. The introduction of new technology to Soviet industry would therefore encourage the emergence of a more technocratic, independent-minded managerial class. The CPSU also faced popular pressure for increased production of consumer goods and improvements in housing and welfare. British diplomats at the Moscow embassy were conscious of the failings of the Soviet economy and the theoretical need for reform; the ambassador, Humphrey Trevelyan, quipped that 'Khrushchev's achievement was to sow wheat in Siberia and harvest it in Canada'. However, Trevelyan's subordinates suspected that, as the minister at the embassy, Thomas Brimelow put it, the 'massive inertia, conservatism and inefficiency of the Soviet system' and the vested interests of the CPSU elite would impede necessary reforms.[21]

The second constraint involved the Sino-Soviet schism, the basic causes of which involved Chinese opposition to *détente*, competition for leadership of the Communist world and mutual contempt between Khrushchev and Mao Zedong. The latter vehemently rejected the Soviet leader's argument that 'socialism' could be spread by peaceful means, and that the end of capitalism did not necessarily entail war between the 'imperialist' and 'socialist' states. As the split became evident to the Western countries in 1963-4, US officials gradually concluded that the PRC had 'usurped the role of the Soviet Union ... as [the USA's] most troublesome adversary'. These percep-

---

19 Service, *Russia*, 349-52, 361-4, 375; G. Hosking, A *history of the Soviet Union, 1917-1991*, London 1992, 352-3, 388-9.
20 NIE11-9-64, 'Soviet foreign policy', 19 Feb. 1964, in 'The Soviet estimate: US analysis of the Soviet Union 1947-1991', LHCMA, MFF15/390-2; 'Trends and implications of Soviet policy: April-November 1964', NS1022/19, FO 371/177670.
21 JIC(64)43, 'The power struggle in the Soviet Union and the problem of succession', 17 Apr. 1964, CAB 158/53; T. Brimelow (Moscow) to E. Orchard (ND), 6 Mar. 1964, NS1015/11, FO 371/177664; H. Trevelyan to P. Gordon-Walker, 1 Jan. 1965, FO 371/182741.

tions were reinforced by the Communist insurgency in Vietnam and the development of the Chinese nuclear programme.[22] From the British perspective, the Sino-Soviet split had three additional consequences. First, rivalry between the USSR and the PRC would intensify Chinese militancy and support for governments and political movements (notably North Vietnam and the Indonesian Communist Party, or PKI) challenging Western interests in Asia. Second, Soviet efforts to develop *détente* would be constrained by China's efforts to supplant the USSR as Communism's ideological hegemon. Third, the Soviet leadership was asserting its 'anti-imperialist' credentials and its support for 'national liberation' movements in response to the Chinese efforts to undermine the USSR's influence in the Third World. While the Soviet state media assailed the UK's East of Suez policy, the USSR provided Indonesia's President, Ahmed Sukarno, with military and moral support for his efforts to destabilise Malaysia, Britain's principal ally in South-East Asia. The Chinese ideological challenge therefore served only to intensify Soviet efforts to weaken Western strategic and economic interests in the underdeveloped world.[23]

De-Stalinisation had significant potential consequences for Soviet dominance over Eastern Europe. The Albanian leader, Enver Hoxha, rejected Soviet 'revisionism' and preserved an orthodox Stalinist system in his country, while the Romanian Communist regime combined rigid domestic totalitarianism with a more assertive, nationalistic approach to intra-bloc relations. In Hungary, after the upheavals of 1956, Janos Kadar introduced socio-economic reforms which led his country to be known as 'the happiest barrack in the Socialist camp'.[24] These developments led the Foreign Office's PUSD to revisit the assumptions it had made on the processes of reform in Eastern Europe. Official British thinking on the future of the Eastern bloc had concluded that the process of political and economic liberalisation depended on the Soviet leadership moderating the harsh ideological line set by Stalinism, and accepting both *détente* with the West and the right of East European 'satellites' to adopt more autonomous socio-economic policies better suited to their own national needs. In a revised assessment produced in January 1964, the PUSD concluded that since 1956 the Warsaw Pact coun-

[22] Moscow to FO, no.711, 17 Apr. 1964, NS1072/23, FO 371/177670; C. Jian and Y. Kuisong, 'Chinese politics and the collapse of the Sino-Soviet alliance', in O. A. Westad (ed.), *Brothers in arms: the rise and fall of the Sino-Soviet alliance, 1945–1963*, Washington, DC 2000, 226–94; M. Jones, '"Groping toward coexistence": US China policy during the Johnson years', *DS* xii/3 (2001), 175

[23] M. Jones, *Conflict and confrontation in South-East Asia, 1961–1965: Britain, the United States and the creation of Malaysia*, Cambridge 2001, 237; H. Smith (ND) to R. A. Butler, 20 Mar. 1964, NS1022/17, and Moscow to FO, no. 608, 3 Apr. 1964, NS1022/22, FO 371/177610.

[24] Crampton, *Eastern Europe*, 307–8, 311–14; V. Tismaneanu, 'Gheorghiu-Dej and the Romanian Workers party: from de-Sovietization to the emergence of national Communism' (CWHIP working paper xxxvii, May 2002).

tries relied less on state terror and overt coercion, and more on improving domestic living standards and working conditions. To fulfil these conditions the East European countries needed Western capital and technology (particularly computers) in order to modernise their economies. The Communist regimes therefore had an incentive to develop less adversarial relations with Western Europe and the USA. Foreign Office officials expected that the Sino-Soviet split would enable the 'satellite' regimes to exercise greater autonomy, and that the Soviets would tolerate limited reforms within the Eastern bloc states in return for their continued allegiance to the USSR and the ideological line set in Moscow. Britain and other NATO powers could tacitly encourage both *détente* and internal reform by developing closer commercial, cultural and scientific contacts with the Warsaw Pact states. British diplomats still regarded anti-Communist risings behind the Iron Curtain as both futile and a threat to continental peace. The processes of *détente* and of the 'liberalisation' of the Soviet bloc were considered to be mutually supporting, and the long-term result would be the erosion of Communist dogma and the relaxation of Cold War tensions. To quote the PUSD Planning Staff's optimistic assessment, 'any weakening of the Soviet hold over the Satellites … will come about through *evolution* rather than *revolution*'.[25]

This concept of 'evolution' provided the basis for Foreign Office proposals to liberalise Britain's trade with bloc states, and also for efforts to improve political relations and develop *détente* with the Warsaw Pact powers. Foreign Office officials argued that it was no longer appropriate to treat the Eastern bloc states as Soviet puppets, and that the British government should be 'ready to discuss seriously with [the East Europeans] our attitude on major policy questions, even if we have little hope of thereby changing their attitude'.[26] Poland was regarded as a strong candidate for bilateral political contacts because of the disarmament initiatives associated with both Gomulka and Rapacki, and the fact that the Polish regime was more 'liberal' than those of other Soviet bloc states. However, Poland's reputation as a comparatively reform-minded state in Eastern Europe proved to be ephemeral, as Gomulka's regime – having ended the collectivisation of agriculture and after granting considerable concessions to the intelligentsia and the Catholic Church – became progressively more authoritarian during the 1960s.[27]

The Planning Staff's report, 'Policy towards the East European satellites', gradually gathered support within Whitehall. The JIC agreed with the

---

25 SC(61)25, 'United Kingdom policy towards the satellites', 27 June 1961, emphasis added, and C. Tickell (Planning Staff) note, 24 Jan. 1964, PLA13/1; SC(64)1; 'Policy towards the East European satellites', 27 Jan. 1964, PLA13/2, FO 371/177821.

26 ND note, 11 June. 1965, and E.Youde (ND), 16 June 1965, FO 371/182529; FO to missions, no. 349 guidance, 1 June 1964, FO 371/177410.

27 Interview with R. Braithwaite, DOHP, transcript, 2; C. Thompson (ND) to J. Whitehead (Washington), 20 Oct. 1964, N1015/22, FO 371/177407; Crampton, *Eastern Europe*, 316–19.

assessment that 'nearly all of the former "satellites" now enjoy some degree of independence from the Soviet Union', although its analysts noted that this 'growing diversity and fluidity within the Soviet bloc' could prove short-lived if *détente* collapsed and East-West rivalries intensified.[28] This consensus received further support from the meeting of British ambassadors to the USSR and Eastern Europe, convened in London in April 1964. A summary of the Foreign Office's views on 'evolution' was forwarded to Patrick Gordon Walker shortly after he became Foreign Secretary in October. This memorandum acknowledged that Khrushchev's downfall had not been anticipated, but concluded that his successors would not crack down on liberalisation within Eastern Europe unless the USSR's supremacy over the region were threatened.[29] The optimistic conclusions of 'Policy towards the East European satellites' were reflected in the works of contemporary academic specialists. It is also worth noting that British officials remained unwilling to contemplate covert action 'to set the governments and peoples of Eastern Europe against the Soviet Union', as practised by the American and British intelligence services in the 1950s, because such an approach would 'be self-defeating', leading only to further repression behind the Iron Curtain and the dangerous intensification of East-West hostilities.[30]

While Foreign Office officials were agreed that the Eastern bloc was gradually becoming less reppressive and less doctrinaire, most tended to be cautious as far as the pace of 'evolution' was concerned. One notable exception was Duncan Wilson, the assistant undersecretary of the Northern Department responsible for Soviet affairs. He argued that the East European leaderships would follow Tito's example, developing their own 'national Communist' policies without interference from Moscow. Other officials were less optimistic. Trevelyan argued that although the USSR was suffering from 'an economic malaise .... [ideology], bureaucracy and the need to maintain the balance of military power' with the USA 'will all exercise a strong conservative influence on Soviet policy' and would forestall internal reforms. The CPSU was determined to maintain its 'leading role' over both Soviet society and the Communist world, and the *Politburo* would tolerate neither political pluralism, or Yugoslav-style 'national Communism', in any of the Warsaw Pact states. Trevelyan also suggested that the Soviet bloc regimes could not introduce limited reforms without inspiring popular demands for

[28] JIC(64)25(Final), 'Relations between the Soviet Union and Communist countries in Eastern Europe', 17 July 1964, CAB 158/52.
[29] 'Conclusions of HM ambassadors' conference on Eastern Europe', 21–3 Apr. 1964, N1015/31, FO 371/177405; H. Smith (ND) to P. Gordon Walker, 19 Oct. 1964, N1051/G, FO 371/177410.
[30] G. Ionescu, *The break-up of the Soviet empire in Eastern Europe*, London 1965, 150–7; G. F. Hudson, *Fifty years of Communism: theory and practice, 1917–1967*, London 1968, 187–8; D. Zagoria, *The Sino-Soviet conflict, 1956–61*, Princeton, NJ 1967, 394–401; SC(64)20, 'Current trends in the policy of Communist powers and implications for our propaganda', 1 May 1964, PLA13/4, FO 371/177821.

more radical changes, provoking future outbreaks of unrest similar to those in East Berlin in 1953, in Poland and Hungary three years later, and in Novocherkassk in 1962.[31]

Over the previous decade the British government had been at odds with the USA and other allied powers over both the interpretation of Soviet policy and developments in the Communist world. Yet by 1964 other Western governments had concluded that the prospects for *détente* had improved. De Gaulle firmly backed Adenauer during the Berlin crisis, but by 1964 the French president spoke of the eventual emergence of a '*Europe totale*', unencumbered by ideological divisions and stretching 'from the Atlantic to the Urals'. De Gaulle argued that 'Russian' national interests would eventually prevail over Communist ideology, and that as the USSR became preoccupied with China, the Soviets would loosen their grip on Eastern Europe. With the disappearance of the 'Soviet threat', NATO would disintegrate, the USA would withdraw from European affairs and France would emerge as Western Europe's spokesman in negotiations with 'Russia', leading the way from East-West *détente* to continental *entente*. De Gaulle considered this outcome to be inevitable, informing the US ambassador to Paris that the growth of East-West trade would soon result in 'the end of Communism as the Soviets now conceive it'.[32]

Johnson inherited the policy of developing *détente* with the USSR which Kennedy had followed before his assassination. The US president alluded to Khrushchev when he told the Soviet ambassador to Washington, Anatolii Dobrynin, that '[we] do not want to bury the Soviet Union, but at the same time we do not want to be buried'. In his 'bridge-building speech' at Lexington, Virginia, in May 1964, the president also advocated the establishment of closer cultural and commercial relations between the USA and Eastern Europe. It was an election year, and Johnson's pro-*détente* policy proved to be more popular with the American public than the hawkish rhetoric of his Republican opponent, Barry Goldwater.[33] Although Goldwater's virulent anti-Communism was criticised by the administration, some of Johnson's officials did suggest that the USA could exploit the Eastern bloc's economic difficulties for political leverage. The prevailing view – as expressed by the Secretary of State, Dean Rusk, and Johnson's special assistant for national security affairs, McGeorge Bundy – was that restric-

---

31 D. Wilson, *Forward from socialism?*, 4 Feb. 1964, FO 371/177404; comments by Trevelyan (Moscow), 27 Feb. 1964, N1015/21, FO 371/177405.

32 G.-H. Soutou, 'De Gaulle's France and the Soviet Union from conflict to *détente*', in Loth, *Cold War and coexistence*, 73–89; Paris to State Dept., no.3517, 11 Dec. 1964, and no. 4359, 2 Feb. 1965, 'Lyndon Johnson national security files: Western Europe, 1963–1969', LHCMA, MF403.

33 NSAM, 304, 3 June 1964, *FRUS*, XVII: *Eastern Europe, 1964–1968*, Washington, DC 1996 12; A. Dobrynin, *In confidence: Moscow's ambassador to America's six Cold War presidents (1962–1986)*, New York 1995, 128–9; T. Schwartz, *Lyndon Johnson and Europe: in the shadow of Vietnam*, Cambridge, MA 2003, 19–20, 43.

tions on 'non-strategic' trade with the Eastern bloc not only undermined the administration's 'bridge-building' pledges, but also gave West European and Japanese firms a free hand in trade with East European countries. A few months after his landslide election victory in November 1964, Johnson established the Miller Committee to examine how the USA could increase its share of non-strategic trade with the Eastern bloc states.[34]

By mid-1964 Foreign Office officials had concluded that the East European states were undergoing a process of 'evolution' from rigid, monolithic Stalinism towards a less oppressive and more autonomous 'polycentric' system, permitting greater scope for reform in individual states. The means available to Western powers to encourage 'evolution' were limited to trade, cultural exchanges and ministerial visits, but these would in the long-term help to develop *détente* and would assist East European efforts to gain greater autonomy from the USSR. Similar conclusions were being reached in Washington and Paris, while in the UK the Labour party and its leader, Harold Wilson, were also assessing the implications of the Eastern bloc's internal political developments, and the impact these would have for party policy.

Wilson, the Labour party and East-West relations, 1947–64

Apart from party-political loyalties, the principal difference between Wilson and his Conservative predecessors was that his pre-parliamentary career in academia and the civil service gave him considerable experience of socio-economic issues, but less interest in diplomatic or military affairs. For example, although he had controversially resigned from the Cabinet in April 1951 over increased defence expenditure, he subsequently played only a peripheral role in Labour debates on military-strategic issues such as unilateral nuclear disarmament and proposals for the disengagement of NATO and Warsaw Pact forces in Europe. Wilson's alignment with the Labour left effectively began with his departure from the Attlee government in April 1951. His relationship with his predecessor as party leader, Hugh Gaitskell, and other leading right-wingers was coloured by intense mutual dislike. Wilson's adversaries within the Labour party did not consider him to be a pro-Communist 'fellow-traveller' but saw him as a shameless opportunist, hence George Brown's bitter comment that '[if] we have to die in the last ditch Harold won't be there. He will have scrambled out'.[35]

This animosity made it all the more noteworthy that, following his election as Labour leader in January 1963, Wilson appointed many of his old

[34] M. Bundy to Johnson, 14 Apr. 1964; NSAM no.324, 9 Mar. 1965, *FRUS*, IX: *International development and economic defense policy: commodities*, Washington, DC 1997, 452–3, 481–2, 484–5.
[35] Pimlott, *Wilson*, 235, 242; *Patrick Gordon Walker: political diaries, 1932–1971*, ed. R. Pearce, London 1991, 267, entry for 2 June 1960.

adversaries to the shadow Cabinet. After October 1964 the right-wingers held the main ministerial posts. Brown became First Secretary of State in the Department of Economic Affairs and James Callaghan was appointed Chancellor of the Exchequer, even though both had stood against Wilson for the party leadership. Douglas Jay was appointed President of the Board of Trade, Patrick Gordon Walker became Foreign Secretary and Denis Healey was Defence Secretary throughout Labour's term in office. Wilson promoted his old enemies to maintain party unity, and also as part of the traditional political tactic of playing ones rivals off against each other. The uneasy relationship between the prime minister and his Cabinet colleagues reinforced what David Bruce, the US ambassador to London, referred to as Wilson's 'lone wolf' tendency. George Ball, Johnson's Under-Secretary of State, likewise observed in December 1964 that Wilson was 'on guard in the presence of his own Cabinet colleagues'. Barbara Castle, a left-wing minister and one of Wilson's allies, noted that the prime minister spoke in 'casual, throwaway tones' in Cabinet meetings, as if to dull the atmosphere and stifle debate. Wilson clearly took considerable care to conceal his thoughts from his colleagues.[36]

None the less, with regards to his impression of the USSR and his view of East-West relations, some conclusions can be drawn from both his career and his public pronouncements. As a junior minister at the Board of Trade, Wilson had travelled to Moscow in April 1947 to negotiate an Anglo-Soviet trade treaty, returning with a reputation as a tough, capable negotiator who had proved a match for his Soviet counterpart, Anastas Mikoyan.[37] As President of the Board of Trade, he suspended commercial relations with Hungary in 1949 after its government imprisoned a British businessman, Edgar Saunders, for espionage. In the same year Wilson also supported the Attlee government's decision to compile a list of items which British firms were forbidden to export to the Eastern bloc, an action which preceded the establishment of COCOM. His support for closer trading relations with Communist countries was therefore not unconditional. Yet following his resignation from the government in April 1951, Wilson's enthusiasm for trade with the Eastern bloc became more pronounced. In his 1952 pamphlet *In place of dollars*, he criticised the strategic embargo on East-West commerce, declaring that Britain needed 'greater freedom to develop trade with the non-dollar' countries, particularly the Eastern bloc states, in order to revive its economy. The

---

36 D. Bruce to R. Neustadt, 6 Dec. 1964, NSF, LBJLIB, UKCF 216; Ball note on conversation with Gordon-Walker and Wilson, 10 Downing St (No.10), 2 Dec. 1964, *FRUS*, XIII: *Western Europe region, 1964–1968*, Washington, DC 1995, 130; B. Castle, *The Castle diaries, 1964–70*, London 1984, 119, entry for 28 Apr. 1966.
37 Pimlott, *Wilson*, 99–102, 111–13; F. Roberts, *Dealing with dictators*, London 1991, 105–6.

author of *In place of dollars* did not, however, acknowledge his own role in imposing controls on exports to the Communist powers in 1949.[38]

After his resignation from Attlee's Cabinet in April 1951 Wilson became an advisor to the timber firm Montague Meyer Ltd, on whose behalf he paid a series of visits to the USSR and other Soviet bloc states until 1959. These visits subsequently provided the basis for the manifestly absurd conspiracy theories alleging that the future prime minister had been suborned by the KGB.[39] They also gave Wilson his life-long interest in East-West trade, and enabled him to portray himself as an expert on Soviet affairs. His visit to Moscow in May 1953 and his otherwise inconsequential meetings with the 'collective leadership' shaped his impressions of the post-Stalinist USSR. Following his return home, Wilson wrote a lengthy report to the prime minister, in which he claimed that Stalin's successors had a 'Bevanite' agenda of easing tensions with the West, reducing military expenditure and concentrating on domestic problems. It is doubtful that Churchill, who followed his own policy of 'easement' towards the Soviets, gave much thought to an opposition MP's unsolicited assessment of developments in the USSR. None the less, Wilson derived from his travels the conviction that the Soviet system was undergoing a long-term process of internal reform. In November 1956 he refused to sign an open letter of protest, drafted by other Labour MPs, which condemned the USSR's intervention in Hungary. Wilson insisted that Khrushchev's actions marked a 'tragic reversal of policy', which did not detract from the gradual liberalisation of the Soviet bloc.[40]

Wilson loathed Communism as an ideology, and in the summer of 1966 he condemned the Communist party of Great Britain for its alleged role in provoking the seamen's strike that year. He was, none the less, among the significant number of Labour politicians who continued to believe that 'Left understands Left', and that it was possible to achieve an amicable relationship with the Soviets without compromising Britain's security or independence. While the majority of Labour MPs were repelled by the political nature of the Soviet system, particularly its repressiveness and its human rights violations, many party members wondered whether the USSR's socio-economic model offered examples for democratic socialism to emulate, and Wilson's 'white heat' speech showed that he shared this view. As a backbencher Wilson opposed West German rearmament and the foundation of SEATO – both of which he regarded as examples of US escalatory policies which

---

[38] Pimlott, *Wilson*, 100–1; Jackson, *Economic Cold War*, 35. Saunders was released in 1953. See J. Rainer, 'The new course in Hungary in 1953' (CWIHP working paper xxxviii, 2002), 47; H. Wilson, *In place of dollars*, London 1952.

[39] Austen Morgan rebuts these conspiracy theories in *Wilson*, 233–7. See also C. Andrew and V. Mitrokhin, *The Mitrokhin archives*, I: *The KGB in Europe and the West*, i, London 1999, 527–8.

[40] R. Crossman, *The backbench diaries of Richard Crossman*, ed. Janet Morgan, London 1981, 249–56, entry for 22 June 1953; Wilson to Churchill, 6 June 1953, NS1631/11, NS1631/12, FO 371/106579; Pimlott, *Wilson*, 199.

were bound to provoke Soviet and Chinese hostility – and he also spoke in favour of recognising the GDR. He also shared the Labour left's hostility to Adenauer, and its impression of the FRG as both a barrier to East-West *rapprochement* and as a potential threat to European stability.[41] During the early 1960s Wilson gradually divested himself of the more extreme Bevanite beliefs. Much to the disgust of the party's hard left, soon after he assumed leadership of Labour he renounced his anti-Americanism and stressed the importance of the alliance ties with the USA. Wilson's visit to Washington in March 1964 was, as Rusk informed Johnson, intended to 'reassure you regarding his *reliability* as an ally'. The Secretary of State's comments showed that the Labour leader faced considerable distrust in official circles within Washington as a result of his left-wing past.[42]

Wilson's visits to the USSR strengthened his interests in East-West trade and also influenced his views on the use of 'democratic planning' as a means of reviving the UK's economy. Although British diplomats in Moscow were aware of the USSR's economic woes, Wilson's speech on the revolutionary nature of technological change at the Labour party conference at Scarborough (October 1963) owed much to his impressions of the apparent effectiveness of Soviet economic planning. The Labour leader made an ambitious pledge to reverse Britain's post-war decline, telling party members that 'those of us who have studied the formidable Soviet challenge … know that our future lies not in military strength alone but in the efforts, the sacrifices and above all the energies which a free people can mobilise for the future greatness of our country'. Wilson's efforts to put 'white heat' rhetoric into practice, and to harness the economic potential of the technological 'revolution', led to the establishment of Mintech and the ill-fated DEA. Although the rise and fall of these ministries lie outside the scope of this study, Wilson's impressions of the supposed successes of the Soviet command economy contributed to their creation and to the abortive 'National Plan' of 1966.[43]

While Wilson had been a Bevanite, his predecessor Gaitskell and the Labour right adhered to the Atlanticist policies established by Attlee and Bevin. Gaitskell was particularly suspicious of 'fellow travellers' within the Labour party and was compared to Senator Joseph McCarthy after he claimed in 1952 that one-sixth of party delegates were 'Communist or Communist-inspired'. The Labour right actually abhorred McCarthyite demagogy as much as the Bevanites did but Gaitskell, like Attlee, was determined to prevent

41 F. Beckett, *Enemy within: the rise and fall of the British Communist party*, London 1998, 156–7; Callaghan, *Foreign policy*, 217–19; Pimlott, *Wilson*, 184–5; Larres, 'Britain, East Germany', 124–5.

42 N. D. Lankford, *The Last American aristocrat: the biography of David K. E. Bruce, 1899–1977*, Boston MA 1996, 329; Dean Rusk to Johnson, 28 Feb. 1964, LHCMA, MF 410, emphasis original.

43 D. Edgerton, *Warfare state: Britain, 1920–1970*, Cambridge 2006, 239–41; Morgan, *People's peace*, 197–200; Callaghan, *Foreign policy*, 198–200.

the CPGB from infiltrating the Labour Party.[44] The Labour right's links with American trade unionists and CIA officials gave rise to the myth that Washington 'called the tune' to which the Labour party 'danced'. Robin Ramsay asserts that due to these contacts Labour right-wingers acquired opinions on the USA which were 'as rational as those held by their equivalents 20 years before, who had seen in the Stalinist Soviet Union the embodiment of their yearnings for a socialist society'. Yet Gaitskell, Healey, Brown and other leading figures of the Labour right were neither as inflexibly anti-Communist nor as slavishly pro-American as their contemporary and scholarly detractors suggest.[45] They were conscious of the ideological hostility of Communism towards rival democratic socialist parties, which was evident when Khrushchev publicly quarrelled with the Labour leadership during his visit to Britain in April 1956. As the party's international secretary during the late 1940s, Healey (a former CPGB member) recalled the grim fate of East European socialists who had refused to collaborate with the pro-Soviet regimes.[46] At the same time the Labour right's anti-Communism did not prevent Gordon Walker from criticising the American trade embargo on Cuba. Nor did it stop Gaitskell and Healey from welcoming the Rapacki plan of 1957, and from adding military disengagement in Europe (under the so-called 'Gaitskell Plan') to Labour's 1959 manifesto, much to the annoyance of the West German government.[47] None the less, after Labour's return to office in 1964 there was a profound difference of outlook between the majority of Wilson's ministers, and the sizeable body of left-wing backbenchers who considered NATO to be obsolete, favoured the unconditional abolition of the British nuclear deterrent, supported recognition of East Germany and were prone to outbursts of anti-Americanism.

Referring to the Labour right, Wilson spoke of 'running a Bolshevik revolution with a Tsarist shadow Cabinet'. Yet both he and his 'Tsarist' rivals agreed that the Soviet threat to Western Europe had diminished, and that the East European regimes were no longer mere puppets of the USSR.[48] The shadow Cabinet was also united in condemning the agreement Macmillan made with Kennedy to purchase the submarine-launched *Polaris* missile system as a replacement for the V bomber force (December 1962), and in

[44] Beckett, *Enemy within*, 114–15, 121; M. Stewart, *Life and Labour: an autobiography*, London 1980, 93–5; P. Deery, '"The secret battalion": Communism in Britain during the Cold War', CBH xiii/4 (1999), 1–28.
[45] R. Ramsay, 'Wilson and the security services', in Coopey, Fielding and Tiratsoo, *Wilson governments*, 152. H. Wilford, *The CIA, the British left and the Cold War, 1945–1960: calling the tune?*, London 2003.
[46] M. Bowker and P. Shearman, 'The Soviet Union and the left in Britain', in A. Pravda and P. Duncan (eds), *Soviet-British relations since the 1970s*, Cambridge 1990, 148–9; Taubman, *Khrushchev*, 357; Healey, *My life*, 85–8.
[47] Healey, *My life*, 178–80; *Gordon Walker diaries*, 290–2, entry for 30 May 1963.
[48] *Crossman's backbench diaries*, 987, entry for 12 Mar. 1963; P. Gordon Walker, 'The Labor party's defense and foreign policy', FA xlii/3 (1964), 390–8.

its opposition to American proposals to create a multi-lateral nuclear force in NATO. Prior to the 1964 election, the Labour party had united behind a pro-disarmament agenda, with an ambiguously-worded pledge to renounce the British deterrent in order to forestall any independent West German nuclear programme. Labour's manifesto proclaimed the party's intention to support the integration of NATO's nuclear weapons (as an alternative to the left's proposals on unilateral disarmament) so that Alliance members had a say in their deployment and control.[49] In addition, Wilson's public praise for Khrushchev's commitment to *détente* and the LTBT did not prevent him from condemning the threat the 'totalitarian Communism of China' posed to world peace.[50]

In his speeches Wilson emphasised the need to establish a 'friendly understanding' with the USSR much as he did the importance of the 'close' Anglo-American relationship. In June 1963 he travelled to Moscow with the shadow Foreign Secretary, the main event of the visit being the meeting between Wilson, Khrushchev, Gordon Walker and the Soviet Foreign Minister, Andrei Gromyko, on 10 June 1963. These talks were dominated by Khrushchev, who alternated between crude jokes at the expense of his visitors, and blustering threats over Berlin. The latter referred to the UK's vulnerability to nuclear attack, and he gave the Labour leader's proposal for Soviet-Western co-operation on Third World development short thrift. Wilson did not distinguish himself by sycophantically comparing Khrushchev with Lenin, and by asserting that '[we] have no respect either for Adenauer or for [Ulbricht]'. A second visit in June 1964 took place with less embarrassment, and the Soviets treated Wilson in a manner befitting a potential prime minister. The Labour leader took with him a 'master plan' for disarmament, involving a halt in the production of nuclear delivery vehicles, a 'bonfire' of obsolete bombers, a non-proliferation treaty and an agreement to 'freeze' the deployment of atomic weapons in Central Europe. Wilson also proposed to convene annual quadripartite summits between the superpowers, the UK and France. This 'master plan' simply amalgamated existing US and Soviet proposals on disarmament and, as expected, the Soviets rejected the first and second proposals, which the Johnson administration had initially raised in early 1964. Khrushchev expressed a vague interest in the annual summit proposal, but given the fact that Labour was still in opposition, the main purpose of the visit was symbolic.[51] When Wilson did eventually become

---

[49] B. Lapping, *The Labour government, 1964–70*, London 1970, 84–5, 93; Peter Catterall, 'Foreign and Commonwealth policy in opposition: the Labour party', in Kaiser and Staerck, *Foreign policy*, 93–4; *Manifestos*, 123–4.

[50] Speech at Bridgeport University, Connecticut, 3 Mar. 1964, in H. Wilson, *The new Britain: Labour's plan: outlined by Harold Wilson*, London 1964, 90–100.

[51] Ibid.; S. Dockrill, *East of Suez*, 45; Gordon-Walker, A. Gromyko, N. Khrushchev and Wilson conversation, Kremlin, 10 June 1963; Moscow to FO, no.1211, 15 June 1963; N. Henderson (FO) to J. O. Wright (No.10), 10 June 1964, PREM 11/4894; Pimlott, *Wilson*, 307–8.

prime minister, he found that he had to pursue his attempts to improve Anglo-Soviet relations with a new leadership in the Kremlin. He also had to address the consequence of China's emergence as a nuclear power for both East-West and Anglo-Soviet relations.

First steps, October 1964–January 1965

Labour's initial objectives, as cited in the queen's speech to parliament on 3 November 1964, included the promotion of multi-lateral negotiations for a nuclear non-proliferation treaty (NPT). This goal became more pressing once China became the world's fifth nuclear power. Douglas-Home was informed that a Chinese nuclear test was imminent when the director of the CIA, John McCone, visited London in September 1964. A month later the PRC conducted a successful test at Lop Nor in Xinjiang Province. American and British intelligence estimates concluded that China was unlikely to develop a short-range delivery capability before 1968, or to acquire long-range missile systems before 1975.[52] The main problem – as far as American and British officials were concerned – was that the Chinese test set a dangerous precedent for other states. India, having lost its border war with China in October 1962, was considered most likely to go nuclear in response. During his visit to London in December 1964 the Indian prime minister, Lal Bahadur Shastri, requested an Anglo-American guarantee to protect non-nuclear states against atomic blackmail. Officials in Whitehall and senior Labour MPs feared that if India became a nuclear power, the result would be widespread proliferation and increased global instability. Furthermore, Britain's East of Suez commitments could be threatened by nuclear-capable enemies.[53] Yet despite Shastri's request the non-aligned Indians later expressed their preference for a US-Soviet guarantee rather than an all-Western commitment, even though the USSR was unwilling to exacerbate its problems with China by agreeing to such a guarantee. In late March 1965 the OPD was advised by OPD(O) that the Western powers should offer no security assurances to Delhi unless 'the only alternative would be an Indian nuclear programme'. For both the USA and UK, this dilemma demonstrated the urgent need to halt the spread of nuclear weapons, although as discussed subsequently the

---

[52] 701.HC.Deb.5s, London 1964, 34–7; J. McCone–Douglas-Home conversation, No.10, 21 Sept. 1964, PREM 11/5147; CC(64)2nd Cabinet conclusions, 24 Oct. 1964, CAB 128/39. The Chinese did develop MRBMs by the mid-1960s, but the deployment of China's first ICBMs was delayed until 1980, by which time the USSR had become Beijing's main adversary: J. Lewis and H. Di, 'China's ballistic missile programs: technologies, strategies, goals', IS xvii/2 (1992), 9–19.

[53] Shastri–Wilson conversation, No.10, 4 Dec. 1964, PREM 13/973; S. Schrafstetter, 'Preventing the "smiling Buddha": British-Indian nuclear relations and the Commonwealth nuclear force, 1964–68', JSS xxv/3 (2002), 87–108.

process of drafting an NPT was hampered both by superpower rivalry and by the intra-Western debate over NATO nuclear sharing.[54]

Unlike the Chinese nuclear test, Khrushchev's downfall was unexpected. On the evening of 14 October 1964 the Soviet leader was summoned to a plenum of the Central Committee of the CPSU, during which he was assailed by the party's ideological chief, Mikhail Suslov, for his mismanagement of the economy and his high-handed treatment of the East Europeans and the Chinese. Other *Politburo* members joined in Suslov's denunciation of Khrushchev's record – '[not] leadership, but a complete merry-go-round!' – condemning the recklessness he had shown over Cuba in 1962. Following this arraignment, the Central Committee voted for Khrushchev's dismissal, consigning him to the political wilderness until his death in 1971. Brezhnev became CPSU Secretary and Kosygin was appointed premier, but there was also a younger generation of *Politburo* members, notably Alexander Shelepin (the former chairman of the KGB) and Dmitrii Polyanskii (appointed deputy premier), who had increased their influence as a result of the *coup*.[55]

The Foreign Office and JIC were aware of the failure of Khrushchev's economic policies, but his overthrow took them by surprise. Trevelyan attributed the Kremlin *coup* to Khrushchev's 'personal idiosyncrasies', the failure of his economic policies and his mishandling of Sino-Soviet relations. Both he and his superiors in the diplomatic corps presumed that there would be no sudden changes in Soviet policy towards East-West relations, and that the prospects for *rapprochement* with China were non-existent.[56] Allied assessments of the succession and its implications were expressed in similar terms, the American view being that Khrushchev's successors would conduct a less reckless foreign policy.[57] The Soviet ambassador to London, Alexei Soldatov, assured Wilson on 18 October that the new leadership would follow Khrushchev's policy on 'peaceful coexistence', and would develop commercial, cultural and scientific co-operation with Britain. However, Trevelyan's dispatches to the new Foreign Secretary expressed reservations as to how far Anglo-Soviet contacts would develop. The ambassador noted that Khrushchev had pursued a contradictory policy, distinguishing between avoiding an East-West 'war of extermination' while supporting 'wars of national liberation' directed against pro-Western regimes in the post-colonial world. By 1963 the Soviet leadership had discovered that increased military expenditure did not enhance security, but instead crippled the Soviet economy. The USSR

---

54 OPD(65)19th meeting, 31 Mar. 1965, CAB 148/18; M. Stewart to Wilson, 3 Mar. 1965, PREM 13/973.

55 Service, *Russia*, 376–9; Taubman, *Khrushchev*, 3–17; P. du Quenoy, 'The role of foreign affairs in the fall of Nikita Khrushchev in October 1964', *IHR* xxv/2 (2003), 334–56.

56 JIC(64)51st meeting, 15 Oct. 1964, CAB 159/42; Moscow to FO, 20 Oct. 1964, N2215; Wright to T. Bridges (FO), 21 Oct. 1964, FO 371/177670.

57 For a French assessment see Moscow to Paris, 16 Oct. 1964, in *DDF, 1964*, ii. 334–6; NATO working group on Soviet policy papers, 25 Nov. 1964, NS1022/75, FO 371/177672.

needed *détente* with the USA and its allies, but this would involve closer contacts between Eastern and Western Europe – which could undermine the Eastern bloc regimes – and would also anger the more militant Chinese. Khrushchev's dilemma was that he wanted to improve East-West relations but was unwilling to remould the USSR's political strategy to achieve this aim. Trevelyan presciently concluded that that Brezhnev and Kosygin would likewise fail to resolve this intractable dilemma.[58]

The Foreign Office advised Wilson that in the short-term the Soviet leadership would 'go slow' on East-West relations. Nevertheless, the prime minister intended to invite Kosygin to London for the spring of 1965, and Trevelyan was instructed to offer this invitation to the Soviet Foreign Ministry on 9 December. Diplomatic protocol stipulated that, following Macmillan's trip to the USSR in 1959, it was the British government's turn to welcome the Soviet premier. However, Trevelyan informed London on the 12 December that the Soviets insisted that Wilson should visit Moscow.[59] The ambassador warned that if the prime minister accepted these terms the Soviet leadership could cross-examine Wilson on NATO nuclear-sharing before any agreement had been reached between member states of the Alliance. Wilson, however, was impatient to travel to the USSR. According to Bruce, the prime minister believed that the new Soviet leadership had to establish its position within the Kremlin first, and that while Kosygin would feel 'inhibited' in London, on home ground he 'would feel more secure and would, hopefully, be more forthcoming' with his visitor.[60]

As Trevelyan noted, if Wilson visited Moscow he could not easily avoid discussing with his hosts the controversy surrounding proposals for NATO nuclear sharing, which revolved around a proposal developed by State Department officials in 1960–1 for a Multilateral Force. The MLF was initially intended to satisfy West German demands for a role in NATO nuclear strategy, and to prevent the FRG from acquiring its own deterrent, either independently or in collaboration with France. However, it provoked serious dissent not only between NATO governments but within the policy-making establishment in Washington too, with the JCS and Department of Defense adamantly opposing the transfer of US nuclear technology to Alliance members.[61] At the Nassau summit between Macmillan and Kennedy in December 1962, both leaders had agreed to 'the development of a multi-

[58] FO to Moscow, No.3822, 18 Oct. 1964, NS1015/65, FO 371/177665; Trevelyan to Gordon-Walker, 2 Nov. 1964 (two parts), NS1022/69,70, FO 371/177671.
[59] OPD(O)(64)16, briefs for Wilson's visit to Washington, 24 Nov. 1964, CAB 148/40; FO to Moscow, no. 4042, 9 Dec. 1964, and Moscow to FO, no. 2612, 12 Dec. 1964, PREM 13/598.
[60] Trevelyan to FO, 13 Dec. 1964, and Averill Harriman–Wilson conversation, No.10, 7 Dec. 1965, PREM 13/598; London to State Dept, no.79, 16 July 1965, MF408; Wright note, 11 Jan. 1965, NS1051/6, FO 371/182761.
[61] J. Young, 'Killing the MLF? The Wilson government and nuclear sharing in Europe, 1964–66', *DS* xiv/2 (2003), 295–324.

lateral NATO nuclear force', yet the Conservative government had been fundamentally opposed to the MLF and intended to keep *Polaris* (once it entered service) under national control. Within Whitehall, the MoD and COS considered the MLF – described by Mountbatten as 'militarily nonsensical' – to be impractical and a threat to Britain's deterrent. Foreign Office officials were concerned that West German participation in a NATO nuclear force would arouse Soviet wrath, while Wilson and other Labour politicians sympathised with what they regarded as the USSR's genuine fear of a 'German figure on the trigger', particularly if the FRG used access to nuclear weapons as a means of pursuing a more assertive agenda on reunification.[62]

During the course of the election campaign Wilson realised that Britain's nuclear status was popular with 'the man in the pub' and he therefore decided, despite Labour's manifesto promise, to retain the deterrent. Following his accession to the premiership Wilson seized on the concept of an 'Atlantic Nuclear Force', as both an alternative to the MLF and a means of justifying Labour's policy reversal. Although Wilson claimed to have thought of the ANF prior to the 1964 election, this proposal bore a striking resemblance to a concept devised by Cabinet Office officials prior to Labour's victory in the polls. The ANF was to consist of the British V bomber force (replaced by *Polaris* submarines once they entered service), an American contingent of equal strength and a mixed-manned element, with the French *force de frappe* being added if, contrary to expectations, de Gaulle agreed to join. Participants would also sign a treaty blocking the dissemination of nuclear weapons to non-nuclear states.[63]

Wilson claimed that the ANF would reinforce interdependence within NATO, thereby obscuring his abrupt U-turn on *Polaris*. National pride would be appeased by the fact that British nuclear weapons would return to sovereign authority if the Alliance collapsed. The ANF concept was also considered by ministers to be less harmful to *détente* – and less provocative to the Soviets – because it diluted the mixed-manned element (with its West German component), and consisted mainly of existing rather than new weapons systems. However, officials approached the issue within the context of NATO relations, and did not believe that the ANF would be any more acceptable to Moscow than the MLF.[64] The West Germans gave a cautious welcome to the ANF, but when Wilson, Gordon-Walker and Healey visited Washington on 7–8 December 1964 they discovered that Johnson was inde-

---

62 COS(64)44th meeting, 30 June 1964, DEFE 4/171; Wilson–Gerhard Schröder (FRG Foreign Minister) conversation, No.10, 11 Dec. 1964, PREM 13/27.
63 Rusk–Wilson conversation, 2 Mar. 1964, NSF, LBJLIB, UKCF 213; Hennessy, *Secret state*, 70–7; MISC11/12, Defence study group report, 9 Nov. 1964, CAB 130/211; S. Schrafstetter and S. Twigge, 'Trick or truth? The British ANF proposal, West Germany and nonproliferation', *DS* xi/2 (2000), 167–9.
64 MISC17/4th meeting, 22 Nov. 1964, CAB 130/213; MISC11/2(Final), 'Atlantic Nuclear Force', 9 Nov. 1964, CAB 130/211.

cisive on the nuclear-sharing issue. The Washington visit concluded with the Americans promising to 'consider' the ANF, and to allow the British time to consult other NATO governments on their proposals.[65]

The MLF had, as Healey later put it, been 'torpedoed', but as Foreign Office and MoD officials had predicted, the Soviet government was as hostile towards the ANF as they had been towards the MLF. Kosygin wrote an angry letter to Wilson on 7 January 1965, accusing him of acquiescing in West German nuclear ambitions, and stating that NATO nuclear-sharing would preclude Moscow's agreement on an NPT. During a visit to London on 17–19 March, Gromyko made similar accusations against the ANF in conversation with Michael Stewart, Gordon Walker's successor as Foreign Secretary, and also stated that Kosygin's visit to the UK would be postponed indefinitely.[66] Wilson's hopes for an early meeting with the Soviet leadership had been dashed, and the escalation of the war in Vietnam during the first months of 1965 served only to complement Anglo-Soviet differences over non-proliferation and nuclear-sharing.

Both the new Labour government and senior officials emphasised the reduction in East-West tensions, but there was a difference in emphasis between Wilson's attitude towards *détente* and developing opinions within the Foreign Office. The latter focused on incremental means employed by the UK and other Western powers (including trade and ministerial-level visits) to promote gradual political change, or 'evolution', within Eastern Europe, while Wilson adopted a Russocentric approach to East-West relations, concentrating less on contacts with the states within the USSR's sphere of influence. The prime minister was also impatient to meet Khrushchev's successors at the earliest available opportunity, ignoring the advice of Trevelyan and other diplomats with first-hand knowledge of the USSR, who argued that the new Soviet leadership was too involved with internal problems and developments within the Communist world to make any immediate progress on East-West *détente*. Underpinning Wilson's intentions was a belief in his own diplomatic skills and in the expertise in Soviet affairs which he had apparently derived from his successive visits to Moscow. He also acted, as Macmillan and Churchill had done, on the assumption that Britain had a positive and unique role to play in promoting *détente*, and that the UK could act both as a loyal ally to the USA and other NATO powers, and as an independent power capable of fostering greater goodwill between the West and the Eastern blocs.[67] This

[65] Memoranda on US-UK talks, 7–8 Dec. 1964, PREM 13/104; conversations at White House on MLF, 6, 8 Dec. 1964, NSF, LBJLIB, UKCF 214.
[66] Healey, My *life*, 305; Schrafstetter and Twigge, 'ANF proposal', 174; Kosygin to Wilson, 7 Jan. 1965, PREM 13/279; Gromyko–Stewart conversation, No.10, 17 Mar. 1965, PREM 13/603.
[67] *Crossman diaries*, ii. 87, entry for 24 Oct. 1966; FO to Washington, 28 Feb.1966, PREM 13/805.

conception was to be tested and ultimately discredited during the course of the late 1960s.

Wilson's conception of Anglo-Soviet relations did not recognise the ideological factors which drove Soviet policy and, in particular, the effect that these had on his chosen interlocutor, Kosygin. As Sergei Radchenko argues, both Brezhnev and Kosygin were neophytes as far as foreign relations were concerned. The premier's background lay in economic planning, while Brezhnev grumpily told one of his aides that throughout his party career 'I never had anything to do with this damn foreign policy and know nothing of it!' The new CPSU Secretary's approach to external affairs was shaped both by his attempts to forge consensus within the *Politburo*, and by his class-based analysis of international affairs, which in his opinion meant solidarity with North Korea, North Vietnam and other 'socialist' states in their struggles against the 'imperialists'. Brezhnev and Kosgyin blamed the decline of Sino-Soviet relations on Khrushchev's incompetence, while Polyanskii and Shelepin were particularly opposed to *détente* and advocated *rapprochement* with the PRC. The result was that Soviet policy in the year following Khrushchev's fall took a decidedly anti-Western slant, as the post-Khrushchev leadership sought to ease tensions with China and to support the North Vietnamese in their war against the USA.[68] Meanwhile, the competing policies of the USSR and Britain over Vietnam were to stall any significant improvements in bilateral relations throughout the first two years of the Wilson government.

---

68 S. Radchenko, 'The China puzzle. Soviet policy towards the People's Republic of China, 1962–1967', unpubl. PhD diss, London 2005, 18, 182–5; R. N. Lebow and J. G. Stein, *We all lost the Cold War*, Princeton 1994, 156–8.

3

The Wilson Government and the Vietnam War, 1965–1968

The first months of 1965 saw an escalation of the civil war in South Vietnam, pitting the Communist-led National Liberation Front (or Viet Cong) against the pro-American government of the Republic of Vietnam. The Kennedy administration provided financial aid and military advisers to assist the South Vietnamese, but the lack of either a coherent counter-insurgency strategy or an effective, competent regime in Saigon meant that such assistance was essentially wasted. As the NLF gradually established control over the South, supported with troops and supplies by the Democratic Republic of Vietnam, the Johnson administration decided to launch air-strikes against the DRV to force it to cease assisting its ideological allies in the South. In March 1965 the first US combat units were sent to South Vietnam, and by May American troops were involved in the war against the Viet Cong and supporting North Vietnamese army units. The USA gradually became drawn into the Vietnam War through its determination to arrest the expansion of Communism in South-East Asia, while the North Vietnamese leadership believed that they had been tricked into accepting partition in the 1954 Geneva conference, and were determined to reunify Vietnam by force.[1]

The war in Vietnam had a damaging effect on East-West relations, stalling superpower *détente* and inflaming Sino-American tensions. The conflict also undermined America's international reputation, as both the bombing campaign against the North (*Rolling Thunder*) and US military operations in the RVN were condemned by non-aligned governments. Vietnam also poisoned the transatlantic relationship, and although de Gaulle was the only allied political leader to openly condemn American policy in South-East Asia, other US allies provided a half-hearted public support for American actions tempered by private unease. NATO governments were fully conscious of the fact that the war was having an inflammatory effect on public opinion in their countries, particularly on the radical left and politically-conscious youth, and throughout Western Europe there was an increasing popular

---

[1] The best analysis of the origins of American involvement remains D. Kaiser's *American tragedy: Kennedy, Johnson, and the origins of the Vietnam War*, Cambridge, MA 2000. See also R. D. Schulzinger, *A time for war: the United States and Vietnam, 1941–1975*, Oxford 1997, 154–81.

sentiment which considered the USA , rather than the USSR, to be a major threat to world peace.[2]

For many of its left-wing critics, the Wilson government's policy on Vietnam represented both a shabby betrayal of Labour's principles, and disgraceful subservience to a war-mongering US president. Britain's support for America's war was denounced by Labour backbenchers, and Wilson and his ministers were often heckled – and at times physically attacked – by protestors when they appeared in public. The satirical journal *Private Eye* reflected widespread disillusionment with Britain's passive response to the Vietnam War when it printed a scurrilous cartoon showing the prime minister on his knees, applying his tongue to Johnson's rear.[3] Of all the controversies arising from the Wilson era, the only foreign policy issues to arouse a similar degree of contemporary partisanship were the government's handling of Rhodesian UDI and (between 1967 and 1970) its support for the Nigerian government's suppression of the Biafran revolt.

Wilson's response to the Vietnam War was strongly influenced by competing pressures. He was obliged to demonstrate diplomatic support for the policies of Britain's most powerful ally, but he was also aware that Labour opposition to America's war in Indochina was spreading from the hard left towards mainstream opinion within the party. Many Labour MPs and party members were both concerned at the prospects of escalation and also concluded that the Viet Cong insurgency was an anti-colonial, rather than a Cold War, issue. Wilson openly endorsed the Johnson administration's actions, but he also faced efforts by American officials to cajole his government into sending British troops to South Vietnam as part of the USA's 'more flags' policy.[4] The war in Vietnam also had significant implications for Wilson's own concept of East-West relations. The prime minister was genuinely worried that the conflict in South-East Asia could eventually provoke a Sino-American or even a global war. He was also frustrated that the war prevented the development of Anglo-Soviet *rapprochement*, owing to the irreconcilably opposed positions that both the British and Soviet leaderships had adopted towards Vietnam. When Wilson did finally meet with Brezhnev and Kosygin (during his visit to Moscow on 21–23 February 1966) he portrayed contacts with the Soviets as a means by which the UK could

2   M. Vaïsse, 'De Gaulle et la Guerre du Vietnam: de la difficulté d'être Cassandre', in C. Goscha and M. Vaïsse (eds), *La Guerre du Vietnam et l'Europe, 1963–1973*, Brussels 2003, 169–78; G. Herring, 'Fighting without allies: the international dimensions of America's defeat in Vietnam', in M. Gilbert (ed.), *Why the North won the Vietnam War*, Basingstoke 2003, 77–82; Sandbrook, *White heat*, 361.
3   Pimlott, *Wilson*, 393, 473; Morgan, *People's peace*, 293–4; J. Young, 'Britain and "LBJ's war", 1964–68', *CWH* ii/3 (2002), 68–9, 76–7.
4   Ellis, *Vietnam War*, passim; Young, *Labour governments*, ch. iii, and '"LBJ's war"', passim; G. Hughes, 'A "missed opportunity" for peace? Harold Wilson, British diplomacy, and the *Sunflower* initiative to end the Vietnam War', *DS* xiv/3 (2003), 106–30; Callaghan, *Foreign policy*, 192–4, 199, 204–13.

act as a valuable interlocutor between the superpowers. Following this visit he expressed to Johnson his conviction 'that [the Soviets] want to maintain an active dialogue with the West', and he maintained that Britain would had a vital role to play in preserving East-West contacts:

> I think that mainly because of Vietnam they see difficulties in the immediate future in having too public a dialogue with you, *but they may be ready to keep it going through us*. But they are in no doubt as I said earlier that they will be negotiating with us as your loyal allies.[5]

The prime minister's belief in his own diplomatic skills, and his conviction that his contacts with the Soviet leadership led him to develop a rapport with 'the Russians', were in themselves important factors influencing his policy towards Vietnam and his attempts to settle the conflict in Indochina. However, in the process he overestimated the significance of his personal relationship with Brezhnev and Kosygin, and misunderstood the effect his attempts at peacemaking would have on officials in Washington. As the conflict in Indochina intensified Wilson's Vietnam policy undermined the prime minister's standing with Johnson, and became one of the Cold War issues (alongside East-West trade, foreign exchange costs for BAOR, the East of Suez withdrawals and nuclear proliferation) which were the cause of policy disputes between the USA and UK.

Vietnam and British foreign policy

At the time of Dien Bien Phu, Wilson accused a 'lunatic fringe' of US politicians of being bent upon waging 'a holy crusade against Communism' in Asia. Yet during the following decade his government publicly supported the USA's efforts to check Communism in Indochina.[6] The most eloquent expression of its support was provided by Stewart's defence of American intervention before a hostile audience at a University of Oxford 'teach-in' in June 1965, during which he insisted that the DRV was the aggressor in Vietnam.[7] The Labour government's endorsement of the war was partly intended to bolster the Anglo-American alliance, and also to ensure American backing for the 'confrontation' against Indonesia. The UK was also reliant on US support for its nuclear deterrent and to preserve sterling against devaluation,

---

[5] Ellis, *Vietnam War*, 71; FO to Washington, 28 Feb. 1966, PREM 13/805, emphasis added; State Dept to London, N5006, 26 Feb. 1966, NARAII, RG 59: 250, 5–7, 2788.
[6] Ellis, *Vietnam War*, 7. See also P. Busch, *All the way with JFK? Britain, the US and the Vietnam War*, Oxford 2003.
[7] Transcript of Oxford University 'teach-in', 16 June 1965, Michael Stewart papers, Churchill College, Cambridge, 12/3/3.Gordon Walker lost his parliamentary seat at Smethick in October 1964, and after losing the Leyton by-election the following January he was replaced by Stewart.

and these factors made it difficult for Britain to openly criticise American actions in Vietnam. An additional factor involved the long-term objectives of British policy in South-East Asia, which were focused upon the reduction of East-West tensions in the region. Since 1954 British officials had hoped to neutralise the region as an arena for Cold War competition, hence the Macmillan government's support for the 1962 international agreement establishing a non-aligned Laotian government, but ongoing civil strife between pro-Western and Communist forces in both Vietnam and Laos thwarted this objective. British policy-makers regarded Chinese-inspired subversion as the main threat to Western strategic and economic interests in South-East Asia. Of particular concern was Indonesia, where Sukarno – having flirted with the USSR – was forging closer ties with both the Chinese leadership and the increasingly powerful PKI. Senior British officials concluded that in the immediate future a Western military presence was needed to bolster local allies (South Vietnam, Thailand, Singapore and Malaysia) until they were stable enough to withstand external threats and internal subversion. Wilson's antipathy to Chinese policy led him to draw a distinction between the anti-Western and radical PRC and the more 'rational' USSR, and British officials initially supported American involvement in Vietnam on the grounds that the USA alone could prevent the expansion of China's influence in South-East Asia.[8]

Yet as was the case with previous Cold War crises, as US officials expanded their country's military commitment in South-East Asia the British government privately feared that the Vietnam War could lead to a major East-West confrontation. When the Johnson administration initiated *Rolling Thunder* in early March 1965, officials in Whitehall wondered whether their American counterparts had defined their strategic objectives in Vietnam, let alone determined how these could be achieved by military means. The COS and Foreign Office diplomats also had few illusions about either the effectiveness of US air power against a pre-industrial state like North Vietnam, or (assuming that the Johnson administration succeeded in forcing the DRV to cease supplying and reinforcing the NLF) the will of the Communist insurgents in the South to fight on despite American intervention. During late 1964 and early 1965 Wilson was worried that the USA would escalate the war, despite the risks of Chinese or Soviet intervention, if it was 'checkmated' in Vietnam.[9]

8 A. Parker, 'International aspects of the Vietnam War', in P. Lowe (ed.), *The Vietnam War*, Manchester 1998, 201; Middeke, 'Global military role', 153; OPD(O)(65)63(Final), 'Defence review studies: Indo-Pacific strategy', 20 Oct. 1965, CAB 148/44; Wilson, *New Britain*, 90–100. Singapore merged with Malaysia in September 1963, but subsequently declared independence on 9 August 1965.
9 COS17th/64, 25 Feb. 1964, DEFE 4/165; JIC(65)14th, 1 Apr. 1965, CAB 159/43; J. Young, 'The Wilson government and the Davies peace mission to North Vietnam, July 1965', *RIS* xxiv/4 (1998), 545–6, 553; *Castle diaries*, 107, entry for 14 Feb. 1966.

Like their Conservative predecessors Labour ministers intended to avoid any military embroilment in the conflict. When Wilson, Gordon-Walker and Healey visited Washington in December 1964, Johnson asked for the deployment of a British contingent to the RVN. The Labour government turned down repeated American requests to send troops to South Vietnam, arguing that the defence of Malaysia stretched British military capabilities in South-East Asia to the limit. Even after the end of 'confrontation' ministers were determined that British forces released from Borneo would not be sent to Vietnam.[10] The prime minister was also aware that his endorsement of US policy in Indochina had enraged the Labour left and, unlike his Australian and New Zealand counterparts, he was unwilling to send even a limited number of troops to Vietnam. Although Wilson was not concerned with protests outside parliament, he knew that if he gave way to Johnson's request to send a token force to war – the proverbial 'platoon of Highlanders with bagpipes' – he would split the Labour party.[11]

Diplomatic activity offered the prime minister the best means of mollifying both backbench criticism of his government's stance on Vietnam and American demands for more overt British support against the DRV and the Viet Cong. It also enabled Wilson to bolster his self-proclaimed credentials as an intermediary between the superpowers. In his telegrams to and conversations with Johnson, Wilson argued that the UK's role as co-chairman of the Geneva conference precluded active participation in the war, and that Britain had to work with the other co-chair, the USSR, to promote a negotiated settlement. The Geneva accords did not grant the co-chairmen a long-term peace-making role, and the 1954 conference could not be reconvened without the consent of all the other participants – the USA, France, China, North and South Vietnam, Laos, Cambodia and the International Control Commission states (Canada, India and Poland). None the less, the Labour government adopted the position that Britain and the USSR could co-operate diplomatically to 'restore peace and stability in Vietnam'.[12] The Geneva accords therefore provided the basis for Wilson's subsequent efforts to initiate peace talks on Vietnam.

While the British government supported American efforts to contain Communist expansion in South-East Asia, policy-makers in Washington and London had differing views on the USSR's policy towards Vietnam. By early 1965 American officials regarded Soviet military aid to the DRV as

---

[10] COS50th/64, 11 Aug. 1964, DEFE 4/171; conversations between Johnson, Wilson and others at White House, 7 Dec. 1964, PREM 13/104; London to State Dept., SECUN14, 14 May 1965, LCHMA, MF 407; OPD(66)29th, 17 June 1966, and OPD(66)31st, 5 July 1966, CAB 148/25.

[11] J. Colman, 'Harold Wilson, Lyndon Johnson and Anglo-American "summit diplomacy"', *Journal of Transatlantic Studies* i/2 (2003), 135; Pimlott, *Wilson*, 391–4.

[12] SEAD memorandum, 4 Dec. 1964, and FO to Washington, no.1212, 17 Feb. 1965, PREM 13/692.

proof that Moscow was complicit in North Vietnamese 'subversion' of South Vietnam.[13] In contrast, British diplomats argued that the Soviet government was competing for supremacy in the Communist world with its Chinese rival, and that the USSR was obliged to support a fellow 'socialist' state against American 'aggression'. Furthermore, the Soviet leaders feared the escalation of war in Indochina not only because they wanted to avoid confrontation with the USA, but also because a prolonged war would radicalise the North Vietnamese and strengthen their ties with China. Ilya Gaiduk's study of Soviet policy on Vietnam supports these Foreign Office assessments, showing that Brezhnev and his *Politburo* peers hoped to exploit the conflict to supplant the PRC as North Vietnam's principal ally. Yet the USSR did not want Vietnam to provide the *casus belli* of a Third World War, and the Soviet leadership privately advised their North Vietnamese counterparts to negotiate with the Americans. However, the USSR had to contend not only with Chinese competition for influence over the DRV, but also with the latter's persistence in seeking a unified, Communist Vietnam.[14]

In summary, the prime minister's Vietnam policy was partly an opportunistic response to left-wing criticism within parliament, but was also influenced by his perception of East-West relations. Wilson wanted to promote peace talks on Vietnam, not only in order to counter left-wing criticism that he was 'the tail-end Charlie in an American bomber', but also because successful Anglo-Soviet diplomatic co-operation could yield the same results as Eden's statesmanship at Geneva in 1954. The prime minister also believed that he could preserve contacts between the superpowers because of Britain's status as America's most dependable ally and, Wilson claimed, because British diplomatic experience and skills were respected by the Soviet leadership.[15] This presumption was, however, invalidated not only by the impact that the Vietnam war had on US-Soviet and East-West relations, but also because the UK could never be a truly impartial 'honest broker' due to its association with US policy in South-East Asia. Furthermore, even if Wilson were able to persuade the American and Soviet governments of his credentials as a mediator, his chances of gaining any leverage over Chinese and North Vietnamese leaders were far less promising. If Brezhnev and Kosygin were unable to encourage the Hanoi regime to modify its war aims, or to mitigate the effects of Mao's anti-Western militancy, then the prospects of the British prime minister being able to achieve the same were non-existent.

13 Policy Planning Council Paper (State Department), 'Soviet policy in the light of the Vietnam crisis', 15 Feb. 1965, NSF, LBJLIB, USSR country file 220.
14 Beijing to FO, no.134, 5 Feb. 1965, NS103196/7, FO 371/182757; Brimelow to A. de la Mare (SEAD), 18 Feb. 1966, N1021/81/2, FO 371/188487; I. Gaiduk, *The Soviet Union and the Vietnam War*, Chicago 1996, 57–61, 64–7.
15 Morgan, *Wilson*, 277; FO to HM embassy, Washington, nos 1212, 2322, 17 Feb., 23 Mar. 1965, PREM 13/692; FO to Washington, no.2237, 28 Feb. 1966, PREM 13/805.

British diplomacy and the escalating war in Vietnam

In early February 1965 the NLF attacked the American military bases at Pleiku and Qui Nhon, providing the pretext for the *Flaming Dart* bombing raids on North Vietnam on 8th and 11th February. Wilson's response demonstrated both his annoyance at the lack of advance notice of US intentions, and also anxiety over the possible escalation of the war in South-East Asia. Much to the US president's displeasure, Wilson telephoned the White House on the night of 10–11 February to propose a visit to Washington for consultations on Vietnam. While Wilson's suggestion consciously emulated Attlee's discussions with Truman on Korea (December 1950), it merely infuriated Johnson, who bluntly told the prime minister that he did not require his advice. Wilson was mollified by pledges from McGeorge Bundy that air-strikes would be restricted to targets south of the 19th parallel, in order not to provoke the Chinese, and that he would be informed in advance of any change in US strategy in Vietnam. None the less, for the sake of his own prestige and that of his country, he needed an opportunity to prove that Britain was not merely an American lackey blindly following President Johnson's lead.[16]

On 16 February Soviet diplomats proposed a joint Anglo-Soviet declaration on the bombing of North Vietnam. Under prompting from Rusk, the British government suggested that the co-chairmen should instead solicit the views of the other signatories of the Geneva accords in order to 'consider what further action they might take'.[17] To Wilson's disappointment, the Soviet leadership delayed its response until 15 March, only to call upon the UK to endorse a statement condemning the USA's 'aggressive actions' in Indochina.[18] The Soviet government rejected attempts to reconvene the Geneva conference, and responded to Wilson's subsequent peace-making gestures (such as the Commonwealth Mission in July 1965) by demanding that the USA unconditionally halt air-strikes against the DRV and accept the 'four points' outlined by the North Vietnamese Premier, Pham Van Dong, on 8 April 1965. The 'four points' called for an American withdrawal from South Vietnam, the denunciation of the American-South Vietnamese military alliance, the adoption of the NLF's political programme in the South

[16] Schulzinger, *Time for war*, 167–8; Johnson–Wilson telephone conversation, 10–11 Feb. 1965, PREM 13/692.
[17] Moscow to FO, no.326, 16 Feb. 1965, PREM 13/692; Dean Rusk and British ambassador conversation, State Department, 18 Feb. 1965, *FRUS*, II: *Vietnam, 1965*, Washington, DC 1996, 319.
[18] FO to Moscow, no.533, 19 Feb. 1865, PREM 13/692; minutes of Cabinet meeting, CC14(65)14th conclusions, 4 Mar. 1965, CAB 128/3; Moscow to FO, nos 546, 550, 551, 15 Mar. 1965, PREM 13/693.

and the peaceful reunification of Vietnam without foreign intervention.[19] These demands were unacceptable to the Johnson administration, as they effectively involved capitulating to NLF and North Vietnamese war aims.

With efforts to promote talks between the USA and DRV stalled by mutual intransigence, British diplomats proposed in mid-April to convene a conference on Cambodian neutrality. Cambodia was at this time still at peace, and Foreign Office officials hoped that a conference could be used to promote 'back door' negotiations on Vietnam. However, the Johnson administration insisted on prior consultations with the Thai and South Vietnamese governments before any conference was announced, on account of the disputed borders Cambodia had with Thailand and the RVN.[20] This response annoyed the normally pro-American Stewart, who complained that if the USA's regional allies were allowed to veto the Cambodian initiative 'the tail would be wagging the dog'. Despite American objections, the British government prepared for a joint announcement with the Soviets in preparation for a Cambodian conference. However on 24 April the Cambodian sovereign, Prince Norodom Sihanouk, declared that he would not participate in any initiative not strictly confined to the issue of Cambodia's neutrality. Sihanouk subsequently refused to have any dealings with the Saigon regime, thereby thwarting any prospects of employing international mediation over Cambodia to facilitate peace talks on Vietnam.[21] The British ambassador to Phnom Penh attributed the prince's stand to a combination of encouragement from Beijing and his own temperamental, 'feminine' personality. Yet the Cambodian monarch's uncompromising opposition to Geneva talks was only partly due to Chinese support; it derived mainly from the historical rivalry between the Vietnamese and Khmers which predated the Cold War by centuries.[22]

As was the case with other third-party initiatives, Wilson's attempts at peace-making were rendered irrelevant by events on the battlefield. In March 1965 the first American combat units were dispatched to South Vietnam, and at the end of July Johnson decided to raise troop levels from 75,000 to 125,000. By early 1968 there were over 500,000 US military personnel in the RVN. The air raids which had begun with 'Flaming Dart' also increased in scale, becoming the fully fledged bombing campaign known as Rolling Thunder. In response to both developments, the Chinese Foreign Minister,

19 Moscow to FO, no.1252, 23 Jun. 1965, PREM 13/690; William Duiker, 'Victory by other means: the foreign policy of the Democratic Republic of Vietnam', in Gilbert, Vietnam War, 63–5.
20 CC26(65)26th conclusions, 27 Apr. 1965, CAB 128/39;Washington to FO, N.1916, 16 Apr. 1965, PREM 13/694.
21 FO to Belgrade, N.247, 20 Apr. 1965, and Phnom Penh to FO, N.172, N.175, 24 Apr. 1965, PREM 13/694; Phnom Penh to FO, N.264–6, 15 May 1965, N.499; and 6 Sept. 1965, PREM 13/102.
22 Q. Zhai, 'Beijing and the Vietnamese peace talks, 1965–68: new evidence from Chinese sources' (CWHIP working paper xviii, 1997), 4–5.

Chen Yi, issued an indirect warning to the US government on 31 May. He told the British *chargé d'affaires* in Beijing, Donald Hopson, that any American invasion of North Vietnam or violation of the PRC's sovereignty would lead to all-out war.[23] The Chinese leadership supported the DRV in order to undermine 'revisionist' Soviet influence in the Third World and to support 'wars of national liberation', but also because it was concerned by the US military build-up in South-East Asia. Between 1965 and 1970 320,000 Chinese troops were deployed to defend North Vietnam, and Chen's comments to Hopson, which were passed on to Washington, were accompanied by efforts to put China on a war footing.[24] The Johnson administration none the less concluded that the PRC would not intervene unless the survival of the Lao Dong (Vietnamese Workers Party) regime in Hanoi was at stake, and that any damage done to US-Soviet relations by the war would be manageable. In London officials of the Foreign Office's South-East Asia Department concluded that there was no 'half-way house' between US and North Vietnamese war aims, and little likelihood of either side accepting defeat. Although British policy favoured a negotiated settlement, Foreign Office officials realised that both sides were bent upon a military resolution to the conflict.[25]

Contrary to Wilson's fears, the war in Vietnam did not deteriorate into a superpower confrontation akin to the Cuban crisis of 1962; the Johnson administration's reaction to Chen Yi's warning showed that US officials were determined to avert a war with the DRV's allies. Yet despite the Foreign Office's pessimistic conclusions, Wilson persisted with his fruitless attempts at peace-making, even though the North Vietnamese government (with the encouragement of its Chinese allies) consistently rejected third party initiatives throughout 1965. Furthermore, Wilson's Soviet interlocutors consistently refused to support his attempts at mediation. This should have come as no surprise to the prime minister, who privately admitted to de Gaulle in April 1965 that if the Soviet leadership supported peace talks they would be open to Chinese propaganda attacks.[26] Above all, Wilson was deluding himself by arguing that he could persuade the US government to accept a negotiated settlement to the war. Not only did Johnson dislike and distrust the prime minister, he also resented his attempts at peacemaking, and had no

[23] D. Anderson, 'The United States and Vietnam', in Lowe, *Vietnam War*, 107; Beijing to FO, N.722, 31 May 1965, PREM 13/695; Bundy to Johnson, 4 June 1965, *FRUS*, XXX: *China*, Washington, DC 1998, 173–4.
[24] C. Jian, *Mao's China and the Cold War*, Chapel Hill, NC 2001, 216–18, 221–9.
[25] NSC 553rd meeting, 27 July 1965; Robert McNamara to Johnson, 30 July 1965; and Rusk to Johnson, 30 Sept. 1965, *FRUS*, III: *Vietnam, 1965*, Washington, DC 1996, 260–3; SEAD memorandum, 'The war in Vietnam', 1 June 1965, PREM 13/695.
[26] Charles de Gaulle–Wilson conversation, Hotel Matignon, Paris, 2 Apr. 1965, *DDF, 1965*, i. 387. See also Wilson-Harriman conversation, No.10, 24 Mar. 1965, PREM 13/693; Moscow to FO, no. 496, 23 Feb. 1966, and FO to Washington, no.2237, 28 Feb. 1966, PREM 13/1273.

comprehension of the dilemmas the Labour government faced over Vietnam, which influenced both its refusal to provide military assistance to the USA and its diplomatic manoeuvrings.[27]

Vietnam and Anglo-Soviet relations: January–November 1966

As both US military operations in the RVN and *Rolling Thunder* intensified, Wilson's efforts to promote Anglo-Soviet concord stagnated, and Kosygin repeatedly declined invitations to visit the UK, citing British support for American 'piracy' in Vietnam as one of many prohibiting factors. The poor state of Anglo-Soviet bilateral contacts was emphasised (much to Wilson's chagrin) by the increasing cordiality characterising Franco-Soviet relations during the course of 1965–6. Wilson was invited to Moscow in late February 1966 – during which he made a failed attempt to establish contact with officials at the North Vietnamese embassy – and paid a second visit to the Soviet capital, ostensibly to attend the British Trade Fair, on 16–18 July.[28] The latter trip took place despite the seamen's strike and the ensuing financial crisis; notwithstanding intense press criticism and a suspected leadership bid by George Brown, the prime minister refused to cancel his visit.[29] While there was an element of diplomatic one-upmanship in his actions, influenced in part by envy over de Gaulle's successful visit to the USSR the previous month, Wilson also intended to have 'frank and private' discussions with Kosygin on Vietnam.[30]

At the beginning of June 1966 the Johnson administration decided to bomb oil storage facilities in Hanoi and the port of Haiphong, both of which were North of the 19th parallel. Having acquiesced in US air attacks on targets below this line, Wilson dissociated Britain from the raids on these two cities, despite Foreign Office advice warning that such a statement would sour Anglo-American relations. Johnson had been forewarned by the prime minister of this statement of dissociation, although this did not assuage his anger over what he regarded as British disloyalty. For his part, Wilson was alarmed by both the extension of *Rolling Thunder* and the North Vietnamese

---

27 J. Colman, 'The London ambassadorship of David K. E. Bruce during the Wilson-Johnson years, 1964–1968', *DS* xv/2 (2004), 327–52; G. Ball, *The past has another pattern: memoirs*, New York 1982, 336.

28 Ellis, *Vietnam War*, 154–5; Wilson–Mikhail Smirnovsky (Soviet ambassador) conversation, No. 10, 18 Apr. 1966, NS1052/23, FO 371/188929; M. Narinski, 'Les Soviétiques et la décision française', in F. Bozo, P. Melandri and M. Vaisse (eds), *La France et l'OTAN, 1949–1996*, Paris 1996, 504–5.

29 M. Palliser to M. MacLehose (FO), 4 July 1966, NS0151/173/G, FO 371/188923; Pimlott, *Wilson*, 419–27; 'Wrong place … wrong time', *The Express*, 18 July 1966.

30 T. Hughes (INR) to Rusk, 15 July 1966, LHCMA, MF 409. For Wilson's envy of de Gaulle see *Castle diaries*, 270, entry for 22 June 1967; FO to Moscow, N.1622, 4 July 1966, NS1051/174, FO 371/188923.

threat to try captured US pilots for war crimes, and was also convinced that Soviet leaders were 'thoroughly worried' that they would end up with a superpower confrontation with the USA. Kosygin privately showed considerable concern over the course of the conflict, telling Wilson shortly after his arrival in Moscow on 16 July that China would intervene overtly on the DRV's behalf.[31] The prime minister tried to play on Kosygin's fears during their discussions in the Kremlin and at the British embassy two days later, asserting that co-operation between the co-chairmen was needed to stop the Vietnam War from provoking a major international crisis. He admitted that the South Vietnamese government was 'not his favourite regime', but he blamed the failure of repeated peace initiatives on the DRV's intransigence. In response, Kosygin berated Wilson over Britain's support for American 'banditry', and he was also dismissive of Wilson's response to the Hanoi and Haiphong raids, pressing the prime minister to dissociate the UK completely from American actions in Vietnam.[32]

Wilson subsequently sought to make the most of the visit, informing Johnson that he was impressed by the Soviet premier's apparent candour over both Chinese intentions and the potential consequences of the Indochina conflict. He also professed himself to be 'more convinced' that the 'unsensational [sic] relationship that is growing up between Kosygin and myself has real – if still largely potential – value'. Wilson also retrospectively claimed the credit when the North Vietnamese government opted not to put American prisoners-of-war on trial. Rodric Braithwaite, the Commercial Secretary at the Moscow embassy and Wilson's interpreter, recalled that when the prime minister raised the issue of US prisoners with Kosygin, the latter was non-committal. Despite this, Wilson gave the Cabinet a wildly inaccurate account of his trip, recorded in Barbara Castle's diary entry for the 21 July:

> Kosygin had talked privately to him in 'a quite fantastic way'. No other Western leader had ever been given such an insight into Russian thinking. Kosygin had confided in him about all his problems. There was nothing he would like more, Harold was sure, than to reconvene the Geneva conference, but he couldn't. [Kosygin was very] afraid of escalation and bitterly critical of the Americans. He believed that Kosygin was anxious for him to carry a message back to Johnson. Kosygin made it clear that he regarded Britain as a valuable go-between. 'If there were another Cuba situation, they would want our services'.[33]

---

[31] Johnson to Wilson, 14 June 1966, FRUS, IV: Vietnam, 1966, Washington 1998, 426–8; FO to Washington, no. 6947, 15 July 1966, NS1051/225, FO 371/188924; Ellis, Vietnam War, 161–73; 'note for the record', 16 July 1966, CAB 164/2.

[32] Alexei Kosygin–Wilson conversations, Kremlin (a.m.), UK embassy (p.m.), 18 July 1966, CAB 164/2.

[33] Wilson, Labour government, 275; FO to Washington, no.7075, 19 July 1966, PREM

If Castle's record of this Cabinet meeting is accurate, then Wilson blatantly embellished his account of his visit to Moscow. The Foreign Office's transcript of the meetings does not contain any statement by Kosygin that his government would seek British mediation in any Cuban-type crisis. The prime minister's claim that the Soviet leadership regarded Britain as 'an intermediary' in contacts with the USA was also challenged by Geoffrey Harrison (Humphrey Trevelyan's successor as ambassador to Moscow), who told his American opposite number that the Soviet leadership did not see the British government as a potential mediator between the superpowers. It is unclear whether the prime minister sought to deceive his ministers, or whether he had in fact deluded himself.[34]

Wilson persistently maintained that his contacts with the Soviet leadership could be used to promote peace in Vietnam, and developments in East-West relations during the autumn of 1966 appeared finally to justify these claims. There were clear signs of a less adversarial Soviet policy towards the Western world and a selective interest in détente, one of which was the progressive development of US-Soviet negotiations for an NPT from October 1966 onwards.[35] The Cultural Revolution in China was, American and British diplomats presumed, an additional factor in moderating the USSR's hostility towards the West, as the Soviet government was becoming increasingly nervous about the radicalising effect the 'revolution' would have on Chinese foreign policy. Paradoxically, the internal turmoil inspired by Mao undermined China's reputation with Communist and non-aligned countries, enabling the Soviets to seek détente with the West. While Foreign Office officials attributed the thawing of East-West relations in part to Kosygin's interest in developing closer trading ties with NATO powers, Johnson and his subordinates concluded by late 1966 that the Soviet government was now genuinely interested in pursuing a negotiated settlement to the war in Indochina.[36] Vietnam was therefore no longer as significant an obstacle to improved US-Soviet or Anglo-Soviet relations as it had been beforehand.

At the end of October 1966 Kosygin finally agreed a date to visit Britain, arranged for early February the following year. Having initially been sceptical of Wilson's personal diplomacy on Vietnam, Harrison was by now convinced that the British government had a role to play as the 'voice of

---

13/1218; Braithwaite interview, DOHP, transcript, 3; *Castle diaries*, 151, entry for 21 July 1966.
34 CC39(66)39th conclusions, 21 July 1966, CAB 128/41; Moscow to State Dept, no.300, 20 July 1966, NSF, LBJLIB, USSRCF 200.
35 O. Bange, 'NATO and the Non-Proliferation Treaty', in A. Wenger, C. Nuenlist and A. Locher (eds), *Transforming NATO in the Cold War: challenges beyond deterrence in the 1960s*, Abingdon 2007, 169–71.
36 KV(67)1, 'Steering brief', 26 Jan. 1967, CAB 133/365; G. Chang, *Friends and enemies: the United States, China and the Soviet Union, 1948–1972*, Stanford, CA 1990, 275; Moscow to State Dept, 28 Nov. 1966, FRUS, XIV: *Soviet Union*, Washington, DC 2001, 434–41; Gaiduk, *Soviet Union*, 93–6.

reason' within the Western world, and that in spite of de Gaulle's overtures towards the USSR the Soviet leadership saw Britain, rather than France, as the more credible partner in the development of *détente*.[37] Similar sentiments were expressed by Brown, who had exchanged portfolios with Stewart in a Cabinet reshuffle in August. The new Foreign Secretary was a far more dynamic and pro-active figure than his predecessor, but was also notoriously inclined to become 'tired and emotional' after a few drinks, with potentially embarrassing diplomatic results – his notorious row with Khrushchev during the latter's visit to Britain in 1956 was alcohol-fuelled. Furthermore, not only did Brown have an uneasy relationship with his Foreign Office subordinates, whom he considered tainted by class prejudice, but he had been a bitter rival of Wilson's ever since he stood against him for the Labour leadership in 1963.[38]

Yet for all his personal hostility towards the prime minister, he too believed that Britain could use its privileged relationship with the USA and its contacts with the USSR to promote peace in Indochina. Prior to his first trip to Moscow (22–25 November 1966) Brown told the US ambassador to London that the UK could exert 'critical influence' on the development of Soviet policy towards the West. The Foreign Secretary's efforts to discuss Vietnam and arms control during his visit in late November proved fruitless, but Bruce observed that Brown's return to London 'with no definite accomplishment' did not 'disturb his ever ready optimism'.[39] This hope was to be tested by the *Sunflower débâcle* of February 1967, in which both his and Wilson's attempts to involve Kosygin in a new peace initiative during the latter's visit to the UK ended with transatlantic acrimony.

Sunflower is planted: British diplomacy and the Vietnam war, June 1966–January 1967

In addition to Wilson, other potential mediators had attempted to promote peace talks between the USA and North Vietnam. These included US allies (notably Canada and Italy), non-aligned states (Ghana and India) and Communist powers (with Hungarian and Polish attempts to encourage negotiations in late 1965 and early 1966).[40] In the summer of 1966 the Polish ICC representative, Janusz Lewandowski, approached the US ambassador to

---

[37] Moscow to FO, no.1958, 29 Oct. 1966, NS1052/45, FO 371/188930; Harrison to G. Brown, 21 Nov. 1966, and Smith to Harrison, 18 Dec. 1966, NS1022/69, FO 371/188906.

[38] Interview with Donald Maitland (FO Private Secretary to Brown), DOHP, transcript, 12; Young, *Labour governments*, 6–7.

[39] London to State Dept, no.3814, 7 Nov. 1966, and no. 4377, 27 Nov. 1966, NARAII, RG 59, 250, 5–7, 2788.

[40] G. Herring (ed.), *The secret diplomacy of the Vietnam War: the negotiating volumes of the Pentagon papers*, Austin, Tx 1983; J. Hershberg, 'Peace probes and the bombing pause:

Saigon, Henry Cabot Lodge, claiming that he was in direct contact with the North Vietnamese leadership. A series of meetings between Lewandowski and Lodge, codenamed *Marigold* by American diplomats, led to discussions in December between Rapacki and the US ambassador to Warsaw, John Gronouski. Concurrently with *Marigold* the State Department established the 'Phase A/B' formula for military disengagement in Vietnam, whereby the USA would halt air attacks on the North, prior to the cessation of both PAVN infiltration and American reinforcements to the South. Gronouski was due to meet a North Vietnamese envoy in Warsaw when, following a US air raid on Hanoi on 15 December, the DRV broke off the *Marigold* negotiations. The initiative collapsed with mutual accusations of bad faith, but provided the background for *Sunflower*, which involved two separate contacts – the approach of the US embassy in Moscow to North Vietnamese diplomats in January 1967, and Wilson's discussions with Kosygin the following month.[41]

Despite *Marigold* and *Sunflower*, Johnson and many of his officials became convinced during the course of 1966 that no settlement was possible without fundamental concessions by North Vietnam's leaders, and as far as the president and his advisers were concerned it was up to the Soviet leadership to persuade their counterparts in Hanoi to come to the negotiating table on the USA's terms. The administration's more intransigent attitude followed Ball's resignation as Under-Secretary of State and Bundy's replacement by Walt Rostow. Both Johnson's new national security advisor and the JCS maintained that the war in South Vietnam could be won, and that the losses the DRV incurred through *Rolling Thunder* would force the North Vietnamese to abandon their support for the NLF. The 'hawks' favoured the escalation of military action against North Vietnam, and Rostow compared Wilson's dissociation from the Hanoi and Haiphong raids to Macmillan's response to the Berlin crisis, commenting with evident disgust that 'we are up against a [British] attitude which, in effect, prefers that we take losses in the free world rather than the risks of sharp confrontation'. Unlike Bundy, Rostow clearly had no sympathy for the competing pressures the Labour government faced over Vietnam, nor did he understand the prime minister's genuine concern over the prospects of a wider war in East Asia. Wilson's attempts at peacemaking would therefore receive an even less accommodating response from the Johnson administration than had previously been the case.[42]

Hungarian and Polish diplomacy during the Vietnam War, December 1965–January 1966', *JCWS* v/2 (2003), 32–67.

41 See J. Hershberg, '"Who murdered *Marigold*"? New evidence on the mysterious failure of Poland's secret initiative to start US–North Vietnamese peace talks' (CWIHP working paper xxvii, 2000).

42 A. E. Goodman, *The search for a negotiated settlement of the Vietnam War*, Berkeley, CA 1986, 19; W. Rostow to Johnson, 5 Apr. 1966, *FRUS* iv. 329–33, and 28 July 1966, LCHMA, MF 411.

Brown took a more active interest in negotiations on Vietnam than his predecessor, and hoped to use his November 1966 visit to Moscow to persuade the Soviets to co-operate with British attempts at mediation. The Foreign Secretary blamed the continuation of the war on North Vietnamese intransigence, but Michael Palliser (Wilson's Private Secretary on foreign affairs) recalled that Brown was 'more worried about the American role' in Indochina than Stewart had been. According to Castle, the Foreign Secretary once told her that he was 'sickened' by the government's policy on Vietnam. Despite this outburst, Brown publicly supported Wilson's position on the war, arguing that complete disassociation from US policy would not only damage the Anglo-American alliance, but would lead an isolationist America to 'follow a sporadic and unpredictable foreign policy, withdrawing here and over-asserting herself there'. China and the USSR could respond to 'unwise temptations' arising from American inconsistency, with disastrous consequences. Brown argued that Britain possessed some influence in Washington and Moscow, and that the British government had 'a duty and a capacity to maintain a continued readiness to act in the cause of peace when asked to do so by one of the combatants'. Although these arguments were advanced nine months after the Kosygin visit, they reflected the attitudes of both Wilson and Brown in early 1967.[43]

When Brown visited Washington in October 1966, he was given the Phase A/B formula but was not informed of the *Marigold* discussions. Rusk told him that Johnson would not end *Rolling Thunder* unless North Vietnam's leaders gave 'substantial advance information' of de-escalation on its part. Despite their doubts about Brown, US officials acquiesced in the Foreign Secretary's involvement on the ground that Anglo-American relations 'would suffer a damaging blow' if the Labour government questioned the USA's commitment towards peace negotiations.[44] In Moscow, Brown apprised Gromyko of Phase A/B, only to be told that the USSR had no authorisation from the Lao Dong leadership to discuss Vietnamese affairs, and that air-strikes against the DRV had to end as a precondition for negotiations. Brown's statement to Gromyko is worth quoting, because it displays British officialdom's interpretation of the US negotiating position:

Consideration might be given to the possibility of the parties agreeing secretly on mutual measures of de-escalation which would be put into effect once the bombing had stopped. *In this the first step would be to stop the bombing and the second step would be further action of de-escalation by the American side to which the North Viet-Namese [sic] and Viet Cong would respond by similar acts of de-escalation; but with both phases forming part of a firm prior understanding.*

[43] Palliser interview, DOHP, transcript, 12; *Castle diaries*, 148, entry for 18 July 1966; C(67)180: 'Vietnam', 15 Nov. 1967, CAB 129/134.
[44] Washington to FO, no. 2835, 17 Oct. 1966, PREM 13/1277; W. Bundy to Rusk, 15 Nov. 1966, NARAII, RG 59, 250, 5–7, 2788; memorandum of meeting at State Department, 10 Nov. 1966, *FRUS* iv. 820–5.

Brown's statement, to which Rusk did not object, clearly stipulated that the USA would make the first move by stopping *Rolling Thunder*, although this would only be on the understanding that North Vietnam would respond by halting PAVN and NLF activity in South Vietnam.[45]

Wilson and Brown were livid when they found out about the *Marigold* initiative in January 1967, claiming that their ignorance of the Polish-American contacts had hampered the Foreign Secretary's discussions with the Soviet leadership.[46] None the less both remained committed to the promotion of peace talks. Wilson later maintained that in early 1967 there were 'straws in the wind' suggesting that negotiations could prove feasible. He referred to a press interview with the DRV's Foreign Minister, Nguyen Duy Trinh, who stated that US-North Vietnamese talks could follow the 'unconditional' end of *Rolling Thunder*. Brown likewise told his Cabinet colleagues on 12 January 1967 that the prospects for a negotiated settlement were 'slightly more hopeful than hitherto', because China's efforts to thwart mediation were forestalled by the Cultural Revolution.[47] American officials were already seeking to establish contacts with their adversaries through the North Vietnamese embassy in Moscow, and this initiative, codenamed *Sunflower* by the State Department, subsequently incorporated Kosygin's visit to London from 6–13 February 1967.

What were the Soviet government's motives for its involvement in *Sunflower*? As the DRV's principal source of military assistance by 1967, the USSR was by no means a disinterested party in the war, but Gaiduk argues persuasively that by the time Kosygin visited London Brezhnev and his peers wanted a political settlement to the conflict in Vietnam, and believed that China's ability to block North Vietnam's involvement in peace talks had diminished. According to Dobrynin, the Soviet premier apparently hoped to achieve a diplomatic success similar to the Tashkent conference (January 1966), during which he brokered a ceasefire concluding the Indo-Pakistani war over Kashmir. Both Dobrynin and Gaiduk retrospectively confirm Gore-Booth's conclusions that the Soviet leadership had an interest in seeing a conclusion to the war in Vietnam before it '[got] out of hand',[48] and Kosygin's involvement in *Sunflower* provided additional confirmation of this assessment. Throughout his visit to London, the Soviet premier was 'in prompt, confidential communication' with the North Vietnamese, and his telephone

[45] Brown–Gromyko conversations, Soviet Foreign Ministry, 23, 25 Nov. 1966, NS1051/290, FO 371/188928, emphasis added; State Dept. to London, 27 Nov. 1966, *FRUS* iv. 865–6.

[46] FO to Washington, N.92, 4 Jan. 1967, and Bruce–Wilson conversation, No.10, 10 Jan. 1967, PREM 13/1917.

[47] Wilson, *Labour government*, 345; Gore-Booth, *With great truth*, 358–9; CC1(67)1st conclusions, 12 Jan. 1967, CAB 128/42.

[48] Gaiduk, *Soviet Union*, 96–7; Dobrynin, *In confidence*, 155–7; Gore-Booth to de la Mare, 23 Jan. 1967, FCO 15/615.

conversations with Brezhnev, intercepted by MI5, suggested that the former saw a chance to achieve a ceasefire.[49]

At Wilson's request Johnson sent Chester Cooper, a National Security Council official, to London to brief the prime minister on the USA's negotiating position.[50] The prime minister regarded the forthcoming Vietnamese New Year (*Tet*) truce – which coincided with Kosgyin's visit – as an opportunity to persuade his guest to recommend the Phase A/B proposal to the North Vietnamese, and he used Cooper as a back-channel to secure American approval for his efforts.[51] Phase A/B was only concerned with military de-escalation which, as Johnson informed Wilson, was intended to lead to 'private and direct' discussions between US and North Vietnamese diplomats. The president also described his terms for de-escalation using language which later proved to be contentious: '[We] are prepared to and plan through established channels to inform Hanoi that *if they will agree to an assured stoppage of infiltration into South Viet Nam, we will stop the bombing of North Viet Nam and stop further augmentation of US forces in South Viet Nam.*'[52]

Following the Soviet premier's arrival in London on 6 February, Wilson sought his endorsement of Phase A/B, claiming that Johnson was under domestic pressure which favoured 'a stronger prosecution of the conflict' in Vietnam. Despite Kosygin's insistence on an unconditional end to *Rolling Thunder*, Wilson was impressed by his guest's anti-Chinese attitude.[53] He assured the US president that Kosygin was showing 'a great sense of urgency' in discussions, which in his opinion reflected the USSR's interest in ending the war and curtailing the PRC's influence in North Vietnam.[54]

At a meeting at 10 Downing Street on 7 February, Kosygin requested a written copy of the Phase A/B proposal, and following this discussion Cooper produced a paper with the assistance of Bruce, Palliser, Burke Trend (the Cabinet Secretary), and a SEAD official, Donald Murray. This document was similar to the one that Brown had taken to Moscow the previous November. The formula defined 'assured stoppage' as involving a halt to the bombing, followed by an end to PAVN infiltration and the American military build-up in the South. Kosygin discussed the disengagement proposals with Wilson and Brown at a meeting in his hotel suite at Claridges on 9

---

[49] Herring, *Secret diplomacy*, 400; T. Benn, *Out of the wilderness: diaries, 1963–67*, London 1987, 468, entry for 6 Feb. 1967; Gaiduk, *Soviet Union*, 100.

[50] C. Cooper, *The lost crusade: the full story of US involvement in Vietnam from Roosevelt to Nixon*, London 1971, 354–5; Herring, *Secret diplomacy*, 430–1.

[51] C. Cooper–Wilson conversation, No.10, 16 Jan. 1967, and Washington to FO, N.321, 1 Feb. 1967, PREM 13/1917.

[52] Johnson to Wilson, CAP67038, 6 July 1967, PREM 13/1917 (emphasis added to original); Herring, *Secret diplomacy*, 436–7.

[53] KV(67)1st meeting, No.10, 6 Feb. 1967, CAB 133/365; Kosygin–Wilson conversations, No.10, 6, 7 Feb. 1967, PREM 13/1917.

[54] Kosygin– Wilson conversation at dinner, No.10, 7 Feb. 1967, PREM 13/1715; Wilson to Johnson, T22/67, 7 Feb. 1967, PREM 13/1917.

February. The Soviet premier was by now more interested in Phase A/B, and he informed Wilson and Brown that he would pass the formula to the North Vietnamese leadership.[55]

Kosygin may have considered the Phase A/B formula to be militarily advantageous to the DRV, as it guaranteed a bombing halt which would enable it to send more troops to the South. However, James Hershberg argues that Kosygin's conduct reflected Soviet policy goals in early 1967, which focused on using private mediation to avert a US-Soviet confrontation over Vietnam. The USSR's leaders had supported *Marigold*, and could have been prepared to see whether Kosygin's talks with Wilson would yield any results. For their part, British officials believed that they had achieved a breakthrough, because previously their Soviet counterparts had flatly refused to co-operate with any peace initiatives. Cooper sent a copy of this text to his superiors in Washington, and considering the lack of a response to indicate approval. An excited Wilson wanted to deliver Phase A/B to Kosygin before the latter left for a weekend tour of Scotland on 10 February, and he told the Soviet premier that all Johnson required was a private assurance from Hanoi that PAVN troop movements to the South would cease if *Rolling Thunder* stopped. The prime minister was delighted, and he enthusiastically informed his ministers that 'the Russians regarded us as the real mediators over Vietnam'.[56] However, Wilson's attitude changed completely once the Johnson administration belatedly responded to the Phase A/B formula Cooper had transmitted to Washington.

Sunflower is uprooted: the end of Phase A/B, 10–13 February 1967

Cooper and his hosts interpreted 'assured stoppage' as an end to *Rolling Thunder*, followed by mutual de-escalation on the ground. Having acted on this assumption, Cooper spent the evening of 10 February at the theatre, only to be summoned backstage halfway through a performance of *Fiddler On The Roof* to receive a telephone call from an enraged Rostow. The NSC official rushed back to the US embassy to receive a new message from Washington, stating that *Rolling Thunder* would end once the Johnson administration was 'assured that infiltration from North Vietnam to South Vietnam *has stopped*'. Not only were both he and the ambassador obliged to inform British officials of this message, but an amended version of Phase A/B had to be hastily drafted and passed on to the Soviet party before it departed for

55 Kosygin–Wilson conversation, Claridges, 9 Feb. 1967, PREM 13/1715; 'The Kosygin visit' (Feb.1967), 10–2, FCO 15/634.
56 London to State Dept, 9 Feb. 1967, *FRUS*, V: *Vietnam, 1967*, Washington, DC 2002, http://www.state.gov/r/pa/ho/frus/johnsonlb/v/13139.htm, downloaded 8 Apr. 2006; Hershberg, *Marigold*, 81–2; Cooper, *Lost crusade*, 356–7; Kosygin–Wilson conversation, No.10, 10 Feb. 1967, PREM 13/1715; *Castle diaries*, 217, entry for 9 Feb. 1967.

Edinburgh.[57] Wilson was furious as he faced a difficult meeting with Kosygin at Chequers on 12 February, and in a blunt telegram to Johnson he asserted that these sudden changes to the Phase A/B formula placed him in 'a hell of a situation'. During an acrimonious meeting with Bruce and Cooper on the evening of the 11th Wilson stated that either the proposals outlined by the latter 'did not reflect American policy or that policy had been changed during the course of the week'. Wilson and Brown threatened outright dissociation from American policy, and questioned the sincerity of the US government's commitment to peace negotiations. With the *Sunflower* initiative in tatters, the tensions between the prime minister and Foreign Secretary also erupted. Cooper recalled that 'Wilson and Brown just went for each other' in front of both himself and the US ambassador to London, and that during the course of this row the Foreign Secretary made repeated threats to resign. As Cooper wryly recalled, '[it] was a pretty rough night'.[58]

In his response to Wilson, Johnson stated that North Vietnam had exploited the Tet bombing pause by infiltrating more troops into the South. He also expressed surprise at the manner in which Cooper and the British government had interpreted the phrase 'assured stoppage'. This transatlantic dispute was not merely a matter of mixed tenses. While Kosygin was in London, the Johnson administration sent a message to Hanoi for Ho Chi Minh on 8 February, calling for bilateral talks and stating that the president would halt both *Rolling Thunder* and troop reinforcements to South Vietnam *'as soon as [he is] assured that infiltration into South Vietnam by land and sea has stopped'*. Wilson, Brown and Foreign Office officials were furious that they had not been informed of the content of this message to Ho.[59] McNamara retrospectively attributed the failure to keep the British government informed to the Johnson administration's inability to co-ordinate its diplomatic approach to the Vietnam War with military operations, in stark contrast with the Lao Dong's strategy of 'fighting while negotiating'. However, Cooper concluded that Johnson and his advisers considered the Kosygin visit to be a 'sideshow', and did not want Wilson to get any credit for a diplomatic breakthrough. The documentary evidence available confirms Cooper's belief that the Johnson administration regarded the Kosygin–Wilson talks with unease. The president displayed little confidence in either the prime minister's efforts to mediate, or the potential for the London talks to achieve a decisive result.[60]

---

[57] Chester Cooper oral history interview III, 7 Aug. 1969, LBJLIB, transcript, 17–19; Rostow to Trend, 10 Feb. 1967, PREM 13/1918 (emphasis added).

[58] Wilson to Johnson, 12 Feb. 1967, and Brown, Bruce, Cooper and Wilson conversation, No.10, 11 Feb. 1967, PREM 13/1918; Lankford, *Last American aristocrat*, 335; Cooper oral history interview, transcript, 21.

[59] Johnson to Wilson, CAP67043, 12 Feb. 1967, PREM 13/1918; Goodman, *Vietnam War*, 26–7; Palliser to Wilson, 23 Mar. 1967, PREM 13/1919.

[60] R. McNamara, *In retrospect*, NY 1995, 250–2; Cooper, *Lost crusade*, 355–6, 367–8; *Secret diplomacy*, 396; telephone conversation between Johnson and Rusk, 9 Feb. 1967,

While Kosygin and Wilson met at Chequers on the 12 February, Cooper discussed with Trend a possible extension to the Tet truce, should the North Vietnamese leadership agree to halt troop movements to the South. He telephoned his superiors with this suggestion, and waited for a response while Wilson tried to stall Kosygin's departure for London. Cooper became convinced that his compatriots were deliberately delaying their response, and dangled his telephone out of a window, so that anyone on the other end of the line could hear Kosygin's police escort revving up their engines. Rostow eventually informed Cooper that Johnson agreed to this proposal, but that the North Vietnamese leadership had to deliver its response by 10.00 a.m., London time, the following day.[61] Wilson tried to persuade Kosygin to accept this proposal early on the morning of the 13th, only for the latter to protest that he had too little time to get an answer from Hanoi. Wilson and Brown countered by commenting on the PAVN build-up in the South and on lack of a response from the DRV to the original Phase A/B proposal. Wilson told Kosygin that 'peace was more important than victory', and the latter eventually passed the PAVN halt/Tet truce extension proposal to the North Vietnamese.[62] Wilson pleaded with Johnson for more time, and was grudgingly granted six more hours, and once these expired Bruce tried in vain to request a further extension from his superiors.[63] The DRV made no response to the proposals Kosygin transmitted, and the Soviet party left Britain on 13 February without a deal being struck.

At a Cabinet meeting the following day Wilson, in Castle's words, 'stressed how near he had been to pulling it off over Vietnam'. He later claimed that White House officials had sabotaged his efforts to achieve a cease-fire while Chinese influence over the DRV was hampered by the Cultural Revolution. Brown likewise blamed American 'hawks', but also criticised Wilson for his excessive optimism. In the aftermath of the Kosygin's visit, Brown concluded that the Soviet leaders would lose interest in mediation, and that the USSR's involvement in *Sunflower* would have antagonised the North Vietnamese leadership, driving them closer to the Chinese in the process.[64] The Foreign Office's assessment was that, despite their military build-up, the Americans were losing the counter-insurgency war in South Vietnam. However, British diplomats were also privately critical of Wilson

---

FRUS, v, http://www.state.gov/r/pa/ho/frus/Johnsonlb/v/13139.htm, downloaded 19 Dec. 2006.

61 *Secret diplomacy*, 471–2; Cooper, *Lost crusade*, 364–5; Johnson to Wilson, CAP67045, 12 Feb. 1967, PREM 13/1918.

62 Brown, Kosygin and Wilson conversation, Claridges, 13 Feb. 1967, PREM 13/1715; Ellis, *Vietnam War*, 237.

63 Johnson to Wilson, CAP67046, 13 Feb. 1967, PREM 13/1918; 'Kosygin visit', 27–8, FCO 15/634; Lankford, *Last American aristocrat*, 336.

64 *Castle diaries*, 220, entry for 14 Feb. 1967; Wilson, *Labour government*, 346–5; George Brown, *In my way*, London 1972, 139–40; memorandum of conversation, State Dept, 19 Apr. 1967, FCO 15/619.

and Brown's conduct. Gore-Booth stated that his political masters overrated their ability to influence American policy, and that peace initiatives were determined by the need to appease domestic criticism rather than by a 'cool estimate' of what British diplomacy could actually achieve.[65] The fact was that Phase A/B only involved military de-escalation, and did not address the practicalities of negotiations. Even if a disengagement formula acceptable to both the USA and North Vietnam had been found, Wilson still had little reason to claim in his memoirs that 'a historic opportunity [for peace] had been missed'.[66]

Like their British counterparts, US officials concluded that after the abortive talks in London, the USSR 'had no alternative but to help Hanoi carry on the war, hoping that changes of attitude in either Hanoi or Washington, or both, will make a [negotiated] solution possible later'. Administration officials attributed the collapse of Phase A/B to the PAVN's violation of the Tet truce, and were also furious that Wilson implicitly blamed them for the failure of his talks with Kosygin.[67] The British ambassador to Washington, Patrick Dean, asserted that the Johnson administration was at fault for neglecting to inform the British of the discrepancy between the letter to Ho and the disengagement proposals agreed in London. Palliser noted Rostow's comment (as reported by Dean) that US officials 'had not thought about [the Phase A/B formula] very much' until they realised that it had been handed to Kosygin as a diplomatic note. This collective lack of interest in Washington was expressed by Rostow in his telephone conversation with Cooper on the night of the 10 February, during which he stated that 'we don't give a Goddamn about you, and we don't give a Goddamn about Wilson!'. When the prime minister met Johnson's national security advisor in London in late February, the latter placed the president's war aims in the context of domestic electoral concerns. Rostow stated that Johnson 'had to achieve a balance between readiness to negotiate and a determination to prosecute the war with firmness but moderation' in order to win a second term in office in 1968. Rostow thus expressed the president's determination to achieve a military victory in Vietnam, and his complete disinterest in third-party efforts to promote peace negotiations. Following *Sunflower* the Americans attempted to use the USSR as a channel for diplomatic contacts with the DRV, excluding would-be mediators such as Britain from any involvement in peace initiatives.[68]

---

[65] Ellis, *Vietnam war*, 112–13; Michael Alexander interview (Foreign Office advisor to CINC Far East, Singapore 1967–8), DOHP, transcript, 20; Gore-Booth to de la Mare, 23 Jan. 1967, FCO 15/615.

[66] Conversation, Claridges, 9 Feb. 1967, PREM 13/1715; 'Kosygin visit', 14, FCO 15/634; Wilson, *Labour government*, 365.

[67] SNIE11–11–67, 'Soviet attitudes and intentions toward the Vietnam War', 4 May. 1967, LCHMA, MFF15–419; Washington to FO, N.469, 16 Feb. 1967, PREM 13/1918; Ellis, *Vietnam War*, 241.

[68] P. Dean to Wilson, 10 Apr. 1967, and Palliser to Wilson, 12 Apr. 1967, PREM

Wilson emerged from the *Marigold* and *Sunflower* fiascos suspecting that hard-line US officials were responsible for the failure of both peace initiatives. Against the Foreign Secretary's advice, he pestered Johnson over the 'apparent failure of communication' which had occurred during Kosygin's visit. During a meeting with Rapacki at 10 Downing Street on 24 February, Wilson suggested that their governments could compare notes on the collapse of *Marigold*.[69] The Foreign Office's collective reluctance to undertake an Anglo-Polish *post mortem* was reflected in Gore-Booth's instructions to Thomas Brimelow, at that time the British ambassador to Warsaw, warning against Polish efforts to stir up Anglo-American discord. Following Brimelow's consultations with Polish diplomats, SEAD officials concluded that the latter did not have 'a sufficiently clear mandate from the North Vietnamese' to act as an intermediary with the US government.[70] Wilson's persistence in requesting a detailed examination of *Marigold* exasperated Murray, who protested that SEAD was 'unwilling to undertake this entirely profitless analysis'. Brown's visit to Moscow in May 1967 eventually deflected the prime minister's attention from *Marigold*. The Foreign Secretary's failure to reach any consensus with Gromyko on Vietnam effectively marked the end of any significant effort by the Labour government to promote a negotiated conclusion to the war.[71]

During his visit to Moscow in January 1968 – the third and last of his premiership – Wilson passed on Johnson's conditions for peace in Vietnam (the so-called 'San Antonio' formula) to his hosts. However because these terms effectively re-stated the American draft of Phase A/B this approach yielded no results. The launching of the Tet offensive (30 January 1968) in South Vietnam by the NLF and PAVN made further efforts at peacemaking nugatory. Although Tet was a military disaster for the Communist side, it undermined the USA's will to continue fighting, and led to Johnson's public announcement of a partial halt to the bombing of the DRV, his refusal on 31 March 1968 to stand for re-election and the convening of peace negotiations in Paris in May 1968. While America's involvement in Vietnam continued until the Paris Peace Accords of January 1973, the wish of US body politic to disengage from Indochina was evident from March 1968 onwards. As a consequence, aside from a brief furore over the US invasion

13/2458; Cooper oral history interview, transcript, 19; Rostow–Wilson conversation, No.10, 24 Feb. 1967, PREM 13/1918; Gaiduk, *Soviet Union*, 156–93.

[69] Brown to Wilson, 14 Mar. 1967, and Wilson to Brown, 17 Mar. 1967, PREM 13/2458; Wilson–Rapacki conversation, No.10, 24 Feb. 1967, PREM 13/1918.

[70] Gore-Booth to Brimelow, 20 Mar. 1967; Brimelow to Gore-Booth, 5 Apr. 1967; and D. Murray (SEAD), 'Vietnam: the Lewandowski affair', 14 Apr. 1967, FCO 15/646.

[71] Palliser to MacLehose, 17 Apr. 1967, and Murray memorandum, n.d., FCO 15/646; Hershberg, *Marigold*, 90–1; Brown–Gromyko conversation, Soviet Foreign Ministry, 24 May 1967, PREM 13/1919.

of Cambodia in April-May 1970, there was a progressive decline in domestic political and public protests against British policy towards Vietnam.[72]

The Vietnam war assumed a major role in Wilson's conduct of foreign affairs because of its implications for both Britain's international position and its domestic politics. The Labour government was caught between demands from Washington for closer association with the US war effort (including requests for the deployment of combat troops), and dissent both from back-benchers and extra-parliamentary opinion over its support for what critics regarded as illegitimate, imperialistic aggression against a Third World nation. Dissent over policy on Vietnam extended to Cabinet level, which explains why Wilson sought to limit ministerial debate on the war, confining policy discussions for the most part to Stewart and Brown. The domestic reaction to the Vietnam War represented in part a fracturing of the 'Cold War consensus' which had bound public opinion on East-West relations. While there had been protests over Suez and British nuclear weapons policy, the USA's intervention in Vietnam inspired both the growth of anti-American sentiment in Britain, and disgust at the Labour government's acquiescence in the actions of the Johnson administration. Wilson's attempts at mediation were therefore intended in part to appease critics within the Labour party. The prime minister resisted left-wing demands for a complete dissociation from US policy, which would have damaged an Anglo-American relationship already strained by defence disputes, conflicting policies over East-West trade and Johnson's own personal distrust of Wilson. Given the importance of US assistance for the UK's strategic and fiscal interests, the British government could not be as overtly critical as de Gaulle of American intervention in Indochina. In spite of Wilson's threats to Bruce and Cooper in February 1967, a complete breach with American policy over Vietnam was never feasible; as the prime minister privately admitted, 'we can't kick our creditors in the balls'. Wilson was, however, able to refuse the US government's requests to send British soldiers to fight in Vietnam, which aroused considerable resentment within the Johnson administration.[73]

Wilson's persistence in pressing the case for peace talks on Vietnam did not derive solely from a need to counterbalance competing pressures from the Johnson administration and the Labour left. While there was a degree of egotism underpinning his personal desire to play peace-maker, his continued commitment reflects Crossman's description of the prime minister as a 'Yorkshire terrier' who 'having got his teeth into an idea … worries at it and never gives it up'. His concerns over escalation were genuine, if misplaced; the Johnson administration showed by its actions that it was far more wary of Chinese or Soviet intervention than its public pronouncements suggested.

---

[72] Schulzinger, *Time for war*, 251; Wilson, *Labour government*, 490–3; Young, *Labour governments*, 80–1; A. J. Banks, 'Britain and the Cambodian crisis of spring 1970', *CWH* v/1 (2005), 87–106.
[73] Callaghan, *Foreign policy*, 271–8; Young, '"LBJ's war"', 77.

He also displayed genuine humanitarian horror at the suffering caused by the conflict in both North and South Vietnam. Wilson's preference for negotiation over confrontation was also demonstrated by his handling of Rhodesian UDI. Crossman noted that the prime minister saw himself as 'a statesman able to achieve what no diplomat could achieve', a comment supported by Wilson's smug comment to Cooper that the Marigold initiative proved that mediation 'was not a task to be entrusted to amateurs'. As Brown subsequently stated, the prime minister believed that 'he had a special ability to negotiate with the Russians' which would enable him to achieve 'a political triumph over Vietnam'.[74]

However, Wilson's efforts at mediation rested on the assumption that Britain could use a self-declared position as the superpower's 'go-between' to encourage negotiations between the USA and North Vietnam. This represented not only personal conceit but also a lack of understanding of the effect his conduct of diplomacy had on the Johnson administration. Wilson's contacts with the Soviet government and his peace initiatives were regarded with a mixture of cynicism and contempt by Johnson, Rusk and other decision-makers in Washington. As the war in Vietnam deteriorated, and as anti-war opposition grew amongst the US public, the President's response to any external criticism, implicit or otherwise, of his administration's handling of Vietnam became increasingly shrill. Both Rusk and Bundy (prior to his resignation in March 1966) privately sought to persuade Johnson that Wilson was doing his utmost to demonstrate his loyalty as an ally, given the domestic political constraints he had to contend with. Yet US officials had few illusions about the practical significance of British diplomacy in resolving the conflict in Vietnam, and there remained a residual sense of grievance over the lack of support from the UK for the American war effort. Rusk's reported outburst to one British journalist – 'When the Russians invade Sussex, don't expect us to come and help you!' – showed that even the Anglophile Secretary of State was not immune to this sentiment.[75]

Of the three Foreign Secretaries during this period, Brown offered the most support to the prime minister's involvement in Vietnam diplomacy, in spite of his personal antipathy towards Wilson. Gordon Walker played no significant role during his short tenure as Foreign Secretary. Stewart backed the prime minister's efforts at mediation loyally, although his advocacy of American policy outraged the Labour left. While Wilson's views on Vietnam did not differ significantly from those of Foreign Office officials, there was friction between the prime minister and the British diplomatic corps, partic-

---

[74] 716 HC.Deb.5s, London 1965, 1123–7; Crossman diaries, i. 120, entry for 4 Jan. 1965; ii. 87, entry for 24 Oct. 1966; Cooper–Wilson conversation, No.10, 18 Jan. 1967, PREM 13/1917; Pimlott, Wilson, 365–81, 449–58; Brown, In my way, 137; draft notes on Vietnam debate in Commons, 7 July 1966, Wilson papers, Bodleian Library, Oxford, MS Wilson, c.1234, fos 157–9.

[75] Ellis, Vietnam War, 100–1, 112–13; Herring, 'Fighting without allies', 80.

ularly regarding attempts by the latter to 'water down' Wilson's statement on the Hanoi and Haiphong raids in July 1966 to avoid offending American sensibilities. Having initially supported the containment of Communist expansion in South-East Asia, British officials regarded the progressive intensification of US operations in Vietnam with concern, concluding that the Americans could not prevail militarily against the DRV and NLF. There was also no great enthusiasm within the Foreign Office, or the MoD, for even a token military commitment on Britain's part. British officials favoured a negotiated settlement which would help to promote the emergence of a stable, neutral South-East Asia, and developments such as the destruction of the PKI, the end of 'confrontation' in 1965–6, and the foundation of ASEAN in 1967 encouraged hopes within Whitehall that the expansion of Communism could be curtailed without a continued Western military presence in the region. However, incessant Sino-Soviet competition for influence over the DRV, and the North Vietnamese leadership's determination to strive for unification regardless of the human and material cost, meant that the British government was unable to achieve the diplomatic success Eden gained in 1954, and was ultimately unable to effect the final denouement of the war in April 1975.[76]

One crucial difference between Wilson and British diplomats was that the officials (with the exception of Harrison) were convinced that the prime minister's involvement in peacemaking initiatives was misconceived, and with the benefit of hindsight it is clear that Wilson overlooked the complexity of the Indochinese crisis. This was demonstrated not only by the interaction of the Vietnam conflict with the concurrent civil war in neighbouring Laos, but also by Cambodia's precarious position in regional politics, as the failed attempt in the spring of 1965 to convene a conference on that country's neutral status showed. Furthermore, Wilson overlooked the autonomy of both the NLF and the South Vietnamese regime as significant actors in the Vietnamese conflict, assuming that their patrons in Hanoi and Washington could automatically assure their co-operation in any peace talks. The crucial fact which Wilson ignored was that prior to the Tet offensive of 1968 both the Americans and North Vietnamese governments believed that a military solution was feasible, and neither side was willing to compromise their war aims with a negotiated settlement. In declaring to Kosygin that 'peace was more important than victory', Wilson failed to recognise that as far as the main belligerents were concerned, victory was far more important than peace.[77]

---

[76] Vickers, 'Foreign policy', 136; H. C. Hainworth (Jakarta) to Stewart, 3 Aug. 1968, and N. Pritchard (Bangkok) to Murray, 4 Sept. 1968, FCO 15/23; Young, *Labour governments*, 74–5; Jones, *Confrontation*, 297–9.
[77] Conversation, Claridges, 13 Feb. 1967, PREM 13/1715; Hughes, '"Missed opportunity"', 125.

The prime minister's own references to Anglo-Soviet co-operation demonstrated a degree of self-delusion. This was evident during the period between the spring of 1965 and the summer of 1966 when it was clear that Brezhnev and Kosygin could not afford to be seen to collaborate diplomatically with the 'imperialists', lest they cede a crucial propaganda advantage to their Chinese rivals, and were therefore obliged to offer the USSR's full support and military assistance to the DRV. Indeed, Wilson himself sought to embarrass his parliamentary critics by reminding them of China's hostility to peace negotiations, enquiring why they did not blame Mao rather than Johnson for the diplomatic impasse over Vietnam. China's ideological challenge to Soviet pre-eminence over the Communist 'international' was certainly a significant constraint on the USSR's foreign policy in general – and its response to Vietnam – until late 1966. Throughout the 1960s Mao sought to promote China as the patron of revolution throughout the Third World, and he cajoled the Soviet government to respond to Vietnam by abandoning *détente* with the Western powers. Throughout 1965 Chinese officials demanded a more confrontational Soviet posture over Berlin and the German question as a reprisal for US military intervention in South-East Asia. While the USSR's leaders rejected such brinkmanship, they were obliged to distance themselves from the USA and other Western powers in order to demonstrate solidarity with North Vietnam. Furthermore, it is now clear that one factor behind Khrushchev's overthrow was his mishandling of relations with China, the consequences of which his successors were determined to repair. Shelepin and Polyanskii favoured a *rapprochement* with the Chinese, and in his efforts to promote unity within the *Politburo* Brezhnev was obliged to accommodate his peers. It was not until late 1965 that Soviet leaders finally accepted that the alliance with the PRC was moribund, and that Mao had decided on a complete breach with the USSR.[78] While this facilitated improved Soviet-Western relations from 1966 onwards, notably contacts with the Johnson administration on non-proliferation and Vietnam, on these issues the Soviet leadership preferred to deal directly with their American counterparts, as was evident with the summit between Johnson and Kosygin in Glassboro on 23 June 1967. Furthermore, although the Soviet premier was prepared to explore the Phase A/B initiative during his visit to London in February 1967, it is conceivable that – as with other aspects of Anglo-Soviet contacts during Wilson's premiership – the USSR's leaders were looking for opportunities to exploit disagreements and to 'drive wedges' between Britain and the USA.[79]

Finally, it should be noted that the Vietnam War also had an indirect effect on British defence policy, not only because of the importance of trans-

---

[78] Dobrynin, *In confidence*, 131; Q. Zhai, *China and the Vietnam Wars, 1950–1975*, Chapel Hill, NC 2000, 3–5, 115–19, 146–51, 175; Radchenko, *China puzzle*, 186–7, 240–7.
[79] D. Day (FO) to Palliser, 15 Dec. 1967, PREM 13/2402; Gaiduk, *Soviet Union*, 120–32.

atlantic military co-operation for the UK, but because of the Johnson administration's support for Britain's East of Suez commitments. American officials
were determined to ensure a continued British military role in South-East
Asia, regarding Vietnam and the British presence in Malaysia and Singapore as part of a general strategy of anti-Communist containment in the
region.[80] The problem was that the UK had to support a number of global
commitments (some of which had an only indirect relevance to Cold War
competition and the Soviet or Chinese 'threat') despite a decreasing financial base, and by 1968 Wilson and his ministers had decided to abandon
Britain's 'world role' in order to focus on NATO responsibilities. The process
by which the Labour government reached this decision, and the effect of
Cold War developments on of British defence policy in the latter half of the
1960s, is the subject of the next chapter.

[80] Healey, My life, 281; Young, Labour governments, 37.

4

British Strategy and Defence Policy, 1964–1968

From October 1964 until January 1968 the Labour government sought to preserve the UK's status as a world power. Its efforts overstretched the British armed forces, which already had to cope with the two conflicts Britain was involved in, in Borneo and South Arabia. Wilson's Cabinet endorsed two crucial decisions affecting British defence policy; the retention of the UK's nuclear deterrent and the introduction of the *Polaris* ballistic missile submarines, and the withdrawal from the Middle East and South-East Asia of all but a token British military presence, in order to focus on NATO's defence.[1] In March 1967 the OPD decided to withdraw half of all British forces from the Persian Gulf and South-East Asia (excluding Hong Kong) by 1970–1, with the remainder leaving both theatres by 1975–6. In the aftermath of the devaluation crisis the Cabinet decided on 15 January 1968 that the military withdrawal would be completed by December 1971. MPs were informed of this decision when Wilson addressed the Commons the following day.[2]

Of these two developments, it was the withdrawals from East of Suez that caused the most controversy. Labour entered office sharing the Conservatives' view that Britain could still act as a global power because of its Commonwealth role and its links with former colonies. Wilson's grandiose statement that Britain's frontiers lay on the Himalayas reflected the priority the new government placed the UK's 'world role'.[3] However, the successive defence reviews undertaken by Labour during its term in office caused contention within Whitehall. The March 1966 review led to the resignation of the Navy Minister, Christopher Mayhew, and the Chief of the Naval Staff, Admiral Sir David Luce, who both argued that the defence cuts (notably the cancellation of the CVA-01 aircraft carrier) rendered the UK's East of Suez role strategically untenable.[4] The content of the 1967 review alarmed

---

1   P. Darby, *British defence policy East of Suez, 1947–1968*, Oxford 1973; S. Dockrill, *East of Suez*, passim; J. Pickering, *Britain's withdrawal from East of Suez: the politics of retrenchment*, Basingstoke 1998.
2   OPD(67)14th meeting, 22 Mar. 1967, CAB 148/30; CC6(68)6th, CC7(68)7th conclusions, 12 Jan. 1968, CAB 128/43.
3   Lapping, *Labour government*, 65; Darby, *Defence policy*, 240–1.
4   C. Mayhew, *Britain's role tomorrow*, London 1967, 135–53; E. Grove, *Vanguard to Trident: British naval policy since World War Two*, Annapolis, MD 1987, 271–7; S. Dockrill, *East of Suez*, 158–9.

the American, Australian and other allied governments with an interest in the retention of Britain's 'world role', and the acceleration of the East of Suez withdrawals in January 1968 was regarded by officials in Washington, Canberra and Singapore as an act of betrayal. During a visit to Washington in January 1968, Brown was told by Rusk that the decision to retrench had 'the acrid aroma of a *fait accompli*', reflecting a loss of will and nerve on the British government's part.[5] Subsequent critiques had a Cold War flavour to them. The Conservatives accused the Wilson government of reducing defence expenditure and overseas commitments despite the expansion of Soviet power worldwide, and these charges were repeated during the 1980s by commentators concerned with the challenge the USSR posed to the West's strategic and economic interests outside the NATO area.[6]

In fact, the Wilson government's defence reviews followed an almost continual post-war process of reduction and retrenchment, influenced by the UK's economic problems. During the 1960s Britain was still devoting a larger proportion of its national expenditure to defence than other West European countries. In 1965 the UK spent 6.3 per cent of its GNP on its armed forces, compared to 5.6 per cent for France, 4.9 per cent for the FRG and 2.9 per cent for Italy. The UK was a member of the NATO, SEATO and CENTO alliances, and had other defence-related obligations to allies such as Malaysia, Singapore and the pro-British sheikhs in South Arabia and the Persian Gulf. Military commitments in the Middle East were related to the need to secure access to oil supplies. Britain maintained bases in Cyprus, Malta, Libya (before the overthrow of King Idris by Colonel Gaddafi in 1969), Aden, the Persian Gulf and Singapore, and also leased the Simonstown naval facility from South Africa. Despite the Labour party's opposition to *apartheid*, the Wilson government did not renounce defence relations with South Africa and sacrificed ethical concerns to the UK's strategic interests. It also inherited from the Conservatives two separate wars which were a further burden on defence expenditure – the 'confrontation' with Indonesia, and a debilitating anti-British insurgency in Aden and South Arabia. By early 1967 the British armed forces were fully stretched across the globe, with 51,800 men (including 37,300 troops) in South-East Asia, 20,300 servicemen in the Mediterranean region, 20,850 in the Middle East and 63,460 personnel in Central Europe, with 55,700 troops committed to BAOR and Berlin. The effectiveness of some of these commitments was questionable;

5 Washington to FO, no. 54, 11 Jan 1968, CAB 129/35; T. T. Petersen, 'Crossing the Rubicon? Britain's withdrawal from the Middle East: a bibliographical review', *IHR* xxii/2 (2000), 318, 339.
6 J. Campbell, *Edward Heath: a biography*, London 1993, 226–7; M. Chichester and J. Wilkinson, *The uncertain ally: British defence policy, 1960–1990*, Aldershot 1982, 28; J. A. B. Kelly, *Arabia, the Gulf and the West*, London 1980; P. Kennedy, *The rise and fall of British naval mastery*, London 1991, 393–8.

Whitehall officials regarded CENTO and SEATO as paper alliances lacking in credibility.[7]

The Labour government's decisions from 1964 to 1968 were themselves shaped by the key tenets of its predecessor between 1945 and 1951; the UK's membership of NATO, Attlee's decision in 1947 to develop nuclear weapons, the continued emphasis on the 'world role' and the close military ties established between Britain and the USA. The latter had its own effect on British defence policy, as policy-makers in Whitehall continued to believe that the UK's SEATO commitment provided it with some means of influencing American policy in the Far East, and of preventing its ally from adopting a more confrontational posture towards China. Wilson went as far as to repeat this claim to sceptical Labour MPs at a stormy meeting in the Commons in July 1966. For its part, the Johnson administration consistently encouraged Wilson to retain the UK's military presence East of Suez, partly because US officials did not want to inherit British defence commitments in the Third World, but also because it gave American forces access to British bases overseas and supported the Anglo-American intelligence alliance. GCHQ had SIGINT posts in the Middle and Far East, while RAF reconnaissance flights were supported by bases in Cyprus, Sharjah, Oman and Singapore as well as the UK. During the Six Day War, the Americans used the British base at Akrotiri, Cyprus, as a staging post for SIGINT and air reconnaissance missions in the Middle East. However, while the Wilson government faced pressure from the US State and Defense Departments to retain British overseas commitments, the traditionally anti-American and anti-imperialist core of the Labour party wanted to reduce defence expenditure, and was wary of the racial and anti-colonial implications of conflicts such as Aden. Foreign Office officials were also aware of the increased importance of Afro-Asian nationalism and the non-aligned movement in world politics, and the antagonising effect that Western military bases could have on local opinion in host countries. The long-term goals of British policy in flashpoints such as South-East Asia was therefore to promote the indigenous defence capabilities of newly-independent, pro-Western countries, although until January 1968 officials in Whitehall intended to preserve the means required for military intervention overseas if allies in the Middle and Far East required assistance against external threats.[8]

7 COS1295/6/6/2/64, 'Record of meeting between CDS and military coordination committee: Persian Gulf', 24 Jan. 1964, DEFE 4/164; COS21st/64, 10 Mar. 1964, DEFE 4/166; OPD(65)28th, 2 June 1965, CAB 148/18; Jones, *Conflict and confrontation*, 291–3; Stewart, *Life and Labour*, 168.
8 Young, *Labour governments*, 37; Easter, *Confrontation*, 9, 114; J. Bamford, *Body of secrets: how America's NSA and Britain's GCHQ eavesdrop on the world*, London 2001, 163–5; London to State Dept., A-3692, 1 June 1968, NSF, LBJLIB, UKCF212; Jones, *Conflict and confrontation*, 297–9; OPD(66)31st, 5 July 1966, CAB 148/25; Callaghan, *Foreign policy*, 268.

The outcome of the Wilson government's defence policy can therefore only be comprehended if one considers the interaction of economic problems, conflicting alliance commitments, Cold War rivalries and calculations of national interest. It was a combination of these factors that influenced both Britain's continued status as a nuclear power and the UK's focus upon continental defence from 1967–8 onwards. This chapter focuses on 'strategy' and 'defence policy', the former concerning the overall objectives of the Wilson government's external policy in the context of the Cold War. These differed little in substance from those of its predecessors, and involved inhibiting Soviet and Chinese expansionism; the maintenance of peace – or the lowest levels of international tension possible; the preservation of Western alliance ties, and the promotion of the UK's declared role as a world power. The maintenance of these goals depended upon the Labour government's ability to sustain the military forces and the alliance relationships they supported, which provided the basis of its defence policy. In the last resort the fourth of these objectives was eventually sacrificed in order to reinforce both the UK's NATO commitments and its status as a nuclear power.

British perceptions of Soviet military power and global policy

Before discussing the circumstances in which the Wilson government conducted its defence policy, it is necessary to summarise official British perceptions of the threat posed by the UK's most powerful adversary. The latter half of the 1960s saw significant changes both in Soviet military strategy and the structure of the USSR's armed forces. Unlike Khrushchev, Brezhnev not only sought parity with the USA's nuclear arsenal, but also to enhance Soviet conventional ground and naval forces.[9] He also inherited his predecessor's desire to improve the USSR's position in the Third World, and to develop closer ties with non-aligned, 'progressive' states. This was an objective complicated by the competition that the Soviets faced from China and Cuba, both of which had more radical agenda focused on promoting revolution in the Third World, and by the determination of leaders such as the Egyptian president, Gamal Abdel Nasser, to prevent their relationship with their Soviet patron from developing into dependency.[10] In dealing with clients such as Egypt, Iraq and Indonesia the Soviet government used arms transfers as a means of fostering influence. The acquisition of sophisticated weaponry by regional adversaries in the Middle and Far East placed an addi-

---

[9] Zaloga, 'Nuclear forces', 209; B. Ranft and G. Till, *The sea in Soviet strategy*, Annapolis, MD 1989, 53–4.

[10] H. Matthews (Moscow) to Brown, 17 Sept. 1966, NS1022/59, FO 371/188906; C. Barclay (IRD), 'Communist activities in Africa', 14 Feb. 1966, FO 371/188487; Westad, *Global Cold War*, 170–80.

tional strain upon the UK's overseas defence burden, making military interventions East of Suez an increasingly risky enterprise for Britain.[11]

Throughout the defence reviews of the 1960s British officials considered China, rather than the USSR, to be the principal menace to Western interests East of Suez. The Soviets themselves had to contend with an emerging strategic threat from China, which aroused atavistic fears reflecting Russia's historical experiences of Mongol and Tartar invasions. While Wilson was impressed by Kosygin's overtly anti-Chinese attitude during his visit to London, US officials also realised that their Soviet counterparts were alarmed by developments within the PRC, especially China's nuclear programme and its successful H-bomb test in May 1967.[12] The Cultural Revolution, the Hong Kong riots and the sacking of the British mission in Beijing by 'Red Guards' in the summer of 1967 made officials in Whitehall question whether Mao could control the revolutionary extremism he had unleashed. The internal turmoil in China in the late 1960s therefore reinforced the American and British perception of the PRC as a potentially irrational and more dangerous international actor than the USSR.[13]

Military discontent with Khrushchev's reductions of Soviet conventional forces contributed to his overthrow in October 1964. In contrast, Brezhnev increased defence expenditure and oversaw a sustained enhancement of the Warsaw Pact's conventional land warfare capabilities, with the introduction of more technologically advanced armoured vehicles and aircraft to its frontline forces. British and American intelligence assessments concluded that despite the deterioration in Sino-Soviet relations, the bulk of the USSR's armed forces were still committed to Europe. According to JIC and DIS estimates, at the beginning of 1967 the USSR had twenty-four front-line divisions (238,000 troops) facing China. By contrast, the Soviets maintained around fifty-eight divisions (748,000 troops) in the Western USSR. In Eastern Europe, the Soviet army had a further twenty divisions (285,000 troops) with the Group of Soviet Forces (GSFG) in the GDR, four divisions in Hungary and two in Poland, all of which were at full strength. JIC estimates noted that Soviet military theorists were starting to develop a 'limited war' doctrine, and were examining the possibility of a conventional conflict with NATO. Furthermore, the combat capabilities of the East European armed forces, in particular those of the GDR, Poland and Czechoslovakia, had improved.[14] Admittedly there were deficiencies in the

11 MISC17/5th meeting on defence, 13 June 1965, CAB 130/213; OPD(O)(65)37 (Revise): 'Defence expenditure review', 2 June 1965, CAB 148/43; Darby, *Defence policy*, 251–2; Healey, *My life*, 279.
12 Wilson to Johnson, T22/67, 7 Feb. 1967, PREM 13/1917; Walt. W. Rostow, oral history interview, 21 Mar. 1969, LBJLIB, transcript, 59; Westad, *Global Cold War*, 165.
13 Trend to Wilson, 24 May. 1967, PREM 13/1458; JIC(67)40th, 7 Sept. 1967, CAB 159/47; Young, *Labour governments*, 63–4.
14 L. Freedman and G. Hughes, 'Strategy', in Dockrill and Hughes, *Cold War*, 48–9; JIC(67)3, 'Soviet bloc war potential', 16 Feb. 1967, CAB158/65.

Eastern bloc forces, notably in training and in equipment, and the weak-nesses in Soviet-built weapons systems were demonstrated during successive Arab-Israeli clashes. None the less, by the end of the 1960s it was evident to Britain and other NATO powers that the Warsaw Pact was no 'cardboard castle', but a fully-functioning and powerful military alliance.[15]

Khrushchev neglected the Soviet navy, but Brezhnev saw it as a means of upholding the USSR's superpower status. Its chief, Admiral Sergei Gorshkov, focused upon the construction of ballistic missile submarines to bolster the Soviet deterrent and to counter the US Navy's *Polaris* fleet, but he also oversaw the expansion of the surface fleet. The emergence of the Soviet navy in both the Norwegian Sea and the Mediterranean posed a potential danger to NATO's flanks: a Soviet amphibious assault on Norway, for example, would threaten the Alliance's maritime control over the Northern Atlantic. By 1968 the Soviets were active in the Indian Ocean and in the same year the Warsaw Pact conducted a major maritime exercise, *Sever* ('North'), in the Baltic, the Atlantic and the Arctic.[16] During the 1960s Gorshkov phased out obsolete vessels, and oversaw the introduction of newer, more sophisti-cated warships. The 1960s also saw the enhancement of Soviet long-range maritime aviation capabilities across the world's oceans. The potential capa-bility of the USSR's naval power was demonstrated in October 1967 when a Soviet-built Egyptian patrol boat sank an Israeli destroyer, the *Eilat*, with a salvo of *Styx* anti-ship missiles. By 1968 NATO commanders feared that the Soviets were acquiring the capability to interdict sea communications between the USA and Europe in wartime.[17]

Officials in London adopted a less alarmist view of the growth in Soviet military and naval power, and its implications for Soviet foreign policy. Throughout the 1960s Brezhnev's *Politburo* tempered the USSR's military expansion with a cautious and non-confrontational approach to East-West relations. The Soviet government was determined to limit the impact of the Vietnam War on its relations with the USA, and East-West flashpoints such as Berlin and Cuba remained quiet throughout the late 1960s. The Soviet and East German armies did undertake a show of force around West Berlin in April 1965, but this was interpreted by the US, British and French govern-ments as a response to the convening of a *Bundestag* session within the city by the West German government. Wilson and officials in Whitehall blamed

[15] DIS(67)5(Final), 'The Arab-Israeli War: June 1967', dated July 1968, DEFE 63/19; V. Mastny and M. Byrne (eds), *A cardboard castle? An inside history of the Warsaw Pact, 1955–1991*, Budapest 2005, 13–34.

[16] DI58(N), 'Naval intelligence report (NIR)', no.18, Winter 1968, DEFE 63/35; Denis Healey to PM, 3 Nov. 1966, DEFE 13/499; S. Maloney, 'Fire brigade or tocsin? NATO's ACE mobile force, flexible response and the Cold War', *JSS* xxvii/4, 590–1.

[17] COS31st/68, 5 June 1968, DEFE 4/228; DI58(N), 'NIR', no.15, Winter 1967, DEFE 63/32; UKDELNATO to FO, no.2(Saving), 26. Jan. 1968, DEFE 13/901.

their counterparts in Bonn, rather than the Soviets, for what they considered to be a pointless provocation.[18]

The USSR's growing maritime presence in the Mediterranean was interpreted by British military and civilian officials as both a response to US *Polaris* patrols in the region, and also as a means of enhancing its prestige with its principal Arab allies. Soviet maritime power was still inferior to the US Navy, and in the Mediterranean the USSR's Fifth Squadron was no match for the American Sixth Fleet. CIA estimates likewise concluded that the USSR was unable 'to apply its conventional power effectively to areas beyond' the frontiers of the Soviet bloc, and that Moscow preferred to support regional proxies rather than take the political risks involved in deploying substantial forces overseas. US military officials, however, adopted a more sinister interpretation of the USSR's intentions, arguing that the Soviet military build-up was intended to support 'the aggressive pursuit of [the Kremlin's] objectives' across the globe.[19] However, recent disclosures from the Soviet archives suggest that during his first years in power Brezhnev perceived that the international balance of power favoured the 'imperialists', as shown by US intervention in Vietnam, the massacre of the PKI by the Indonesian military (1965–6), and Israel's triumph in the Six Day War of 1967. The Soviet government's nervousness over Vietnam reflected in part this perception that the global 'correlation of forces' did not favour the 'progressive' and 'socialist' side. It was not until the mid-1970s that the USSR had the confidence to embark on an a more ambitious global policy involving greater intervention in the Third World.[20]

The Six Day War (5–11 June 1967) inspired conflicting interpretations of the role in that conflict of the USSR, the principal supplier of arms and military assistance to two of Israel's enemies, Egypt and Syria. The Israeli government, in addition to the more hawkish US officials, concluded that the Soviet leadership deliberately provoked the war by issuing false claims of Israeli mobilisation against Syria, thereby sparking an Arab military build-up on Israel's borders. According to this school of thought, the Soviet motive was to force the Johnson administration to intervene on Israel's behalf, adding to the economic and military pressures on the USA caused by Vietnam, and

18 COS27th/68, 14 May 1968, DEFE 4/228; Bonn to FO, no.387–8, 5 Apr. 1965, PREM 13/343; COS65/18th, 6 Apr. 1965, DEFE 4/182; FO to Bonn, no.724, 13 Apr. 1965, and annotated comment by Wilson on letter from Bridges (FO) to Wright, 12 Apr. 1965, PREM 13/343.
19 DIS report DI4(N)119, 'The Soviet naval presence in the Mediterranean', 1 Jan. 1967, FCO 28/455; CIA memorandum, 'Soviet military policy in 1967', 14 June 1967, LCHMA, MF 343; NIE11–6-67, 'Soviet strategy and intentions in the Mediterranean basin', 1 June 1967, NARAII, RG 263, 190, 28, 16–17.
20 Brezhnev's report to the CPSU Central Committee, 20 June 1967, in U. Bar-Noi, 'The Soviet Union and the Six Day War', CWIHP e-dossier no. viii, http://wwics.si.edu/ downloaded 23 Jan. 2007; Westad, *Global Cold War*, 207–87.

inflicting irreparable damage on American-Arab relations.[21] In contrast, officials in London focused on attempts by Brezhnev and Kosygin to restrain their Arab allies prior to the outbreak of the war, and concluded that while the USSR had a vested interest in stirring up regional tensions (directing the anger of the Arab 'street' against Israel and its Western backers), the Soviet government did not want to start a Middle Eastern war which could end in a superpower confrontation. The Soviet leadership's appeals to Nasser for restraint had the unintended consequence of leaving Egypt open to a pre-emptive Israeli attack on 5 June.[22] Israel's overwhelming victory in the ensuing war was regarded by British officials as a disaster for the USSR. Reporting from Moscow, Harrison stated that the Soviet government's 'total underestimation of Israel's capabilities and over-estimation of the Arabs' has left them in a position where their *protégés* have been disastrously defeated without their lifting a finger'.[23] While British military chiefs were aware of the growth of Soviet air and naval presence in Egypt after June 1967, JIC analyses concluded that Soviet-Arab ties would be handicapped by the volatility of the USSR's client regimes (notably Syria), Arab nationalist opposition to all forms of foreign influence and the ideological tensions between Communism and Islam. To some extent this judgement was vindicated after Nasser's death, as his successor Anwar Sadat sought to end his country's dependency on Soviet aid and to realign Egypt with the West.[24]

Policy-makers in Whitehall thus saw the growth of Soviet military capabilities as part of the USSR's intention to demonstrate its prestige as a superpower. JIC, MoD and Foreign Office assessments also concluded, correctly, that the bulk of the Soviet armed forces faced Western Europe, and the primary threat to Western interests overseas was posed by states other than the USSR, such as China, Egypt and (prior to the end of 'confrontation' in August 1966) Indonesia. The Labour government and Whitehall officials generally regarded the USSR as a more 'moderate' and rational actor in global affairs than the PRC. Soviet intervention in Third World affairs was far more selective than was the case in the following decade, and certain aspects of Soviet diplomacy (such as Kosygin's mediation to end the Indo-Pakistani war of 1965, and the USSR's interest in a peace settlement in Vietnam) were not inimical to Western interests. British policy-makers therefore perceived no imminent danger from Soviet external policy, only a

---

[21] M. Oren, *Six days of war*, Oxford 2002; Levi Eshkol (Israeli PM)–Wilson conversation, No.10, 17 Jan. 1968, PREM 13/2213; Dean to Brown, 12 May 1967, FCO 15/667.
[22] G. Golan, *Soviet policies in the Middle East: from World War Two to Gorbachev*, Cambridge 1990, 58, 61–3; Murray to Palliser, 28 May 1967, PREM 13/1618; Washington to FO, no.1949–50, 6 June 1967, PREM 13/1620; Oren, *Six days*, 54–5.
[23] OPD(O)(67)5th meeting, 16 June 1967, CAB 148/80; Moscow to FO, no.1005, 10 June 1967, FCO 28/31; Harrison to Brown, 20 July 1967, PREM 13/1622.
[24] Vice-Chief of Air Staff to Healey, 20 Dec. 1967, TNA, AIR 20/12134; JIC(68)34 (Final), 'Soviet intentions in the Mediterranean', 20 May. 1968, and JIC(68)19(Final), 'Soviet policy in the Middle East and North Africa', 4 June 1968, PREM 13/2959.

latent threat to the security of the UK and other Western powers that had existed since the late 1940s. Officials in Whitehall were also aware that the USSR had to contend with a new security threat on its Eastern frontier, as demonstrated by the Sino-Soviet border clashes of 1969 and the subsequent build-up of Soviet military power in Siberia and Central Asia.[25] The Labour government, Foreign Office and MoD were therefore confident that the potential for conflict with the USSR was limited, and while the decision to retain the UK's strategic nuclear force was justified on the grounds that it contributed to the deterrence of aggression against the West, there were other calculations (involving considerations of prestige, financial cost and the problems of proliferation) which influenced the Wilson government's nuclear policy.

The Labour government and the nuclear deterrent

Although the Attlee government made the crucial decision to develop the British deterrent, the Labour party's attitude to nuclear weapons remained ambivalent. While the left of the party continually demanded unilateral disarmament, throughout his leadership of Labour Gaitskell followed a more nuanced policy, adamantly resisting Bevanite demands for withdrawal from NATO and the eviction of US nuclear forces from British soil, but proposing the dismantling of the V bomber force. Gaitskell's proposal was intended to reinforce the UK's reliance on the American 'nuclear umbrella' and deprive the FRG of any pretext to develop its own deterrent.[26] Labour's 1964 election manifesto contained a pledge to 'renegotiate' the Nassau agreement, and to place the UK's nuclear forces under NATO control. However, on 11 November, Wilson, Gordon-Walker and Healey agreed to retain *Polaris*, a decision which was endorsed at the conference of ministers, senior civil servants and the COS at Chequers the following week. The Conservatives had planned to build five *Polaris* missile submarines, but in January 1965 the OPD decided that Britain could only afford four.[27] *Polaris* was regarded by the Foreign Office, MoD and COS as insurance against both the emergence of new nuclear threats East of Suez and a return to isolationism by the USA. Although Wilson toyed with the idea of stationing the British deterrent in the Indian Ocean, he was informed by MoD officials that the *Polaris* fleet

---

25 CC(66)2nd Cabinet conclusions, 20 Jan. 1966, CAB128/41; D. Wilson to Stewart, 9 Apr. 1969, *DPBO III*, i. 127–9; OPD(O)(LT)(69)2, 'The Sino-Soviet dispute', 4 Dec. 1969, FCO 49/255.
26 D. Keohane, *Labour party defence policy since 1945*, Leicester 1993, 1–23; L. Scott, 'Labour and the bomb: the first 80 years', IA lxxxii/4 (2006), 685–700.
27 MISC11/16, Gordon Walker, Healey and Wilson conversation, No.10, 11 Nov. 1964, CAB 130/212; MISC17/2nd meeting, 21 Nov. 1964, CAB 130/213; OPD(65)5th meeting, 29 Jan. 1965, CAB 148/18.

could be based either in the NATO area or East of Suez, but could not be deployed simultaneously against both the USSR and China.[28] In strategic terms, the UK's *Polaris* fleet was therefore not only overshadowed by the superpower nuclear arsenals, but its ability to support Britain's overseas commitments was debatable.

The Wilson government's decision to retain the British deterrent coexisted with a determination to prevent other states from developing nuclear weapons. The implicit concern underlying Britain's support for an NPT was that West Germany could develop its own nuclear programme, and this was one of the reasons why the Wilson government had offered the ANF as an alternative to proposals for a multilateral NATO nuclear force. Although the FRG had formally renounced NBC weapons in 1955, the leadership of the Christian Democratic Party and Christian Social Union (CDU-CSU) intended to keep their options open, and some senior conservative politicians – notably Franz-Josef Strauss – envisaged the eventual acquisition of nuclear weapons by West Germany.[29] Such a prospect was not only anathema to the USSR and Warsaw Pact powers, but was adamantly opposed by the FRG's West European allies. Wilson himself regarded Soviet propaganda attacks on German 'revanchism' as a symptom of genuine concern about the unrestricted growth of the FRG's power in Europe. In a private conversation with Kosygin during his visit to the UK, Wilson asserted that Britain and other Western powers were intent upon containing any resurgence of German nationalism, that 'President Johnson feared the Germans, de Gaulle despised and hated them and so long as he himself was in power there would be no question of the Germans being allowed a finger on the nuclear trigger'. Although these comments reflected underlying concerns about the future course of German policy in allied capitals, they could have soured the UK's ties with its NATO partners if disclosed, and as a consequence the record of this conversation was heavily edited before its release to Whitehall departments. Wilson's willingness to express his misgivings about an ally so bluntly, particularly to the premier of the UK's main Cold War adversary, was an astonishing lapse of diplomatic judgement.[30]

Ironically, the prime minister's anti-German comments to Kosygin were uttered as the prospect of the FRG acquiring nuclear weapons through a multilateral NATO arrangement was gradually diminishing. Throughout 1965 the nuclear-sharing issue was the source of a three-way dispute between the US,

---

[28] COS278/64(Annex); 'The British strategic nuclear capability', 14 Oct. 1964, DEFE 5/154; Heuser, *NATO*, 85–8; OPD(65)5th, 19th meetings, 29 Jan., 31 Mar. 1965, CAB 148/18.

[29] Moscow to FCO, N.2595–6, 30 Nov. 1965, PREM 13/805; Bange, 'Non-Proliferation Treaty', 162–80; Wright to Wilson, 2 Dec. 1964, PREM 13/103.

[30] Notes on Kosygin–Wilson conversation at dinner, No.10, 7 Feb. 1967, with annotations by Palliser, PREM 13/1715. Johnson's concerns over Germany were evident in his conversation with Wilson at Adenauer's funeral: Palliser to MacLehose, 28 Apr. 1967, PREM 13/1455.

British and West German governments. Although the Erhard government favoured a solution which gave the FRG a role in NATO nuclear deterrence, the chancellor was more wary than his colleagues in expressing this view. Officials of the Johnson administration had become disillusioned with the MLF, but there was still a lingering concern within Washington that without a nuclear-sharing solution West German resentment towards its allies would lead to a catastrophic breach between the FRG and NATO.[31] Having presented the ANF as an alternative to the MLF in December 1964, the Wilson government effectively abandoned this concept during the following year, and eventually expressed support for a consultative ('software') solution to the nuclear-sharing problem, as outlined by McNamara with his May 1965 proposal for a 'special committee' on NATO's nuclear weapons policies. This allowed the Alliance's non-nuclear members (including the FRG) to be fully appraised of developments in US nuclear strategy and doctrine, and provided the basis for the establishment of the NATO Nuclear Planning Group's (NPG) the following year.[32] Although scholars disagree as to whether the ANF was a genuine effort to resolve NATO's nuclear-sharing dispute, or a tactical ploy to undermine the creation of a multilateral deterrent, the Labour government had no regrets over the ANF's eventual demise. Wilson, Healey and MoD officials paid lip service to 'internationalisation', but were determined to retain national control over the UK's deterrent forces. It was this factor – as well as concerns over a 'German finger on the trigger' and the impact that this development would have on East-West relations – which influenced the British government's support for institutionalised consultative arrangements within NATO, as opposed to a multinational force which would give non-nuclear states access to nuclear technology.[33]

The Soviet government was initially as hostile towards proposals for consultative arrangements on nuclear policy within NATO as it had been towards the ANF, denouncing both as an indirect form of proliferation on West Germany's behalf. However, in late 1966, Soviet officials abandoned their opposition to a 'software' solution to NATO's nuclear dilemma, renewing negotiations with their American counterparts on a draft NPT. Brezhnev and his peers had effectively made *détente* with the USA – and a non-proliferation agreement banning German access to nuclear weapons – a priority. As the treaty evolved the Johnson administration had more difficulties coming to agreement on its terms with NATO allies (notably West

31 Heuser, NATO, 130–2; Schwartz, Johnson and Europe, 51–2; conversation between US and British officials, No.10, 26 Nov. 1965, PREM 13/805; note from British government to Soviet embassy, London, 11 Feb. 1967, PREM 13/1840.
32 J. P. G. Freeman, *Britain's nuclear arms control policy in the context of Anglo-American relations, 1957–1968*, New York 1986, 213–19; Schröder–Stewart conversation, FO, 16 Mar. 1966, PREM 13/805.
33 See Schrafstetter and Twigge, 'ANF proposal', and Young, 'Killing the MLF?', passim; COS63rd/65, 18 Nov. 1965; H. Cleveland (US representative, NAC)–Wilson conversation, 19 Oct. 1964, PREM 13/671.

Germany and Italy) than with its Soviet interlocutors. Both superpowers also concurred in seeing no role for Britain in the negotiations. American officials preferred to avoid mediating between the competing demands of the UK, FRG and other European allies, opting to refine the draft text with the Soviets before presenting it to NATO allies. The Soviet government in turn ignored Wilson's proposal for tripartite discussions on non-proliferation during his February 1966 visit, and subsequently treated the NPT as a bilateral superpower matter. The Labour government's attempt to promote talks between the USA, USSR and UK on a Comprehensive Test Ban Treaty also evoked little interest on the part of its Soviet counterpart. Brown failed to interest Gromyko in a proposal for trilateral scientific contacts on means of providing verification for a CTBT (including the shared use of seismic technology to detect underground nuclear tests) during his visit to Moscow in November 1966. As was the case with the NPT negotiations, the Soviet government preferred to deal directly with its American opposite number, and saw no need to include the UK in major arms control negotiations.[34]

The establishment of the NPG in 1966 assuaged West German demands for a greater say in NATO strategy, and the 'grand coalition' government which took power in Bonn in December 1966 was also less interested in pursuing nuclear sharing than its CDU-CSU predecessor. Although these changes in German policy were welcomed by the Labour government, Wilson and his ministers were obliged to contend with another threat to the UK's nuclear status. The prospective development of anti-ballistic missile defences by the superpowers threatened to render *Polaris* obsolete before it entered service in 1968. The Soviet military built a network of ABMs around Moscow and deployed a new missile system, known as *Tallinn*, in the north-west of the USSR, thereby provoking a debate within the US government as to whether its Soviet rival was planning a comprehensive ABM defence. The CIA argued that *Tallinn* was a surface-to-air missile (SAM) system, but the Pentagon concluded that it could be upgraded as part of a country-wide missile defence network. While the JCS, with some support from Congress, advocated the development of a national ABM system, McNamara believed that a 'thick' anti-missile deployment would not only be prohibitively expensive, but would also encourage Soviet efforts to build up their ICBM arsenal, thereby escalating the arms race. McNamara won a temporary victory when Johnson decided in December 1966 that while ABM research would continue, the USA would seek agreement with the USSR to limit the development of anti-missile systems. The US ambassador to Moscow, Llewellyn Thompson, passed a letter from Johnson to Kosygin in January 1967, proposing a superpower summit to discuss ABMs, but the

[34] Bange, 'Non-Proliferation Treaty', 169–71, 174–6; Brown–Gromyko conversation, New York, 8, 10 Oct. 1966, NS1052/39, FO 371/188930; Kosygin–Wilson conversation, Kremlin, 24 Feb. 1966, CAB 164/2; CC62(66)62nd conclusions, 1 Dec. 1966, CAB 128/41.

Soviets delayed their response. From the British perspective, anti-missile systems had the potential to intensify the superpower arms race, while a Soviet missile defence system would consign the *Polaris* fleet to impotence soon after its first submarine (HMS *Resolution*) became operational in 1968. Enhanced Soviet ABM defences would remove the UK's ability to fulfil what MoD officials called the 'Moscow criterion', Britain's theoretical ability to destroy the USSR's capital in the event of nuclear war.[35]

The problem was that Kosygin – both during his visit to the UK and the Glassboro summit – refused to acknowledge that the development of ABMs would lead to a renewed arms race. So, on 19 September, McNamara announced that the USA would build a 'thin' ABM force, ostensibly to counter the emerging Chinese nuclear threat. Although McNamara informed Healey in advance of his decision, British officials protested that they and other NATO allies had been presented with a *fait accompli*.[36] The Wilson government had already ruled out purchasing *Poseidon*, the next generation of American SLBM which was designed to beat ABM defences, and so McNamara's announcement forced Whitehall to address the issue of whether *Polaris* should be upgraded. ABM systems worked by detonating nuclear warheads in the earth's outer atmosphere, thereby destroying or rendering ineffective incoming missiles. The MoD and Foreign Office argued that *Polaris*'s warheads needed to be 'hardened' to withstand exo-atmospheric nuclear explosions, and to be fitted with dummy 'penetration aids' in order to breach the USSR's anti-missile defences. The Treasury and DEA, however, stated that Britain could not afford to upgrade *Polaris*, particularly since the devaluation of the pound in November 1967 had added an extra £50m to the costs of defence. Wilson's chief scientific advisor, Sir Solly Zuckerman, also argued that the MoD's proposals were strategic nonsense, as it was inconceivable that the UK would wage nuclear war alone against the USSR.[37]

During the winter of 1967–8, at the height of the devaluation crisis, Wilson conducted a debate on *Polaris* which was confined to the Cabinet's PN Committee, excluding the majority of ministers from the decision-making process. Of all PN's members, Healey was the most vociferous in supporting the retention of *Polaris*. The Defence Secretary argued that the prospects of further proliferation, and the political consequences of leaving de Gaulle's France as the only nuclear power in Western Europe, necessitated the reten-

35 NIE11–3-65, 'Soviet strategic air and missile defenses', 18 Nov. 1965, NARAII, RG 263:190, 28, 16–17; L. Freedman, *US intelligence and the Soviet strategic threat*, Basingstoke 1986, 97–128; KV(67)2d, 'Disarmament: anti-ballistic missiles', 26 Jan. 1967, CAB 133/365.

36 KV(67)5th meeting between Brown, Kosygin and Wilson, No.10, 10 Feb. 1967, CAB 133/365; J. Newhouse, *Cold dawn: the story of SALT*, Toronto 1973, 89–99; McNamara to Healey, 14 Sept. 1967, and Brown to Wilson, 15 Sept. 1967, DEFE 13/733.

37 OPD(O)(67)16, 'British nuclear weapons policy', 10 Oct. 1967, CAB 148/81; J. Baylis and K. Stoddart, 'Britain and the Chevaline project: the hidden nuclear programme, 1967–1982', JSS xxvi/4 (2003), 124–55.

tion of a credible deterrent. He also hinted at a future return to isolationism by the USA and the long-term reliability of the American nuclear umbrella, arguing that the USSR 'might only be deterred from such an attack on our cities if we ourselves had the capability to inflict heavy damage on her'. On 5 January 1968 the majority of the PN, including Wilson, sided with Healey, authorising further studies to upgrade the British deterrent.[38] Having all but promised to abolish Britain's nuclear forces in 1964, four years later the Labour government had effectively assured their retention. In December 1973 its Conservative successor commissioned the upgrading of *Polaris*, and the costs of this programme – known as *Chevaline* – subsequently spiralled out of control during the following decade.[39]

The conclusion of the NPT in June 1968 and the foundation of the NPG (with the FRG as a permanent member) provided additional guarantees against a nuclear-armed West Germany, and also reaffirmed Britain's status as one of the five recognised nuclear powers. While these were favourable outcomes for the Wilson government, in contrast with the LTBT of 1963 Britain could claim no role in the negotiation of the non-proliferation agreement. Moreover, while the NPT averted the emergence of additional nuclear powers East of Suez until the post-Cold War period, there was an unresolved dichotomy between its endorsement by the Labour government and the latter's decision – despite its 1964 manifesto pledge and the financial crisis caused by the pound's devaluation – to preserve Britain's nuclear force. The retention of the deterrent and the quiet abandonment of the ANF showed that Wilson and Healey had given up any pretence that the UK would renounce nuclear weapons as a means of preventing global proliferation. As was the case with previous prime ministers, Wilson recognised the 'importance of being nuclear' as a means of mitigating the decline of Britain's influence in the international arena. Furthermore, the Labour government's readiness to upgrade *Polaris* – and to sanction the policy process which led to *Chevaline* – contravened the UK's pledge (as a signatory the NPT) to progressively reduce and eventually scrap its nuclear arsenal. The tension between Britain's declared policy on arms control and its determination to preserve deterrent forces therefore remained unresolved.[40]

[38] PN(67)4th meeting, 5 Dec. 1967, CAB 134/3120; E. Rose (Cabinet Office) to Trend, 18 Jan. 1968, CAB 165/310. The actual minutes of the PN meeting on 5 Jan. 1968 remain classified.
[39] Baylis and Stoddart, 'Chevaline', passim; Healey, *My life*, 313.
[40] This phrase is taken from the title of Hennessy, *Secret state*, ch. ii. See Scott, 'Labour and the bomb', 689–90, and J. Stocker, *The United Kingdom and nuclear deterrence*, Abingdon 2007.

NATO, BAOR and the offsets crisis, 1964–8

Polaris was not the only policy reversal the Wilson government made on defence. In opposition the Labour front-bench had advocated the disengagement of NATO and Warsaw Pact forces in Central Europe. Prior to October 1964 the Conservatives envisaged force reductions in Germany which would enable the UK to concentrate on East of Suez. The increasing burden of defence expenditure led the Douglas-Home government to establish the OPD(O)'s Long-Term Study Group in May 1964. Their conclusions were debated at the Chequers conference on 21–22 November 1964. Both Brown and Callaghan were concerned by the pound's weakness, and persuaded their Cabinet colleagues to reduce military expenditure from £2,400m. to £2,000m. by the end of the decade.[41] The Long-Term Study Group reported that reduced tensions in Europe theoretically enabled the reductions in BAOR (nominally 55,000 strong but actually under-strength by 3,000) and the RAF contingent in Germany. WEU arrangements allowed for the temporary withdrawal of troops from the NATO area: the British used their forces in Germany as a strategic reserve, deploying units overseas whenever crises erupted East of Suez. However, the study group noted that a permanent unilateral reduction of BAOR would encourage the USA to cut its forces (262,000 strong) in West Germany, and could undermine both NATO's solidarity and the Anglo-American alliance. Moreover, if Britain reneged on the London agreement of 1954 the FRG would have a pretext to renounce its pledge not to develop NBC weapons.[42]

Wilson's comments at Chequers reflected both the Labour left's suspicion of West German policy, and the private view in London and other West European capitals that NATO's role was to 'keep the Americans in, the Russians out, and the Germans down'. Wilson told his interlocutors that 'there was no longer the risk of war with the Soviet Union so long as NATO solidarity lasted', and that Alliance force levels were unrealistically high. Yet the reduction of BAOR 'will not only lessen our own political influence in Europe' but would 'lead to a predominating German influence on European defence'. The CDU-CSU government still regarded reunification as a precondition for *détente*, and Wilson expressed the concern that the FRG's growing military power could give the West German government the means to dominate NATO politically and distort the Alliance's defensive agenda. The Chequers meeting ended with agreement not to reduce the strength of either BAOR or the RAF units committed to the 2nd Allied Tactical Air Force (2ATAF), but ministers hoped that British forces in Germany could be

41 M. Middeke, 'Britain's global military role, conventional defence and Anglo-American interdependence after Nassau', *JSS* xxiv/1, 143–64; S. Dockrill, *East of Suez*, 49–59; MISC17/1st meeting, 21 Nov. 1964, CAB 130/213.
42 OPD(O)(64)6; 'Regional study on Europe', 23 Oct. 1964, CAB 148/40; Darby, *Defence policy*, 239.

reduced in future, either through a review of NATO strategy, an agreement on mutual force reductions with the USSR, or by unilateral means.[43]

Interest in reducing the UK's NATO commitments was revived in 1966, shortly after de Gaulle withdrew France from NATO's command structure (7 March). This step came as no surprise to the US and British governments, who had witnessed a continual weakening of military ties between France and NATO since 1958. Although France remained a signatory of the North Atlantic Treaty, and maintained its garrison in the FRG, the French president's actions posed a challenge to NATO's integrity, raising contemporary fears amongst member governments that the Alliance would expire before its twentieth anniversary in 1969. The Wilson government responded to French withdrawal by publicly reaffirming the UK's commitment to NATO,[44] but it also renewed its demands for West German assistance to alleviate the foreign exchange costs of British forces in Germany. Ever since the FRG's admission to NATO and the formal end of the allied occupation in 1955, the financial burden incurred by US and British forces stationed in Germany had been a source of contention between the three NATO members involved. In July 1966 the British government demanded that Bonn should offset all BAOR's foreign exchange costs, or accept the withdrawal of troops and RAF squadrons to the UK.[45] The financial crisis that month reinforced Wilson's conviction – shared by Callaghan and Healey – that Britain was carrying a disproportionate share of the Western defence burden, maintaining by its own means commitments in the Middle and Far East which served allied interests as a whole. Although Indonesia's decision in August 1966 to end the 'confrontation' permitted the reduction of British forces in Malaysia and Singapore, the UK still had to balance its NATO and East of Suez commitments. Labour Ministers claimed that Britain was 'subsidising' West Germany's defence at an estimated cost of £90 million, but the Erhard government maintained – with some justification, according to Gore-Booth – that BAOR contributed to NATO's collective defence. The FRG could not afford to cover the foreign exchange costs of both American and British forces, and West German officials were unwilling to pay for BAOR and the RAF contingent in Germany if the British government were planning to reduce its military commitments to NATO in any case.[46] The offsets crisis

[43] A. Wenger, C. Nuenlist and A. Locher, 'New perspectives on NATO history', in Wenger, Nuenlist and Locher, *Transforming NATO*, 3; MISC17/4th meeting, 22 Nov. 1964, CAB 130/213; OPD(65)12th meeting, 3 Mar. 1965, CAB 148/48; Duffield, *Power rules*, 174.

[44] F. Bozo, *La France et l'OTAN: de la guerre froide au nouvel ordre européen*, Paris 1991, 79–81, 233–4; J. Ellison, 'Defeating the General: Anglo-American relations, Europe, and the NATO crisis of 1966', *CWH* vi/1 (2006), 85–111.

[45] Zimmerman, 'Sour fruits', 225–34; CC38(66)38th conclusions, 20 July 1966, CAB 128/41; MISC17/1st-4th meetings, 21–22 Nov. 1964, CAB 130/213.

[46] Wilson–Rusk conversation, No.10, 14 May. 1965, *FRUS*, XII: *Western Europe*, Washington 2001, 488–9; Catterall, 'East of Suez', 619–20, 622; FRG ambassador–Wilson

had financial roots, but it also had serious implications for NATO unity and the East-West military balance.

At the end of August, Johnson cajoled Wilson into agreeing to trilateral talks to resolve the dispute, and negotiations between the Americans, British and West Germans began two months later. The Johnson administration subsequently offered to purchase UK military supplies to the value of $35m. in order to prevent the unilateral withdrawal of British personnel from Germany. Although the president told Wilson that reductions in BAOR would lead to 'a chain-reaction' of troop cuts which would demolish NATO, his administration contributed to the Alliance's problems by transferring 40,000 US servicemen from West Germany to Vietnam, significantly hampering the combat readiness of US forces based in Europe.[47] While officials in the Departments of State and Defense complained that NATO allies should be contributing more to their defence, Senator Mike Mansfield's call for a reduced US military presence in Europe was acquiring growing Congressional support.[48] McNamara argued that improvements in air transportation permitted the timely transfer of US reinforcements across the Atlantic in a crisis, and the Pentagon planned for the 'rotational' deployment of American forces in Germany, with some army and air force units being based in the USA. British officials suggested that 'rotation' was more applicable to the UK's armed forces as units quartered in Britain were geographically closer to NATO's front-line, and this was one example of how official pronouncements from Washington affected the British position on offsets and NATO force levels. Although Rusk was more concerned than McNamara with the strategic implications of force reductions, in their conversations with Wilson, Healey and Stewart both he and the Secretary for Defense complicated matters by indicating to Labour ministers that the UK's commitments East of Suez were more important than the British military presence in Germany.[49]

Britain's economic problems shaped Wilson's approach to the offsets issue, and he returned from his visits to Moscow in February and July 1966 believing that the Soviets would agree to informal NATO and Warsaw Pact force reductions[50] However, Kosygin only said that mutual troop cuts provided

conversation, No.10, 1 Aug. 1966, and Bonn to FO, N.1153, 7 Aug. 1966, CAB 164/88; Gore-Booth to Trend, 21 May 1966, CAB 164/88.
47 Johnson to Wilson, CAP66583, 28 Aug. 1966, CAB 164/89; Schwartz, *Johnson and Europe*, 123–5, 143–59.
48 NSC566th meeting, 13 Dec. 1966, IV, 48, NSF, NSC meetings 1–2, LBJLIB; P. Williams, *The senate and US troops in Europe*, Basingstoke 1985, 139–48.
49 OPD(O)(66)19th meeting, 3 Aug. 1966, CAB 148/68; Rusk–Stewart conversation, Bruce's residence, London, 2 Aug. 1966, PREM 13/902. See also *Crossman diaries*, i. 95, entry for 11 Dec.1964.
50 CC39(66)39th conclusions, 21 July 1966, CAB 128/41; E. Rostow (US Assistant Secretary of State for Political Affairs)–Wilson conversation, No.10, 21 Nov. 1966, PREM 13/808.

'an interesting avenue for discussion' on 22 February, and was hardly more effusive during Wilson's second visit.[51] The prime minister also neglected the strategic implications of British policy on offsets, as any reduction of the UK's military presence in West Germany undermined the North Atlantic Treaty's ethos of mutual defence. The military rationale for redeploying units from Germany was also questionable. In July 1966 the COS expressed their concerns over the implications of any unilateral reductions, particularly as this could encourage further American troop cuts. Yet by November the chiefs acquiesced in the Wilson government's determination to recover foreign exchange costs from the FRG. Each of the three armed services, according to Healey, saw 'our East of Suez role as an opportunity to gain a greater share of the defence cake', and it seems that the COS considered operations in the Middle East and South-East Asia to be a higher priority than NATO commitments. Following de Gaulle's actions in March 1966, the Defence Secretary had originally argued that reducing BAOR and 2ATAF would cause irreparable damage to NATO. However, being convinced that Soviet aggression against the West was unlikely, Healey subsequently sought to utilise the trilateral talks as a means of persuading the USA and FRG – and through them the rest of NATO – that the Alliance could afford to reduce its force levels in Central Europe.[52]

The Labour government's approach to the offsets negotiations relied on the JIC's assessment that, despite the impact of Vietnam on East-West relations, the Soviets were still unlikely to risk a war with NATO. The JIC confidently maintained that NATO would receive several weeks 'political warning' if the USSR adopted a more hostile attitude towards the West, and would receive four to nine days 'military warning' of any Warsaw Pact attack. Intelligence officials ruled out a surprise (or 'standing start') attack, concluding that during the period of 'political warning' the USA and UK would be able to send reinforcements to bolster NATO's defences. The JIC's assessment theoretically supported BAOR's reduction, provided that other allied powers agreed to this measure.[53] However, this assessment was challenged by the commander of NATO's Northern Army Group (NORTHAG), General Sir John Hackett. Hackett's warning that indicators of Soviet bloc aggression – for example, troop movements from the Western USSR to East Germany and Poland – could be misinterpreted as routine military exercises was disregarded by his superiors. Yet he had a valid point in arguing that the concept of 'political warning' was problematic as it relied on a subjective estimate of Soviet intentions, and an assumption that the USSR would not revert to a more confrontational policy towards the West in the immediate

[51] Kosygin and Wilson, Kremlin, 22 Feb. 1966, PREM 13/805; Kosygin and Wilson, Kremlin and UK embassy, 18 July 1966, CAB 164/2.
[52] COS34th/66, 17 July 1966, DEFE 4/202; COS60th/66, 8 Nov. 1966, DEFE 4/208; Catterall, 'East of Suez', 623, 634; Healey, My life, 293, 309.
[53] JIC(66)57, 'Tripartite talks', 4 Nov. 1966, CAB 158/64.

future. 'Political warning' provided the justification for the US and British governments to 'redeploy' troops from Germany, but the presumption was that in an East-West crisis situation NATO governments would be resolute enough to order a higher state of military readiness. Furthermore, even if the Warsaw Pact and the NATO powers agreed to mutual force reductions, Soviet divisions located in Ukraine and the Baltic States were still geographically closer to NATO's central front than domestically-based American and British units.[54]

By early 1967 the Wilson government found itself obliged to reappraise its policy on BAOR. This was due firstly to a belated recognition by ministers that a unilateral withdrawal of British forces from Germany would encourage other allies, notably Belgium, Canada and the USA, to follow suit, thereby shattering NATO. Given Wilson's earlier concerns for West German military preponderance in Western Europe, it was also ironic that the FRG was considering reductions to the *Bundeswehr*. There was a clear danger that NATO's capacity for collective defence could be fatally undermined at a time when the Warsaw Pact's combat power was being both quantitatively and qualitatively enhanced. Secondly, Kosygin made it clear during his 1967 visit to London that his government was not interested in mutual force reductions in Central Europe, thereby undermining Wilson's hopes for a NATO-Warsaw Pact agreement on cuts in their respective militaries. Thirdly, the UK's political and economic interests increasingly lay with improved Anglo-German relations, which necessitated a compromise by the British government on the offsets issue. The Labour government decided in April 1967 to make a second attempt at gaining membership of the EEC for Britain, so Wilson's Cabinet was therefore obliged to be more conciliatory in their dealings with the West German leadership. This process was assisted by the efforts the CDU-SPD 'grand coalition' government made to improve relations with the Warsaw Pact states. British officials supported the CDU-SPD government's early efforts at *Ostpolitik*, which they considered to be a welcome reversal of its predecessor's stance on reunification and its equivocal attitude to *détente*.[55] Both West German support for EEC and Anglo-German policy co-ordination on East-West relations influenced the Wilson government's abandonment of demands on both offsets, and its hopes for a significant reduction in the UK's military commitment to NATO.

The trilateral negotiations ended on 27–28 April, with the UK being permitted to repatriate one brigade from BAOR and two squadrons from

---

54 General J. Hackett (NORTHAG) to General J. Cassels (Chief of the General Staff), 21 Dec. 1966, DEFE 13/635; P. Cradock, *Know your enemy: how the Joint Intelligence Committee saw the world*, London 2002, 255; Duffield, *Power rules*, 179–81.
55 KV(67)5th meeting between Brown, Kosygin and Wilson, No.10, 10 Feb. 1967, CAB 133/365; OPD(67)28th meeting, 28 July 1967, CAB 148/30; F. Roberts (Bonn) to Brown, 13 July 1967, PREM 13/1526; A. Stark (Bonn) to P. Hayman (ND), 1 May 1967, and H. Smith (ND) to Hayman, 19 May 1967, FCO 28/29.

2ATAF (5,000 servicemen in total). In return, the Labour government gave up demands for complete repayment of foreign exchange costs. The Americans redeployed two army brigades (35,000 men) and ninety-six warplanes back to the USA, rather than the two complete divisions that McNamara had originally envisaged. The outcome of the trilateral negotiations showed that all three powers recognised the danger that NATO would 'unravel', and as a consequence neither the British nor the Americans could undertake extensive troop cuts.[56] Just as the trilateral talks represented a compromise solution, the eventual outcome of the NATO strategic review, following the adoption of MC14/3 in December 1967, effectively ratified existing force levels. While there was a close resemblance between MoD concepts of NATO strategy and MC14/3's doctrine of a 'symmetrical response' to any Warsaw Pact assault, of 'controlled escalation', and of delaying an all-out nuclear response to Soviet aggression, the Alliance's defence strategy also attempted to smooth over disputes between its members over the forces required both to deter aggression, and to withstand any Warsaw Pact onslaught by non-nuclear means. MC14/3 ruled out a conventional build-up which no NATO power was prepared to undertake, but it also marked the end of Labour's intention to persuade NATO allies to agree to substantial cuts in the Western military presence in Germany.[57]

The Wilson government was not solely responsible for the internal crisis which threatened NATO's survival in 1966–7. The Johnson administration contributed by transferring thousands of US troops from Central Europe to Vietnam, and by placing upon the FRG its own demands for compensation for the foreign exchange costs of American forces in West Germany. France had threatened the integrity of an alliance which protected its own security as well as those of its neighbours by departing from NATO's command structure in March 1966. None the less, by indulging with the West German government in brinkmanship over the financial costs incurred by British forces in the FRG, Wilson and his Cabinet were guilty of poor timing. By mid-1966 NATO was threatened not only by the Gaullist challenge to its role, but by a growing popular sentiment in Western Europe that the Soviet threat had all but disappeared, and by the rise of anti-Americanism caused by the Vietnam War. It took the Czechoslovak crisis of 1968 for NATO member states to revive their collective interest in common defence. Both British and American policy-makers were foolish to assume that they had

---

[56] CC26(67)26th conclusions, 30 Apr. 1967, CAB 128/42; OPD(67)24th meeting, 26 June 1967, CAB 148/30; final report on trilateral talks, (undated), *FRUS* xiii. 562–70; F. Gavin, 'The myth of flexible response: United States strategy in Europe during the 1960s', *IHR* xxvii/4 (2001), 866–71; S. Dockrill, *East of Suez*, 228–9.

[57] J. Stromseth, *The origins of flexible response: NATO's debate over strategy in the 1960s*, Basingstoke 1988, 175–2; C. Bluth, 'Reconciling the irreconcilable: alliance politics and the paradox of extended deterrence in the 1960s', *CWH* i/2 (2001), 97–8; Heuser, *NATO*, 52–4.

the right to reduce their military presence in Germany (through rotational deployments or other expedients) without encouraging other member states to take the same course of action. The conclusion to the trilateral talks in April 1967 therefore represented an understanding by both the Johnson administration and the Labour government that there was a genuine danger that NATO could 'unravel' if they did not modify their initial demands.[58] In addition, Wilson himself placed too much emphasis on Kosygin's elliptical references on East-West force reductions, overlooking the Soviet premier's ominous comment that *détente* depended upon a reduced US presence in Europe. Brezhnev's *Politburo* would not have been displeased to see NATO crippled by 'contradictions' between its members, but also had no fundamental interest in troop cuts which would weaken Soviet power in Eastern Europe. This was evident in the USSR's rejection of the NATO declaration on force reductions following its summit in Reykjavik in June 1968, and the lack of progress in the NATO-Warsaw Pact Mutual Balanced Force Reduction (MBFR) negotiations in the 1970s and 1980s.[59]

Although Labour ministers and officials of the Foreign Office, MoD and COS assumed that potential Soviet aggression against Western Europe would be deterred as long as NATO remained united and had sufficient means to withstand a Warsaw Pact onslaught, the Wilson government jeopardised NATO's cohesion and its capacity for deterrence by attempting significant reductions of both BAOR and the RAF component of 2ATAF. While some Foreign Office officials and military commanders recognised that British forces in Germany did not 'subsidise' the FRG's defence, but contributed to the collective security of Western Europe, Wilson remained oblivious to these concerns. The reversal of policy on offsets in early 1967 did make strategic sense, but even in this case it was influenced more by political and economic concerns, notably the potential benefits of Anglo-German *rapprochement* as far as British attempts to join the EEC were concerned, than any calculations on the effect the dispute over US and British force levels was having on the internal stability of NATO. The outcome of both the trilateral talks and British acceptance of MC14/3 showed that the Labour government had abandoned any intention of alleviating the financial costs of defence policy by reducing the UK's commitment to European defence. The reductions in military expenditure necessitated by Britain's parlous economic condition would therefore have to be met elsewhere.

[58] C. Wiebes and B. Zeeman, '"I don't need your handkerchiefs": Holland's experience of crisis consultation in NATO', *IA* lxvi/1 (1990), 101; Wilson to Stewart, 15 Mar. 1966, CAB 164/28; Herring, 'Fighting without allies', 86.
[59] Kosygin and Wilson, Kremlin, 22 Feb. 1966, PREM 13/805; Dobrynin, *In confidence*, 146, 169; Garthoff, *Détente and confrontation*, 533–7.

The East of Suez withdrawals and policy towards Europe, April 1967–January 1968

The March 1966 defence review announced that British forces would leave Aden and South Arabia by 1968, and reduced the UK's military presence in the Mediterranean. Following the sterling crisis of July 1966 the Treasury demanded further reductions, which in turn shaped a contentious inter-departmental debate leading to the Labour government's announcement the following March of a phased withdrawal from Britain's East of Suez commitments, to be completed by 1975. The gradual shift towards a defence policy with a Eurocentric focus was by no means smooth. During the acrimonious Cabinet debate which preceded Wilson's decision to accelerate the East of Suez withdrawals in January 1968 a minority of ministers argued that the UK could maintain both an enhanced NATO role and a residual presence in the Middle and Far East. Some of Wilson's colleagues feared that Britain's allies in the Arab world would not long survive the departure of British troops from the region. None the less, when the Labour government was forced by devaluation to chose between ending the UK's global role or cutting the NATO commitment, ministers opted for the former.[60]

The Labour government's new-found Europhilia derived in part from institutional pressures from both Westminster and Whitehall. Its back-benchers, both from the left and the pro-EEC lobby, regarded the 'world role' as an unsustainable fantasy, while there was an influential lobby within the Foreign Office encouraging a more Eurocentric approach to external policy. The 'confrontation' sapped the will of British officials and senior military commanders to maintain overseas commitments. The low-level war in Borneo had drawn away troops, warships and RAF squadrons from Germany and other operational theatres, and even though Indonesia eventually conceded defeat the 'confrontation' made ministers and officials more determined to shed commitments that the UK could no longer afford.[61] By the spring of 1967 ministers had become increasingly convinced that Britain's future economic and foreign policy interests were best served by closer integration with the UK's European neighbours. The Labour leadership's turn towards Europe also reflected increasing disillusionment with the Commonwealth. Wilson's hopes of employing its institutions to preserve Britain's influence in the post-imperial world were undermined by the hostility that the UK's policies towards Rhodesia and Vietnam aroused amongst its Afro-Asian members. While Wilson – hitherto an opponent of European integration – became an avid proponent of EEC membership during the

---

[60] Young, *Labour governments*, 44–7; CC6(68)6th-7th conclusions, CAB 128/43; S. Dockrill, *East of Suez*, 202–8; A. Priest, *Kennedy, Johnson and NATO: Britain, America and the dynamics of alliance, 1962–68*, Abingdon 2006, 145–51.

[61] H. Parr, 'The Foreign Office and Harold Wilson's policy towards the EEC, 1964–1970', in Daddow, *EEC*, 87–90; Easter, *Confrontation*, 114, 197–9.

course of 1967, Healey also displayed a greater interest in enhancing the UK's role in European defence. Brown had declared during the July 1966 sterling crisis that the Labour government should 'pull the troops out: all of them. I don't want them out of Germany. I want them out of East of Suez'. After he replaced Callaghan as Chancellor in December 1967, Roy Jenkins – a long-standing proponent of EEC membership – played an important role in shaping the decisions on defence that the Wilson government made the following January.[62]

An additional factor in influencing the end of 'East of Suez' concerned the souring of Anglo-American relations, the catalyst being the failure of the *Sunflower* initiative in February. While the Johnson administration was dismayed by the withdrawal of British forces from the Middle and Far East and the devaluation of the pound, Labour ministers were worried by the intensification of the Vietnam War and the American decision to develop 'thin' ABM defences. Wilson's argument that Britain's Far Eastern commitments gave its government a say in American policies had been discredited by Vietnam.[63] British officials also resented American insensitivity to the concerns of their European allies, as shown by the Johnson administration's handling of NPT negotiations, and its readiness to exclude the British government from any role in non-proliferation talks. The Cabinet's debate on EEC membership echoed the debates within the Attlee government between the Atlanticist and 'Third force' schools of thought, with some ministers arguing that EEC membership would 'provide the political stimulus formerly given by our imperial role', and limit the influence the USA exerted on British policy:

> We must not in any event allow ourselves to become totally dependent on the United States nor on the other hand could we contemplate aligning our policies with the Soviet bloc: joining [the EEC] was essential if we were to avoid finding ourselves increasingly isolated and powerless in world affairs.

Although the Labour government's attempt to take Britain into EEC was vetoed by de Gaulle in December 1967,[64] the decision to apply for membership the previous April derived from a belief that this would curtail excessive American influence on British policy. Having heeded Johnson, Rusk and McNamara's requests that Britain retain both its NATO and East of Suez commitments, by the spring of 1967 Wilson's Cabinet was less prepared to pay heed to US protests against defence cuts. The prime minister expressed

---

62 Catterall, 'East of Suez', 635–7; *Castle diaries*, 148, entry for 18 July 1966; Pimlott, *Wilson*, 434–5, 437–42; S. Dockrill, *East of Suez*, 200–8.
63 Palliser to MacLehose, 28 Apr. 1967, PREM 13/1455; Brown and E. Rostow, FO, FCO 7/767; Healey, *My life*, 312–13.
64 CC(67)26th conclusions, 30 Apr. 1967, CAB 128/42; K. Bohmer, '"We too mean business": Germany and the Second British application to the EEC, 1966–67', in Daddow, *EEC*, 216–33.

his own views on the changed nature of the 'special relationship' in Cabinet on 12 January 1968, stating that since the Johnson administration consulted the USA's own fiscal and strategic interests ahead of those of its allies, its officials were not entitled to complain if the British government did the same.[65] Having began his term in office by affirming the UK's status as a global power, Wilson had come full circle by 1968, adopting a position similar to that which caused him to resign from the Attlee government in 1951 over rearmament. In this case, however, it was the proponents of financial and economic retrenchment who ultimately prevailed in the debate over the viability of Britain's defence commitments overseas.

The East of Suez decision was made only after a prolonged and at times bitter Cabinet debate, with some ministers agonising over the consequences of withdrawal for Britain's overseas allies, and the impact retrenchment would have on Anglo-American relations. Wilson seemed less perturbed by the end of the 'world role', or by the consequences of the defence cuts he had overseen. In his 'white heat' speech of 1963 he had expressed the view that Britain's position in world affairs rested on economic and technological – rather than military – prowess, and he displayed a similar attitude when addressing the Labour party conference at Scarborough five years later. For all his rhetoric on East of Suez, Wilson showed little substantial interest in defence issues, and he left the details of the reviews to Healey, a strong-willed, intellectually high-powered politician never lacking in either self-confidence or ambition. His relationship with Wilson was uneasy, but his uninterrupted service as Defence Secretary from October 1964 to June 1970 reflected his central role in implementing Labour's defence policy. If Conservatives were correct in arguing that Wilson showed negligence in reducing military expenditure, then Healey too deserves some of the blame. Yet it is worth noting that Cabinet critics of the defence cuts hardly referred to the USSR as a growing threat, while officials in Whitehall concentrated more on regional adversaries (notably Egypt, Iraq and Sukarno's Indonesia), and on developments in China.[66] Brown retrospectively asserted that he supported the sale of naval arms to South Africa in December 1967 because of 'the growing Russian advance in the Indian Ocean', but he made no reference to this threat at either the OPD or Cabinet meetings. Wilson himself continued to regard the PRC, rather than the more 'conservative' USSR, as the main danger to Western interests East of Suez.[67]

---

[65] Dean to Brown, 23 Jan. 1967, FCO 7/767; Gavin, 'Flexible response', 869–70; CC26(67)26th conclusions, 30 Apr. 1967, CAB 128/42; CC6(68)6th conclusions, CAB 128/43.
[66] Wilson, *Labour government*, 433–4; Healey, *My life*, 299, 324–5, 331; HC Deb5s, 756, London 1968, 1973–2084; OPD(68)58, *The Czechoslovak crisis and British defence policy*, 20 Sept. 1968, CAB 148/38.
[67] Brown, *My way*, 163–4; OPD(67)39th meeting, 8 Dec. 1967, CAB 148/30;

Outside official circles there was a widespread belief amongst informed opinion that Britain did not need a military presence to protect its economic interests overseas, while contemporary academic specialists generally favoured withdrawal from East of Suez and concentration on a European role.[68] Following the January 1968 decisions the leader of the opposition, Edward Heath, did pledge to restore Britain's East of Suez role as soon as the Conservatives returned to office, and he was perturbed by the expansion of Soviet maritime power. However, although Heath oversaw a limited reversal of his predecessor's cuts, in the form of discreet British military involvement in the campaign against left-wing insurgents in Oman from 1970 to 1976, even the Conservatives accepted that the UK no longer had the capability for major, independent interventions in the Middle or Far East. The Heath government could not answer the question of how Britain could maintain a 'world role' with its weak economy, and in cases where (as in Aden) the deployment of British forces was opposed by both local and non-aligned opinion within the UN. As the Soviets themselves discovered when they were expelled from Egypt in 1972, a military presence in any country did not necessarily ensure lasting influence, and both the Vietnam War and the USSR's subsequent failed intervention in Afghanistan from 1979–89 demonstrated that even a superpower could not use force indefinitely to protect a weak client regime against strong indigenous opposition.[69]

One crucial factor behind the East of Suez decision was the prevailing consensus within Whitehall that the UK's military role in the Middle East and South-East Asia were no longer necessary or in Britain's interests. Once Indonesia had abandoned its attempts to subvert Malaysia, and after Sukarno had been replaced by a pro-Western *junta* in March 1967, there was no real imperative to keep a substantial British force in the Far East. Officials in London were concerned to reduce the UK's defence burden in the region once the 'confrontation' was over. British policy-makers also looked to the neutralisation of South-East Asia, and to develop the capabilities of regional allies to defend themselves with minimum external assistance; this was an approach that Richard Nixon subsequently echoed with the 'Guam Doctrine' of 1969. Furthermore, the UK's CENTO and SEATO commitments were undermined by the fact that members states were more concerned with parochial quarrels – for example, Pakistan's feud with India, and Iranian-Arab rivalry in the Persian Gulf – than with any notion of containing the expan-

CC70(67)70th, CC71(67)71st conclusions, 14, 15 Dec. 1967, CAB 128/42; E. Youde (No.10), Nixon–Wilson conversation, RAF Mildenhall, 3 Aug. 1969, PREM 13/3009/1.
68 Lapping, *Labour government*, 73; Mayhew, *Britain's role*, 51–6. See also A. Buchan, 'Britain in the Indian Ocean', and M. Howard, 'Britain's strategic problem East of Suez', *IA* xlii/2 (1966), 184–93, 179–83.
69 Campbell, *Heath*, 226–7; P. Moon (PM's office) to B. Norbury (Cabinet Office), 15 Sept. 1971, PREM 15/674; B. Reed and G. Williams, *Denis Healey and the politics of power*, London 1971, 8–9.

sion of Soviet or Chinese influence.[70] As both CENTO and SEATO lacked the credibility or cohesion to make them sustainable, it made no strategic sense for Britain to provide token support for reluctant allies.

Although NATO military commanders were alarmed by the growth of the USSR's interest in the Third World, and in particular the enhancement of Soviet maritime power, the governments of Western Europe showed little interest in developments outside the Alliance's sphere. De Gaulle's France, the only other West European power with any pretensions to pursuing a 'world role', was a reluctant member of SEATO, and showed no interest in Soviet activities in the Third World.[71] Although the Johnson administration was vehemently opposed to the East of Suez withdrawals, neither it nor its successor were willing to replace the British military presence in the Persian Gulf or South-East Asia. Nixon's Guam Doctrine and his administration's support for allies such as Iran, General Suharto's regime in Indonesia and Saudi Arabia showed that in the wake of Vietnam the USA hoped to use regional proxies to preserve Western influence in the Third World. The substance of the Wilson government's defence policy reflected a paradox within the so-called 'special relationship'. While British foreign and defence policy was still founded on alliance ties with the USA, the Labour government surrendered Britain's East of Suez commitments despite protests from Washington. Furthermore, the fact that Wilson and his colleagues decided to retain the British deterrent was based in part on implicit concerns as to whether the US nuclear shield over Western Europe could be relied upon in the future, as well as considerations of UK prestige. Just as Churchill concluded that possession of a hydrogen bomb was the price Britain had to pay 'to sit at the top table', the Labour government could not afford politically to either make the UK entirely dependent on the US nuclear umbrella, or to allow French military leadership of Europe. The *Polaris* fleet – despite its small size in comparison with the superpowers' strategic nuclear arsenals – also became a substitute for a capacity for independent global power projection which Britain had lost by 1968.[72]

In the same way that Labour reversed its pre-1964 pledge to 'renegotiate' the Nassau treaty, the Wilson government reneged on its earlier objective to uphold Britain's commitments East of Suez. The ending of the 'world role' should not be viewed solely through the prism of Anglo-American

[70] Easter, *Confrontation*, 176–7, 188; OPD(65)28th, 2 June 1965, CAB 148/18; OPD(65)174, CAB 148/25; Golan, *Soviet policies*, 179–80; JIC(67)11, CAB158/66.
[71] UKDELNATO to FO, 26 Jan. 1968, DEFE 13/901; DI58(N), 'NIR', no.16, Spring 1968, DEFE 63/33; G. Millard (UKDELNATO) to E. Barnes (FO), 25 Aug. 1967, FCO 46/2; de Gaulle–Wilson conversation, Versailles, 19 June 1967, PREM 13/1622.
[72] Ball, Healey, McNamara and Stewart conversation, No.10, 26 Nov. 1965, PREM 13/799; D. Swan, *Anglo-American relations*, 4 Dec. 1967, FCO 7/775; Petersen, 'Crossing the Rubicon', 334, 339–40; W. Bundy, *A tangled web: the making of foreign policy in the Nixon presidency*, New York 1998, 133–6, 329; Hennessy, *Secret state*, 44.

relations, but was due to an interaction of political, economic and strategic factors. Ultimately, both the USSR's military posture and the UK's Cold War interests at that time (notably the relationship between NATO and the growing importance of Anglo-German relations) mandated a continentally-oriented defence policy. As Wilson informed the Commons on 16 January 1968, Britain's future security interests '[lay] fundamentally in Europe and must be based on the North Atlantic Alliance'. Although the prime minister had also considered deploying the *Polaris* submarines East of Suez once they entered service, following the abandonment of Middle and Far Eastern commitments the UK's deterrent was officially committed to the NATO area.[73] The decision to focus on continental defence was made when the Alliance had been weakened by the internal disputes of 1966–7, and as the Labour leadership made a fresh bid for EEC membership. A Europe-oriented strategy also suited the UK's political objectives as far as East-West relations were concerned. The British government could not persuade its partners within NATO to adopt the promotion of *détente* as a parallel mission to deterrence if – through its intentions to cut BAOR – it was considering actions which jeopardised the Alliance's cohesion and capacity for collective defence. Furthermore, efforts to forge closer ties with the FRG were likely to be hampered if British ministers haggled over the costs in foreign exchange of a continental military commitment which served Britain's interests as it did West Germany's.

However, whatever its underlying motives, the Labour government's conduct of defence policy was not governed by an appraisal of where the UK's interests lay, but through a process of 'muddling through'. In the process, Wilson and his ministers myopically sought limited financial gains over long-term interests in their quest to offset the costs of stationing British forces in Germany. While the withdrawal from East of Suez did have a strategic rationale in recognising that European security and economic engagement with the EEC were crucial interests to the UK, their management under grave economic pressures had all the characteristics of a 'scuttle'. The decision to end the 'world role' was not so much the result of a strategic reappraisal, but the action of a government mired in a series of political and fiscal crises, reacting to events beyond its control. In Kenneth Morgan's words, after 1967 Britain was regarded at home and abroad as a weak power, 'unheeded in Europe, a token head of the Commonwealth, a largely powerless client of the Americans, unable to retain what had for so long been its own'.[74] This impression of decrepitude contributed between late 1967 and early 1968 to the deterioration of Anglo-Soviet relations, which is discussed in the following chapter.

---

[73] *Strategic survey, 1968*, London 1968, 13; Barker, *Divided Europe*, 213–15; Heuser, *NATO*, 85–8.
[74] Grove, *Vanguard*, 305; Young, *Labour governments*, 226; Morgan, *People's peace*, 283.

5

Détente, Trade and Espionage, 1966–1968

In early February 1967 Wilson achieved what he regarded as his greatest triumph in Anglo-Soviet relations when Kosygin visited the UK. The trip was a public relations success, and was certainly more cordial than Khrushchev and Bulganin's troubled visit the previous decade. Aside from sporadic protests by Hungarian and Baltic States *émigrés*, the Soviet premier was generally welcomed by public and press alike.[1] Gore-Booth was none the less incensed that Kosygin used his speech at the Guildhall on 8 February to condemn both West German 'militarism' and American intervention in Indochina. Crossman, hardly the most right-wing of Wilson's ministers, was astonished that when Kosygin attacked British policy on Vietnam during his visit to the House of Commons on the 9th, many Labour MPs applauded him. Yet, according to Castle, after Kosygin returned home Wilson 'rhapsodised about the [close relationship] he had built up' with the man he had publicly called 'Moy starii droog' ('My old friend').[2]

Although hopes that both premiers could broker a ceasefire in Vietnam (in the form of the Phase A/B initiative) had been dashed, the prime minister stated in a televised address to the British public that his talks with Kosygin represented a 'new high water-mark in Anglo-Russian understanding'. Wilson informed viewers that the Soviet and British governments would conclude a 'friendship treaty' to improve trade relations and establish a framework for increased co-operation and contacts in the fields of science, commerce and cultural relations. However, his visit to Moscow in January 1968 was a sterile affair, and outside 10 Downing Street few in the British government believed that it had achieved any positive results. The 'friendship treaty' proved to be a dead letter, while the Soviet leadership repeatedly attacked the UK's foreign policy record. The devaluation crisis of 1967 and the subsequent decisions on defence retrenchment were also greeted with ill-concealed glee by the USSR's state media, and the Foreign Office concluded

---

[1] 'He who never smiles, smiles', *The Express*, 9 Feb. 1967; 'It's a really British welcome', *The Mirror*, 7 Feb. 1967; 'Why Mr Kosygin's visit to Britain is important', *The Times*, 6 Feb. 1967.
[2] 'Kosygin alarm on Germany', *The Times*, 9 Feb. 1967; FO/CRO to missions, no.20, 14 Feb. 1967, FCO 28/389; Gore-Booth, *With great truth*, 358; *Crossman diaries*, ii. 231, entry for 9 Feb. 1967; *Castle diaries*, 220, entry for 14 Feb. 1967; Loory and Kraslow, *Diplomacy of chaos*, 188–9.

that efforts made by the Wilson government to develop Anglo-Soviet relations had been rejected by Brezhnev's *Politburo*.[3]

This chapter will examine the Labour government's policy towards the USSR and East-West relations in the context of both the bilateral and multilateral efforts of Western powers to develop *détente*. British officials and politicians generally concluded that Cold War tensions in Europe had eased since the Berlin and Cuban crises, and NATO powers sought to build upon this development by establishing less adversarial relations with the Warsaw Pact states. Although there were predictions – notably towards the left of the political spectrum – that the Cold War had 'ended', officials in Western capitals did not believe that a complete *rapprochement* with the Eastern bloc was likely. Issues such as the German question defied an easy resolution, because of unease in both Eastern and Western Europe as to the implications of a reunited Germany for the stability of continental Europe. However, there were aspects of East-West relations where progress towards *détente* could be measured, in the form of arms control agreements, NATO-Warsaw Pact force reductions and increased trade and reduced restrictions for transnational contacts (for example, tourism and reciprocal cultural and educational exchanges) across the Iron Curtain. Strategic arms control talks had become monopolised by the superpowers during the course of the 1960s. Of the other indices of *détente*, some could be developed through bilateral relationships between NATO and Warsaw Pact states, although multilateral and alliance interests could not be entirely neglected by the governments involved. For example, as far as East-West trade were concerned Western countries had to balance their commercial interests with the COCOM embargo, while East European states were restricted by their own multilateral economic ties with the USSR and each other.

While the French government's policy towards *détente* was intended to challenge the *status quo* in Europe, notably the USA's role in continental security and Western Europe's military integration within NATO, that of Britain was intended to complement and support the Atlantic Alliance, although the offsets dispute with the FRG showed that there were cases where the UK's declared policy ran counter to its actual conduct. This chapter will therefore compare and contrast the Labour government's approach to *détente* with those of its allied counterparts, notably the USA, France and the FRG, and examine why apparently positive developments such as the Kosygin visit and the Anglo-Soviet technological agreement of January 1968 gained Wilson little as far as East-West *rapprochement* was concerned.

---

3   Transcript of TV broadcast, 14 Feb. 1967, Wilson papers, C.1237, fos 157–9; Gore-Booth to W. Rodgers, 16 Jan. 1968, Gore-Booth papers, Bodleian Library, Oxford, MS Gore-Booth, 93, fos 95–6; Walden, *Lucky George*, 171.

Détente, European security and the 'declaration of principles'

During the latter half of the 1960s European members of NATO became more proactive in seeking *rapprochement* with the Eastern bloc. Their efforts included both multilateral (in the form of the Harmel report), and bilateral initiatives (most notably those of de Gaulle, Adenauer's successors and the Belgian government's informal contacts with its Polish counterparts) intended to improve East-West ties. The motives behind *détente*-related policies differed according to the government involved. Some were primarily commercial, notably the Soviet-Italian agreement which saw Fiat build a car factory in the USSR. De Gaulle's policies on East-West relations constituted a fundamental challenge to transatlantic alliance ties and the USA's role in European security, while West Germany's gradual process of *Ostpolitik* represented a tacit awareness on the part of Erhard, Kiesinger and Willy Brandt (the Foreign Minister from December 1966 to September 1969) that the FRG was out of step with its allies as far as East-West relations was concerned.[4] West European governments were also aware of the growing sentiment amongst their electorates that the Soviet 'threat' was vanishing, and that NATO was becoming increasingly irrelevant to the interests of its members. For example, the Belgian government had to placate public opposition to the relocation of NATO's military headquarters (SHAPE) from the outskirts of Paris to Mons following 1966. While de Gaulle sought to capitalise on this development, other Western leaders sought to persuade domestic opinion that the Atlantic Alliance could provide both military security and the political means of fostering closer ties with the Communist East.[5]

On the surface Franco-Soviet relations flourished during the 1960s. De Gaulle and the Soviet leadership took identical positions on the MLF and Vietnam, and as traditional victims of German aggression both France and the USSR regarded the FRG's future intentions with apprehension.[6] The French president allegedly justified the Franco-German treaty of 1963 by stating privately that '[we] extend our hand to the Germans so that we could at least be sure they were not holding a knife in theirs', and he caused consternation during his visit to Poland in September 1967, when he appeared to openly endorse the Oder-Neisse frontier. Although the USSR sought to exploit the 'contradictions' between France and other Western powers,

[4] P. Hanson, *Trade and technology in Soviet-Western relations*, Basingstoke 1981, 107–8; F. Bozo, '*Détente* versus alliance: France, the United States and the politics of the Harmel report (1964–1968)', *CEH* vii/3 (1998), 343–66; Hanrieder, *Germany. America, Europe*, 176–94.
[5] L. Kaplan, *NATO divided, NATO united: the evolution of an alliance*, New York 2004, 47–8; V. Dujardin, 'Go-between: Belgium and *détente*, 1961–1973', *CWH* vii/1 (2007), 102.
[6] SNIE11–11–65, 'Soviet attitudes towards the US', 26 May 1965, *FRUS* xiv. 273–85, 289–90.

there were limits to how far the Franco-Soviet relationship could develop. Despite his personal contempt for the FRG de Gaulle realised that his plan to make France pre-eminent in Europe would not survive a complete rift with West Germany. Furthermore, the logical implication of the Gaullist concept of 'Europe totale' was the eventual end of both Soviet authority and the Communist order in Eastern Europe, and it was this outcome which Gomulka publicly denounced during de Gaulle's Polish visit. The Czecho-slovak crisis of 1968 demonstrated the complete ideological opposition of the Soviet leadership – and that of other Warsaw Pact states – to chal-lenges to the *status quo*, and ultimately that the French president's concept of Europe's future was incompatible with the USSR's continued supremacy over its Eastern half.[7]

None the less, when de Gaulle withdrew France from NATO's military structure in March 1966, Foreign Office officials feared a French diplomatic offensive which would complement Soviet efforts to undermine the cohe-sion of the Alliance. The Labour government responded by encouraging the other thirteen member states to reaffirm their commitment to the North Atlantic Treaty.[8] Yet de Gaulle's actions threatened, as the British ambas-sador to the NAC noted, to reinforce the French government's portrayal of NATO as a 'ponderous and rigid organisation' incapable of adapting to 'changing political circumstances and military needs'. British officials feared that de Gaulle's pronouncements on NATO's obsolescence, combined with improved bilateral ties between France and the USSR, could create discord between the USA and its European allies, while other Alliance members could also decide to emulate France's actions of March 1966. Norway and Denmark were both wary of antagonising the USSR, and were susceptible to both Soviet propaganda attacks against their alignment with the USA and public opinion questioning the validity of their membership of NATO. Greece and Turkey were both embroiled in an intractable feud over the future of Cyprus. These four countries on NATO's Northern and Southern flanks could be tempted to sever ties with the Atlantic Alliance, with unpre-dictable political and strategic consequences for the Western world.[9]

From the Labour government's perspective, de Gaulle was not only a threat to Western unity, but the exponent of a rival version of *détente*. Following

---

7   Andrew and Mitrokhin, *The Mitrokhin archive*, i. 605; P. Reilly (Paris) to Stewart, 18 Mar. 1965, PREM 13/324; T. Wolton, *La France sous influence: Paris–Moscou: 30 ans de relations secrets*, Paris 1997, 388–90; G. Martin, 'Grandeur et dépendances: the dilemmas of Gaullist foreign policy, 1967–1968', in N. P. Ludlow (ed.), *European integration and the Cold War*, Abingdon 2007, 37–9.

8   CC(66)16, 'France', Stewart memorandum, 23 Mar. 1966, CAB129/124; B. Heuser and C. Buffet, 'Résister à la tempête: les reactions britanniques au départ de la France de l'intégration militaire de l'OTAN', in Bozo, Mélandri and Vaïsse, *France et l'OTAN*, 447–8.

9   E. Shuckburgh to Stewart, 23 Mar. 1966, CAB 164/28; OPD(66)44: 'France and NATO', Trend memorandum, 1 Apr. 1966, CAB 148/27.

the advice he had received from Oliver Wright, his Foreign Office Private Secretary, Wilson decided that Britain could play a crucial role in rallying allies around NATO and promoting *détente*. In the aftermath of France's withdrawal, Wilson told Stewart (then Foreign Secretary) that while de Gaulle's visceral anti-Americanism and 'rogue elephant tactics' were deplorable, some of his views on East-West developments 'may be more up to date and in tune with the times than our own'. While British objectives in NATO – collective deterrence against Soviet aggression, a US military presence in Europe and the suppression of German nationalism – remained valid, it was also necessary to 'parley' with the Eastern bloc powers.[10] Stewart and other ministers were receptive to these arguments. The Foreign Secretary observed that de Gaulle's view that the Soviet threat had receded had widespread support within Western Europe, and there was a consensus within Whitehall that, in order to preserve the NATO alliance against the Gaullist challenge, member states were obliged to adopt a collective approach to improve relations with the USSR and the East European states.[11]

Wilson and his ministers therefore saw French withdrawal from NATO as an opportunity for a fresh start in the transatlantic relationship. The prime minister later expressed his views to Rusk in June, stating that the difference between the French and the Anglo-American conceptions of East-West relations 'is not over ends but over means'. If other Western powers emulated France, 'far from *détente* a truly dangerous situation would be created in Europe', as the Alliance would be split. One way of reinforcing NATO's 'solidarity of purpose' was to recognise popular support for *détente* within Western Europe, and the prime minister maintained that Britain would play an important role in promoting *rapprochement* with the East. In his opinion, the USSR's leaders were 'realists' who were aware that de Gaulle's 'real influence in the world, and above all on the conduct of United States policy, was marginal'. In contrast, Britain still had a role to play in terms of its global influence and its close relationship with the USA, and that 'when it came to practical politics rather than propaganda ... the Russians would rather talk to us'.[12]

There was, however, a stark difference between the Wilson government's declared intention to encourage a collective Western approach to *détente*, and its lack of substantial action, excluding the abortive attempt to promote a 'statement of principles and proposals governing European affairs and relations'. This initiative originated with a conversation between Stewart and

---

[10] Ellison, 'Defeating the General', 93–7; J. O. Wright to PM, 11 Mar. 1966, PREM 13/1043; PM to Stewart, 15 Mar. 1966, CAB 164/28.
[11] Schroeder–Stewart conversation, 16 Mar. 1966, PREM 13/927; Shuckburgh to Stewart, CAB 164/28; OPD(66)18th meeting, CAB 148/25; OPD(O)(66)6th, 7th meetings, 18, 28 Mar. 1966, CAB 148/68.
[12] Palliser to MacLehose, 4 June 1966, PREM 13/902; Wilson–Rusk conversation, No.10, 10 June 1966, PREM 13/2264.

the Czechoslovak ambassador on 17 March 1966. The Foreign Secretary was handed a document calling upon European powers to respect the sovereignty and territorial rights of other states, and to avoid taking 'any steps which might result in aggravating international tensions'. Stewart concluded that while these clauses were directed against West Germany, the paper's references to trade, cultural agreements and technological co-operation had some merit. Although there were concerns within the Foreign Office that the declaration was a 'platitudinous' document which the Czechoslovak government had concocted purely for 'wedge-driving' purposes, Northern Department officials proposed that a draft declaration be prepared for NATO allies to endorse.[13] The OPD approved a copy of the declaration – a bland document containing broad statements on bilateral and multilateral co-operation in trade, scientific co-operation and on mutual respect for sovereignty and non-interference in internal affairs – at the beginning of July. Stewart conceded that the draft made no substantial recommendations, but was 'the kind of general declaration to which eastern European countries attached importance', and he claimed that 'the reiterated renunciation of the use of force to settle disputes' would be welcomed by the FRG's Warsaw Pact neighbours.[14]

The OPD approved the draft, but the FRG's representative to the NAC complained that it contained no reference to German reunification. US State Department officials objected that the draft overlooked 'the essential role of the United States in [negotiating] a European settlement', while Harlan Cleveland, the American representative to the NAC, supported his West German colleague's objections. The Foreign Office proposed that the declaration be approved within NATO, then presented to 'one or more countries in Eastern Europe' (thereby avoiding a joint Warsaw Pact statement which would involve the GDR), but American officials preferred a joint declaration 'without either joint or individual subscription by the countries of the Warsaw Pact'.[15] Although Johnson reaffirmed his administration's interest in 'bridge-building' in a speech on 7 October, Rusk and his State Department subordinates argued that ill-timed diplomatic approaches to the Eastern bloc would exacerbate intra-NATO problems and undermine efforts to reinforce Western unity in the aftermath of March 1966.[16] Despite American concerns, the NAC approved the British decision to pass the

13 Gore-Booth, 'A declaration on Europe', 2 May 1966, and annotation by Greenhill, 3 May 1966, N1075/11; Stewart to Shuckburgh, 12 May 1966, N1075/13, FO 371/188497.

14 OPD(66)76: FO memorandum, 'East/West relations; a declaration', 1 July 1966, CAB148/28; OPD(66)31st meeting, 5 July 1966, CAB 148/25.

15 Lord Hood (Western Organisations Department) to Shuckburgh, 1 July 1966, N1075/27, FO 371/188498; Washington to FO, no. 2118, 19 July 1966, and Sutherland to Greenhill, 21 July 1966, N1075/50, FO 371/188499.

16 F. Costigliola, '"Not a normal French government": la réaction Américaine au retrait de la France de l'OTAN', in Bozo, Mélandri and Vaïsse, France et l'OTAN, 411, 415;

draft to the Czechoslovak Foreign Ministry, and William Barker, the UK's ambassador to Prague, presented it on 12 December. However, the Czecho-slovak government rejected the declaration the following month because it did not acknowledge *de jure* either the GDR or Germany's eastern borders. Czechoslovak officials also informed their British counterparts that the document was purely bilateral, thereby defeating the original purpose of the exercise.[17]

Having concluded by the spring of 1966 that Britain could rally NATO and influence both the Alliance's strategic doctrine and its approach to *détente*, Wilson's government actually devoted far less time to this effort than to the offsets dispute with West Germany. To paraphrase the prime minister's remarks to Rusk in June 1966, this hardly contributed to the task of establishing 'solidarity of purpose' within NATO in the aftermath of France's departure from the Alliance's military framework. It was left to the Belgian government to take the lead in promoting a review of NATO's policy towards *détente*. This, and its concluding report, published in December 1967 and named after the Belgian Foreign Minister, Pierre Harmel, established mutual defence and the promotion of *détente* as the 'two pillars' of NATO policy. The Wilson government supported the Belgian initiative because its conclusions reflected its view that, as Brown put it, NATO was not waging 'an old-style Cold War crusade against a Communist attack which may never come', but was 'constructive in terms of *détente* as well as watertight in terms of defence and deterrence'. In this respect, there was a clear convergence between Belgian and British concepts of NATO's role as both an organisation devoted to the mutual security of its member states, and as a means of promoting collective diplomatic dialogue with the Warsaw Pact powers. However, the argument that both the Soviet menace and East-West tensions had diminished had been used to justify efforts to reduce BAOR, and ministers were aware that other NATO powers would have regarded a British version of the Harmel report as a pretext for the reduction of the UK's commitment to West European defence.[18]

While France, Britain and other West European powers were keen to develop *détente*, their respective roles in any East-West rapprochement would count for little without the development of the FRG's *Ostpolitik*. The policies of Adenauer's successors were crucial because the division of Germany remained the principal issue underpinning the Cold War in Europe. East-West

J. Ellison, 'Stabilising the West and looking to the East: Anglo-American relations, Europe and *détente*, 1965 to 1967', in Ludlow, *Integration*, 115.

[17] Brown to Brimelow, 23 Mar. 1967, and D. Tonkin (Warsaw) to Rhodes, 17 Aug. 1967, FCO 28/271; Smith to Hayman, 13 Jan. 1967, and FO to Prague, no. 31, 17 Jan. 1967, FCO 28/1.

[18] OPD(67)38th meeting, 28 Nov. 1967, CAB 148/30; OPD(67)87, 'France and the Atlantic Alliance', by Brown, 20 Nov. 1967, CAB 148/34; Dujardin, 'Belgium and *détente*', 97–101.

politics were polarised by the GDR's claim to sovereignty, which undermined the FRG's claim to be the sole representative of the German people, and by the obligation that the Warsaw Pact and NATO powers had to support the claims of their respective allies. Within West German politics there was also entrenched hostility within the CDU-CSU against any compromise on reunification, the Hallstein doctrine and Germany's eastern borders. Yet a growing body of West German public opinion recognised that reunification was an impossibility, and that the Hallstein doctrine was increasingly untenable (given the number of Third World states establishing relations with East Germany). Furthermore, the more pragmatic politicians in Bonn also realised that the FRG was obliged to overcome a legacy of suspicion and fear – both East and West of the Iron Curtain – arising from Nazi aggression and crimes against humanity during the Second World War.[19] The Erhard government implicitly recognised that reunification could not occur without West German engagement in *détente*, and oversaw a policy known as *Bewegung* (gradual movement). The FRG's 'peace note' of 25 March, condescendingly described by Foreign Office officials as 'a move in the right direction', reiterated Bonn's pledge not to develop NBC weapons, declared that the Munich settlement had 'no territorial significance' and offered the USSR, Poland and Czechoslovakia an agreement on the mutual renunciation of force. Following a policy dubbed *Neue Ostpolitik*, Kiesinger and Brandt made further efforts to improve relations with its eastern neighbours, effectively abandoning the Hallstein doctrine in the process. While Romania was the only East European country to recognise the FRG (in January 1967), the West German government established trade missions with all the other Warsaw Pact states except East Germany.[20]

Although British officials welcomed the FRG's more flexible approach towards East-West relations, the response from Eastern bloc countries was less positive. The *communiqué* issued following a meeting of the Warsaw Pact Consultative Committee in Bucharest in July 1966 rejected the West German peace note.[21] The Bucharest declaration was a show of unity from a pact affected by Polish and Czechoslovak demands for an alliance similar to that of NATO, with a greater role for the East Europeans in the Soviet-dominated military structure. The East German regime was also nervous about

19 W. G. Gray, *Germany's Cold War: the global campaign to isolate East Germany, 1949–1969*, Chapel Hill, NC 2003; H. O. Froland, 'Distrust, dependency and *détente*: Norway, the two Germanys and "the German question", 1945–1973', CEH xv/4 (2006), 495–517; A. Willens, 'New *Ostpolitik* and European integration: concepts and policies in the Brandt era', in Ludlow, *Integration*, 71.
20 D. Bark and D. Gress, *A history of West Germany, II: Democracy and its discontents, 1963–1988*, London 1989, 90–122; MacLehose to Wright, 24 Mar. 1966, PREM 13/928.
21 T. Wolfe, *Soviet power and Europe, 1945–1970*, Baltimore, MD 1970, 285–7; Nation, *Red star*, 247; Bucharest to FO, no. 215, 8 July 1966, PREM 13/902; Garton Ash, *Europe's name*, 55–6.

the FRG's overtures to its allies, and insisted (with the USSR's support) that no East European state should open diplomatic relations with West Germany unless it recognised the GDR's sovereignty. Yet aside from concerns over security and East German statehood, there was an inflexibility within the Warsaw Pact alliance, demonstrated by its collective proposal for a European security conference which specifically excluded the USA. During his talks with Wilson and Brown the following February, Kosygin combined invective against the FRG's 'threat' to European security and the CDU-SPD coalition's 'revanchist' attitudes with a verbal assault on NATO, and reiterated that the USSR and its allies would not permit American involvement in European security negotiations. The conference of the European Communist movement in Karlovy Vary, Czechoslovakia, in April 1967, saw repeated denunciations of *Neue Ostpolitik* by the CPSU and other East European parties. Far from contributing to East-West dialogue, the FRG's attempts to alleviate tensions with the Eastern bloc aroused as much hostility as did Adenauer's policies.[22]

The absence of a Warsaw Pact response to both the Harmel Report, and the declaration by NATO's Foreign and Defence Ministers on mutual force reduction negotiations after the Reykjavik summit of June 1968, testified to the unwillingness of most of its members (excluding Romania) to undertake reciprocal gestures of *rapprochement* with the West. In the case of Poland, previously considered by the Foreign Office to be the most *détente*-minded of East European states, the ruling regime was by 1967 one of the most rigid defenders of the *status quo*, and both *Bewegung* and *Neue Ostpolitik* had little effect on Gomulka's almost pathological Germanophobia. The extent to which continental *détente* could develop was restricted in part by the intractability of the German question, notably traditional fears of German nationalism in Eastern Europe and the FRG's refusal, supported by its NATO allies, to recognise the GDR. Yet by the late 1960s Foreign Office officials concluded that Western attempts to foster better relations with the Eastern bloc were being rejected by the Soviet government and its clients, which required the existence of an illusory external security threat to reinforce the legitimacy of their own regimes.[23]

Although the FRG still served a useful purpose as a 'revanchist' adversary for the Soviet, Polish and Czechoslovak governments in particular, in commercial terms West Germany was also emerging as a significant trading partner for the Eastern bloc regimes. By the end of the decade, the volume

[22] Mastny and Byrne, *Cardboard castle*, 29–32; NIE11–15–66, 'Reliability of the USSR's East European allies', 4 Aug. 1966, LCHMA, MFF 15/412; DI3/1/14, 'Defence developments in Eastern Europe', 23 Sept. 1966, CAB163/57; KV(67)5th meeting, CAB133/365.
[23] A. Stark to Smith, 22 Feb. 1966, N103118/1, FO 371/188477; Brown to Brimelow, 23 Mar. 1967, FCO 28/271; V. Mastny, 'Was 1968 a strategic watershed of the Cold War?', *Diplomatic History* xxix/1 (2005), 156.

of West German trade with the USSR and Eastern Europe exceeded that of any other NATO power. The development of trading links provided a contrast to the political impasse affecting East-West relations in Europe, and the Labour government's approach to this issue reflected not only Wilson's long-standing enthusiasm for commercial contacts with the Eastern bloc, but policies followed by his Conservative predecessors.[24]

British policy towards East-West trade

Conservative and Labour governments alike supported the development of non-strategic trade with the Eastern bloc, while Foreign Office officials argued that East-West commercial ties would encourage *détente* and 'evolution' in Eastern Europe. The Douglas-Home government cut quotas on East European imports, securing reciprocal agreements from Bulgaria, Czechoslovakia, Hungary and Poland to increase their own imports of British products. The Conservatives also approved the sale of buses to Cuba, thereby disregarding the trade embargo that the USA had imposed on Castro's regime.[25] British policy on East-West trade derived from the UK's traditional economic dependence on overseas commerce, the belief of British policymakers that ideological or diplomatic differences should not be a barrier to 'normal' trading contacts between nations, and a concern within Whitehall and Westminster at the economic growth and favourable trade balances of commercial rivals such as France, the FRG and Italy.[26] There were, however, several constraints which restricted the development of Britain's commercial contacts with the Eastern bloc states during the 1960s.

The first concerned the Co-ordinating Committee (COCOM), founded in 1950 by the NATO powers (excluding Iceland) and Japan, which proscribed the export to the Communist powers of a series of goods and raw materials covered by the Munitions, Atomic Energy and International ('I') lists. After the Korean War, COCOM's members maintained a stricter embargo on China until 1957, when the UK unilaterally renounced the 'China differential', on the grounds that the USSR and its East European allies could supply the Chinese with embargoed goods. The following year COCOM abolished the China differential, adopting uniform restrictions for Western trade with the 'Sino-Soviet bloc'. Ironically, a decade later Britain argued that the Sino-Soviet split undermined the rationale for a uniform

---

24 Garton-Ash, *Europe's name*, 651; J. Kronsten, 'East-West trade: myth and matter', *IA* xl/2 (1967), 275.
25 Report by Official Committee on Commercial Policy, 'East-West trade policy', 11 Aug. 1967, FCO 28/59; State Dept. to missions, no. 9634, 5 Jan. 1964, NSF, LBJLIB, UKCF 206; CM(64) Cabinet conclusions, 30 Apr. 1964, CAB 128/38.
26 A. Pravda and P. Duncan, 'Introduction', and M. Kaser, 'Trade relations', in Pravda and Duncan, *Soviet-British relations*, 5–7, 208–9; White, *Britain, détente*, 167–9.

embargo on the Communist world. Within COCOM, there were frequent transatlantic quarrels over the USA's attempts to tighten the embargo. The 'I' list was the main source of contention because it covered 'dual use' raw materials and manufactured goods (notably computers and machine tools) with military as well as civilian applications.[27]

COCOM was criticised within parliament and the British business community, where there was widespread suspicion that West European competitors were flouting the embargo's rules.[28] However, COCOM was also a significant factor in Anglo-American relations, not least because the British information technology industry was dependent upon American-manufactured components, thereby restricting the British government's capacity to approve unilateral sales of computer equipment to the Eastern bloc. This would have been less problematic if the Johnson administration had succeeded in its efforts to use trade to promote 'bridge-building' with Eastern Europe, as recommended by the Miller Committee. However, many Congressmen opposed closer commercial ties with the Soviet bloc states because of their assistance to North Vietnam, and efforts to pass the East-West Trade Relations Bill in Congress (May 1966) came to grief. Furthermore, American attitudes to British and West European trading relations with China were coloured by concerns that exports of Western technology could enhance the Chinese nuclear programme. In a critical analysis of British policy towards COCOM, the US ambassador to London observed that while the UK supported the strategic embargo in principle, it adopted 'a liberal, and frankly commercial, view towards the question of what could be considered strategic'. Britain's livelihood depended upon foreign trade, and the UK was less inclined than the USA 'to sacrifice export earnings for what we may consider to be the greater good'. Bruce recognised that British official and parliamentary opinion suspected that the USA was using COCOM to bar its competitors from markets it was unable, or unwilling, to exploit, and acknowledged that the USA's allies also thought that the Johnson administration was 'crying wolf' over Chinese military capabilities.[29] Officials in Whitehall and Labour MPs therefore viewed US protests at British trade policy as being motivated by mercenary as well as ideological considerations.

An additional constraint upon the development of Britain's trade relations with the Eastern bloc concerned the nature of the latter's command economies. There were proposals from within the Communist elites to reform the

[27] I. Jackson, 'Economics', in Dockrill and Hughes, Cold War, 171–4; ESC(65)8, 'Memorandum for ministerial committee on strategic exports', 3 Mar. 1965, CAB 134/1906.
[28] Kronsten, 'East-West trade', 273–4; T. Benn, Office without power: diaries, 1968–1972, London 1998, 7–18; KV(67)2nd meeting between Benn, Peter Jay, Kosygin and Wilson, No.10, 7 Feb. 1967, CAB 133/365.
[29] Schwartz, Johnson and Europe, 83–4; London to State Dept., 9 Feb. 1966, FRUS ix. 525–8; Newhouse, Cold dawn, 81–6.

Eastern bloc's decrepit economies, including Kosygin's plans to liberalise the USSR's economic planning. In 1966 the Hungarian regime introduced the New Economic Mechanism (NEM) permitting private enterprise, and the Czechoslovak deputy premier, Ota Sik, argued the case for similar reforms in his country with the leadership of the ruling party (the CPCS). Yet although the Eastern bloc required Western technology to modernise its industries, the ideological orthodoxy of the ruling parties, and the devotion of considerable resources to defence, limited the scope for East-West trade. Furthermore, the Warsaw Pact states co-ordinated their economic planning through the Council for Mutual Economic Assistance (CMEA, or *Comecon*). East European states were therefore bound by restrictive bilateral trade agreements with the USSR and each other.[30] East-West trade was constrained by hard currency shortages, the inflexibility of the national five-year plans and the *Comecon's* multilateral structure. Furthermore, while the USSR's state-owned import-export companies favoured long-term fixed trade agreements, British firms wanted to preserve their freedom of action to respond to frequent fluctuations within the global market, and to avoid being constrained by potentially unprofitable long-term deals with Soviet bloc states.[31]

The challenges involved in developing trade relations with the USSR and Eastern Europe meant that Foreign Office officials fought an uphill battle to persuade other Whitehall departments of the need to remove trade quotas on Eastern bloc exports in order to encourage 'evolution' behind the Iron Curtain. The CRO and the Ministry of Agriculture supported protectionist measures which, respectively, favoured Commonwealth imports to the UK and British farmers,[32] while the BoT wanted to alleviate the UK's balance of payments deficit, using quotas to force the Warsaw Pact states to balance their trade deficits with Britain. It was not until 1970 that the majority of quotas on Eastern bloc imports were revoked by the British government, although there remained a net imbalance between British exports to the USSR and Eastern Europe, which were exceeded by the UK's purchase of materials and goods from Warsaw Pact powers.[33]

Throughout his premiership Wilson was frustrated by the BoT's lukewarm attitude towards East-West commerce, and he regarded Kosygin's visit to London in February 1967 as the opportunity for a 'striking new initiative' on bilateral trade, preferably an equivalent of the Franco-Soviet 'Grand

---

[30] Crampton, *Eastern Europe*, 316–17, 321; Service, *Russia*, 379–80; R. Braithwaite (Moscow) to M. Fretwell (ND), 15 Nov. 1965, NS1102/51, FO 371/182778; Parrott to Stewart, 8 Feb. 1965, FO 371/182511.
[31] Kronsten, 'East-West trade', 265–81; BoT memorandum, STT(67)11, (no date), BT11/6600.
[32] R. Wall (Ministry of Agriculture) to D. Allen (DEA), 4 May 1965, and A. Welch (BoT) to S. Charles (DEA), 4 May 1965, N1151/39, FO 371/182514.
[33] Moscow to FO, no. 2288, 29 Oct. 1964, PREM 13/1863; Jay to Wilson, 15 Feb. 1966, PREM 13/1863. See also Morgan, *People's peace*, 243–6, and Barker, *Divided Europe*, 270.

Commission' on scientific and technological co-operation established following Kosygin's visit to Paris in December 1966. He was persuaded by the BoT and the Foreign Office to settle for ministerial discussions between Douglas Jay and the Minister of Technology, Tony Benn, and their Soviet counterparts, which took place at 10 Downing Street on 7 February 1967.[34] Benn subsequently concluded a technological agreement with his opposite number, V. A. Kirillin, when the latter visited London on 19 January 1968, arousing a hostile response from US policy-makers. Dean informed London in early March that Pentagon officials and Congressmen were threatening to curtail defence co-operation with Britain, on the grounds that Anglo-Soviet technological collaboration undermined COCOM. Both Wilson and senior Foreign Office officials rejected these arguments, asserting that the Benn-Kirillin agreement was restricted to civil co-operation. As Bruce had suggested to his superiors in the State Department, British officials suspected that the USA had an ulterior motive in restricting Britain's trade with the USSR and Eastern Europe until – once Congressional restrictions on US trade had been lifted – American businesses had greater access to the Eastern bloc market.[35]

The Anglo-American dispute over technological transfers affected the Labour government's proposals to liberalise the strategic embargo. The 1966 COCOM review had, according to officials in the ESC(O) (the Cabinet Office's Strategic Exports Committee), been hampered by the US government's refusal to share intelligence information justifying its opposition to proposed reductions in the embargo lists. Furthermore, ESC(O) officials noted that 'some valuable markets in Russia and Eastern Europe were denied to us because the United States did not want certain items', namely computers and telecommunications equipment, 'to be exported to China'.[36] The failure of the 1966 review reinforced the Wilson government's proposal to reintroduce the 'China differential'. Although the BoT and the CRO were concerned that overt discrimination against trade with the People's Republic of China would have dangerous consequences for Sino-British relations, particularly as the Cultural Revolution continued, the ESC(O) devised a compromise formula which formed the basis of the Wilson governments' approach to the next COCOM review, which was due in October 1968. The UK would accept the present restrictions as applicable to China, but would privately propose a reduced list for the Soviet bloc countries on the grounds that '[not]

34 T. Balogh (No.10) to Wilson, 9 Feb. 1966, and Wright to W. Nicoll (BoT), 10 Feb. 1966, PREM 13/1863; Paris to FO, no.137, 2 Feb. 1967, and annotated comment by Wilson, PREM 13/2406; MISC136(67)1st meeting at House of Commons, 30 Jan. 1967, CAB 130/311.
35 Dean to Greenhill, 2 Mar. 1968, *DBPO III*, i. 28–30; Greenhill to Dean, 19 Mar. 1968, FCO 28/372; Wilson–S. Zuckerman conversation, No.10, 8 Apr. 1968, CAB 168/39; Greenhill to Dean, 15 May 1968, FCO 28/373.
36 ESC(O)(66)2nd meeting, 15 Dec. 1966, CAB 134/2798; ESC(O)(67)13; 'International strategic embargo: review of policy', 2 Mar. 1967, CAB 134/2799.

only do we now regard Soviet aggression as [unlikely]', but that the technological progress of the Warsaw Pact powers invalidated the existing restrictions. Ministers approved these proposals, acknowledging that although the
UK would face greater Western competition for Soviet bloc markets, one
source of contention in East-West relations would be removed.[37]

Yet Anglo-American discussions on the review in May 1968 ended in
deadlock, because while British officials wanted to reduce the embargo lists,
their American counterparts proposed to block fifty-eight more items from
being exported to the Soviet bloc and the PRC. British proposals for a
'China differential' were also opposed by Japan, whose government refused
to jeopardise Sino-Japanese commercial ties by discriminating against trade
with the PRC. The strategic embargo was in danger of collapsing, and some
ministers in Wilson's Cabinet were prepared to see COCOM disintegrate.
The prime minister himself criticised what he called the 'indefensible and
anomalous restrictions on trade with Eastern Europe', and Benn subsequently
asserted that British commerce had been handicapped by its adherence to
COCOM rules. Wilson and Benn had an ally in Anthony Crosland, became
President of the Board of Trade when Jay was sacked in August 1967 for
opposing EEC entry. Despite being a leading member of the Labour right,
Crosland proposed that Britain should reserve the right to export items (such
as computers) to the Eastern bloc, regardless of the 'I' list, even if such a
policy led to the collapse of COCOM and a rift with the USA.[38]

The issue of COCOM reform was further complicated by the debate
within Whitehall in May-June 1968 over proposals by one British firm, ICL,
to export computers to the USSR and Romania. Benn argued that ICL's
machines had a purely civilian application, but the DIS reported that they
could help the USSR bridge the technological gap separating the Eastern
bloc from the West. Furthermore, as Dean noted, computer sales by ICL
would encourage American suspicions concerning the Anglo-Soviet technological agreement, and establish the impression within US policy-making
circles that Britain was an unreliable ally. In response, Mintech officials
argued that the financial gains from computer sales outweighed any consideration of the Johnson administration's concerns, and this sentiment was
shared by the UK's ambassadors to the Eastern bloc states.[39]

Yet despite widespread support for ICL's proposed sales, Cabinet disunity
and widespread concerns within Whitehall at the Anglo-American quarrel

---

37 ESC(67)9; 'International strategic embargo: review of policy', 6 June 1967, CAB
134/2795; ESC(67)3rd meeting, 12 July 1967, CAB 134/2795; Jay to Wilson, 15 June
1967, PREM 13/1863.
38 OPD(68)19, 'International strategic embargo', 14 Mar. 1968, CAB 148/36;
OPD(68)6th meeting, 21 Mar. 1968, CAB 148/35.
39 ESC(68)9, 'COCOM and computers for Eastern Europe', 28 June 1968, CAB
134/2796; Benn, *Office without power*, 89, 94–5 entries for 10 July, 1 Aug. 1968; 'Conference of HM representatives in East European countries. 7–10 May 1968', 7th meeting,
10 May 1968, FCO 28/45.

caused by COCOM hampered efforts to approve the computer deals with the USSR and Romania. Whereas Benn wanted to overrule US objections, and both the prime minister and Crosland envisaged the disintegration of COCOM, most ESC(O) officials feared that the collapse of the strategic embargo would have serious consequences. If the UK withdrew from COCOM, any commercial advantage for British firms would soon be lost once other Western European countries denounced the embargo. The Soviet and Chinese governments would exploit COCOM's collapse and build up their military and technological capabilities. Above all, Britain's withdrawal from the strategic embargo would enrage American officials, thereby damaging the alliance ties which were crucial to Britain's security interests. An additional problem for Mintech and other advocates of ICL's export plans was that Wilson and Crosland, despite their common position on COCOM, were working at cross purposes. Wilson suspected that the President of the Board of Trade (one of Gaitskell's former *protégés*) was plotting to unseat him, and Crosland himself proved to be a diffident and indecisive minister, renowned for 'contributing an idea in Cabinet but not a policy or a decision'.[40] Proponents of caution within the British policy-making establishment were therefore able to delay any decision on computer exports to the Eastern bloc, and the issue remained unresolved until after the Czechoslovak crisis of August 1968.

During the ambassadors' conference Harrison told his colleagues that parliamentary hostility to COCOM reflected widespread popular scepticism concerning 'the present nature of the Soviet threat'. He concluded that USSR technological prowess was only marginally inferior to that of the West, and that Soviet spies could easily buy, or steal, industrial secrets from Western companies to make good this inferiority. Wittingly or not, Harrison had made an accurate observation, as industrial espionage was one of the KGB's principal roles during the Cold War. He also alluded to the increasingly negative impact of Soviet (and Eastern European) espionage on relations between the UK and USSR.[41]

The Wilson government and Eastern bloc espionage, 1964–8

Christopher Andrew argues that previous studies of Soviet history overlooked an important aspect of the USSR's foreign policy, namely the KGB's operations against Western countries, including Britain. Although the KGB did use 'illegals' (operatives working without the protection offered

---

[40] K. Jefferys, *Anthony Crosland: a new biography*, London 2000, 129–35; ESC(O)(68)6th meeting, 6 Aug. 1968, CAB 134/2800; OPD(68)51, 'Future of COCOM', 10 July 1968, CAB 148/38.
[41] 'Conference of HM representatives', 7th meeting, FCO 28/45; Andrew and Mitrokhin, *Mitrokhin archive*, i. 244–7, 553.

by diplomatic immunity) in its external operations, it was common practice for NATO and Warsaw Pact intelligence services to conduct their foreign espionage operations from diplomatic missions, even though this violated the 1961 Vienna Treaty on diplomatic protocols. Throughout the Cold War the UK was a significant intelligence target for the USSR, due to its role in NATO and its alliance ties with the USA, and the exposure of Soviet spies such as Philby, Maclean and George Blake (who escaped imprisonment in 1966 and subsequently made his way to the USSR) embarrassed MI5 and SIS. Given the importance of intelligence co-operation for Anglo-American relations, the effect these spy scandals had on US officialdom's perception of British security was particularly significant. The growth of KGB activity in the UK during the 1960s, under the cover of an expanded Soviet diplomatic presence, led US officials to wonder why the Foreign Office and MI5 was unable to curtail an espionage threat which was detrimental to Western security.[42]

KGB operations were supplemented by those of the GRU (Soviet military intelligence), as well as the Cuban and Warsaw Pact security services. The Czechoslovak StB had a high profile in Whitehall because of its activities in Britain, and enjoyed some success in suborning a handful of trade unionists and Labour MPs. Throughout the 1960s and early 1970s the KGB and the GRU continued to recruit agents within the British government and armed forces, but these tended to be of a lesser calibre than the likes of Philby or Blake. It was also becoming progressively less easy for Soviet bloc intelligence services to operate in Britain and other Western countries, much to the annoyance of Yuri Andropov, chairman of the KGB from 1967 to 1982. In his May 1968 report to Brezhnev, Andropov complained that 'agent access to governmental, military, intelligence and ideological centres of the enemy' was unsatisfactory and needed to be improved.[43] Andropov's conviction that the scope of KGB operations overseas was inadequate contributed to its increased involvement in espionage in the West during the late 1960s, although Vassili Mitrokhin, a former KGB officer, maintained that the continued expansion of the Soviet diplomatic presence in Britain was specifically intended to 'swamp the overstretched MI5 with more intelligence officers than they could hope to keep under surveillance'. The Security Service grew frustrated by what it regarded as the unrestricted build-up of the Soviet diplomatic presence in Britain. Nine 'watchers' were needed to keep one diplomat under surveillance, and officers in MI5's K (counter-

---

42 Andrew and Mitrokhin, *Archive*, i. 715–18; T. Bower, *The perfect English spy: Sir Dick White and the secret war, 1935–90*, London 1995, 307, 330–3; Aldrich, *Hidden hand*, 429–30.

43 C. Parrott (Prague) to Stewart, 2 Apr. 1966, N1075/10, FO 371/188497; R. Garthoff and A. Knight, 'New evidence on Soviet intelligence: the KGB's 1967 annual report', *CWIHP Bulletin* x (1998), 211–19.

intelligence) Branch felt that they could not cope with the expansion in their adversaries' numbers.[44]

In contrast, the Labour government and, until 1967–8, Foreign Office officials did not consider the problem of Eastern bloc espionage in Britain to be significant. Labour MPs tended to dismiss references to Soviet-inspired subversion as manifestations of anti-Communist hysteria, and the party had an instinctive distrust of the British intelligence services dating from the Zinoviev letter scandal of 1924.[45] The Wilson government and the Foreign Office demonstrated their lack of concern by concluding the Anglo-Soviet consular agreement of December 1965, which gave both parties reciprocal rights to consular officials, including diplomatic immunity. This agreement was concluded despite protests from Conservative backbenchers over the activities of Warsaw Pact intelligence officers operating under diplomatic cover. The most outspoken of the MPs, Commander Anthony Courtney, proposed to limit the number of Eastern bloc embassy and commercial staff in Britain, and to deprive them of diplomatic privileges, courier and cipher services. The Foreign Office regarded Courtney's suggestions as 'impractical and unhelpful', arguing that the existing system protected British embassy and consular officials in Communist countries from police harassment. Wilson told Courtney that if his proposals were implemented British diplomats would be expelled from Warsaw Pact states, and he maintained that MI5 had sufficient personnel to keep suspected intelligence officers under surveillance. While Wilson and the Foreign Office concluded that Courtney was crying wolf, the KGB considered that his campaign against Eastern bloc spies warranted 'active measures' to discredit him with smears concerning his private life.[46]

The espionage problem became interlinked with the case of Gerald Brooke, a British lecturer sentenced to five years imprisonment in the USSR in July 1965. Brooke was caught smuggling propaganda material produced by the NTS, an anti-Communist Russian émigré group, and the Soviet government responded to British appeals for clemency by demanding the release of two KGB 'illegals' imprisoned in the UK in 1961, Peter and Helen Kroger (also known as Morris and Lona Cohen). Much to Wilson's discomfort, Brooke's treatment in prison aroused furious protests from parliament and the press. During his visit to Moscow in January 1968 Wilson pleaded in vain with Gromyko and the Soviet president, Nikolai Podgorny, for increased consular

---

[44] Andrew and Mitrokhin, *Archive*, i. 538–9; Walden, *Lucky George*, 144.

[45] Dorril and Ramsay, *Smear!*, 65–9; *Crossman diaries*, iii. 913, entry for 7 May 1970. Many Labour politicians believe that MI5 forged a letter from Grigori Zinoviev, the chairman of *Comintern*, to undermine Ramsay McDonald's government prior to the 1924 elections: A. Thorpe, *A history of the British Labour party*, Basingstoke 1997, 60.

[46] P. Wright (Private Secretary to Gore-Booth) note, 24 June 1965, N1905/5/G, FO 371/182525; T. Bridges (FO) to M. Reid (No.10), 18 June 1965, and conversation between Cdr A. Courtney and Wilson, 29 June 1965, PREM 13/483; Andrew and Mitrokhin, *Mitrokhin archive*, i. 531.

access to Brooke, stating that public opinion was appalled by the punishment the authorities had inflicted on this 'foolish young man'. Brooke was eventually released in July 1969 in exchange for the Krogers, who were freed three months later. Denis Greenhill, who served as Permanent Under-Secretary of the Foreign and Commonwealth Office after February 1969, subsequently stated that British officials had reluctantly agreed to an exchange between Brooke and the Krogers on compassionate grounds, and also to facilitate 'a small improvement in Anglo-Soviet relations'. However, the fact that the British government had given way to Soviet pressure aroused misgivings within Whitehall. In Greenhill's words, the image of 'a defiant Mrs Kroger' boarding 'a homeward bound *Aeroflot* plane at Heathrow made me wonder … whether we had not let our hearts run away with our heads'.[47]

By early 1968 Foreign Office officials had become far less tolerant of Soviet and Eastern bloc espionage in the UK, and the deterioration of bilateral relations between the UK and USSR compounded a growing sense of outrage in Whitehall at increased Soviet intelligence activity in Britain. By this time there were an estimated 120 KGB and GRU officers under diplomatic cover at the embassy and trade mission in London.[48] Two weeks after Wilson's visit to Moscow one of these officers, V. A. Drozdov, was caught by the police at a 'dead letter-box' (a location for concealing sensitive materials) in London. While the Northern Department wanted to publicise the affair, Brown was disinclined to make much of it, pointing out that SIS officers in the Eastern bloc also employed diplomatic cover. The Foreign Secretary referred to the case of Adam Karamczyk, a Polish Defence Ministry clerk recruited by SIS who was executed in late 1967, causing the expulsion of one SIS officer from the Warsaw embassy. Brown implied that there was no alternative to the *status quo*, and argued that if the UK and USSR engaged in tit-for-tat expulsions of embassy personnel then Britain, with its smaller diplomatic corps, would come off worse. Brown also commented on the 'contradiction between the [Foreign] Office's wish on the one hand to bring home to Parliament and public the iniquities of the KGB and, on the other, to increase *détente* with the Russians in every possible field'.[49] Although Brown was reluctant to adopt a tougher line towards the USSR, Stewart (who returned to the Foreign Office in mid-March 1968) supported his subordinates' view that Britain had been 'over-enthusiastic' in its efforts

---

[47] Conversation between Gromyko, Podgorny and Wilson, Kremlin, 24 Jan. 1968 (a.m.), *DBPO III*, i. 14–21; CC(69)30th conclusions, 26 June 1969, CAB 128/44; Greenhill, *More by accident*, 128–9.

[48] Greenhill to Gore-Booth, 29 Jan. 1968, and Gore-Booth to Brown, 31 Jan. 1968, FCO 28/402; 'Conference of ambassadors on Eastern Europe', 27 Apr.–2 May 1966, FO 371/188510.

[49] D. Maitland (FO) to Gore-Booth, 12 Feb. 1968, FCO 28/372; note in *DBPO III*, i. 28; Urban, *UK eyes alpha*, 100.

to enhance contacts with the USSR, and was obliged to reassess its conduct of Anglo-Soviet relations.[50]

What was evident throughout the 1960s was that British politicians and officials underestimated the KGB's role in the making of Soviet foreign as well as domestic policy. The JIC had reported in April 1964 that the Soviet security service had only 'an advisory role' in decision-making, but the elevation of Andropov to the *Politburo* in June 1967 symbolised the KGB's increased importance in Soviet politics.[51] Harrison was one of the few British diplomats to appreciate the growth in the KGB's influence within the CPSU hierarchy, writing in January 1968 that '[if] it is true that party control over the KGB has been strengthened in recent times, the movement may go the other way; these closer links may ... strengthen the influence of the KGB inside the party'. The ambassador to Moscow predicted that this trend would reinforce the Kremlin's suspicions of Western 'subversion', making the Kremlin less receptive towards *détente*. Indeed, in his report to Brezhnev in May 1968, the KGB Chairman warned that '[the] governments and intelligence services of the USA and other imperialist states have intensified their aggressive policies and subversive activities with respect to the socialist countries'. Andropov also encouraged his *Politburo* colleagues' paranoia over 'bridge-building', thereby contributing to the lack of a Soviet response to Western efforts to promote *détente* during the latter half of the 1960s, and to the deterioration of Anglo-Soviet relations which followed Kosygin's visit to the UK in 1967.[52]

Anglo-Soviet relations after the Kosygin visit, February 1967–June 1968

Harrison wrote in March 1967 that after over two years of acrimony, the 'spirit of Kosygin' had a beneficial impact on bilateral relations. The Foreign Office's sense of optimism in the spring of 1967 was reflected by its request to the MoD that RAF SIGINT aircraft should follow flight paths further from the USSR's airspace, so as not to disturb the tentative improvement in bilateral relations.[53] Wilson thought that he had finally established a working

---

[50] Hayman to Harrison, 27 Feb. 1968, *DBPO III*, i. 25–8; minute by Maitland, 23 Feb. 1968.; Harrison to Hayman, 6 Mar. 1968; and Smith to Hayman, 1 Apr. 1968, FCO 28/372; OPD(68)45, 'Relations with the Soviet Union and Eastern Europe', 17 June 1968, CAB 148/37.

[51] Gore-Booth, *With great truth*, 412; JIC(64)43, 'The power structure in the Soviet Union', 17 Apr. 1964, CAB 158/53; Service, *Russia*, 385.

[52] Harrison to Brown, 11 Jan. 1968; memorandum by Giffard, 22 Feb. 1968, and Smith to Harrison, 11 Mar. 1968, FCO 28/325; Yuri Andropov to Leonid Brezhnev, in Garthoff and Knight, 'Soviet intelligence', passim.

[53] Moscow to FO, nos 322, 347, 3, 7 Mar. 1967, FCO 28/371; G. Thomson (FO Minister of State) to Healey, 1 Mar. 1967, DEFE 13/499.

relationship with the Soviet leadership, and he considered Kosygin's suggestion that he should attend the commemoration of the fiftieth anniversary of the Russian revolution in November 1967. This prospect horrified Brown and his officials, who felt that 'a Social Democratic Prime Minister' could not be seen at a 'celebration of a Communist *coup d'etat*'. At the end of 1967 the Soviet government agreed to invite the prime minister to visit Moscow for a third time, on 22–24 January 1968.[54] By this time, the 'spirit of Kosygin' to which Harrison had earlier referred had evaporated.

Wilson's talks with Kosygin led to the establishment of a 'hot-line' between the Kremlin and 10 Downing Street, an act of tokenism which conveyed the image of Britain as a major player on the world stage, but which would have been of little significance in a major East-West crisis, where the key dialogue would have been between the US and Soviet leaderships. Wilson was also pleased with the outcome of the discussions on trade and technological co-operation on 7 February, and regarded the draft Foreign Office *communiqué*'s treatment of these issues as 'quite unsatisfactory'. Wilson informed Brown that both premiers agreed to a treaty of 'friendship and peaceful co-operation' regulating cultural, commercial and scientific contacts, which would be compatible with the existing alliance commitments of their respective countries. The Foreign Office's reluctant response to this proposal annoyed the prime minister, who wanted to see the 'friendship treaty' implemented.[55]

Wilson was focusing on symbolism, rather than substance. France and the USSR had concluded an agreement on technological co-operation in December 1966, so Wilson needed the 'friendship treaty' in order to cap de Gaulle.[56] However, this proposed 'treaty' aroused controversy within NATO although – in the interests of Anglo-German concord, and in contrast with the 'declaration of principles' – the West German Foreign Ministry was shown the text in advance. Wilson attempted to reassure Johnson, stating that he and Brown saw 'no particular harm' in the proposed treaty, and the OPD endorsed the Foreign Office's draft text in early April.[57] Despite the misgivings of the USA and other allied governments, British officials pressed ahead with the treaty, with Greenhill travelling to Moscow in mid-April to present the draft text to Soviet officials. This draft, which focused on fostering bilateral commercial, cultural and scientific ties, was greeted with little enthusiasm by the Soviet Foreign Ministry, whose diplomats told

---

54 Gore-Booth to Hood and Hayman, 20 Apr. 1967; Moscow to FO, no. 2050, 8 Dec. 1967, and FO to Moscow, 4 Jan. 1968, FCO 28/398; Smith to Palliser, 8 Feb. 1967, and Gore-Booth to Hayman, 13 Feb. 1967, FCO 28/371.

55 Wilson to Brown, and Palliser to MacLehose, 11 Feb. 1967, PREM 13/1842.

56 On the Franco-Soviet technological agreement see KV(67)1, 'Steering brief', 26 Jan. 1967, CAB 133/365. See also Kosygin to Wilson, 31 Oct. 1967, FCO 28/371.

57 Wilson to Johnson, PMUK003/11, 11 Feb. 1967, PREM 13/2114; A. Goodison (Bonn) to A. Campbell (Western Department), 9 Mar. 1967, FCO 28/376; OPD(67)25, 'Anglo-Soviet treaty of friendship and peaceful co-operation', 4 Apr. 1967, CAB 148/34.

Greenhill that it needed to address additional, but unspecified, issues beyond bilateral relations. The Soviet government subsequently delayed its response for nine months.[58] During his second visit to Moscow, on 23–26 May, Brown requested a Soviet response to the draft text. Although Gromyko promised that his subordinates would soon produce the USSR's own version, the Foreign Secretary returned home empty-handed.[59]

Brown's visit to Moscow was overshadowed by escalating tensions between Egypt and Israel, which eventually led to the outbreak of war on 5 June. His conversations with Kosygin and Gromyko revolved around the Middle Eastern crisis, which his hosts blamed on Israel. In his analysis of the visit, Harrison told Brown that in his opinion Brezhnev and the CPSU ideologues – 'temperamentally probably more suspicious of the West, less pragmatical [sic], tougher and more dogmatic than Kosygin' – had assumed a more active role in the making of foreign policy. Nevertheless, he again drew comfort from the apparent readiness of the Soviet leadership to maintain links with their British counterparts. However, the head of the Northern Department, Howard Smith, concluded that Britain had been too eager to develop contacts with the USSR. The 'treaty of friendship' was in limbo, and the *Politburo*'s stance on Germany, Vietnam, the Arab-Israeli crisis and the Brooke case remained uncompromising. Smith suggested that Britain should wait and see what concessions the Soviet government was prepared to make for the sake of improved relations with the West.[60] These comments reflected the growing sense of frustration within the Foreign Office over the stagnation of Anglo-Soviet relations. While diplomats at the Moscow embassy thought that Brezhnev and the *Politburo* were obliged to denounce America and Britain after the Six Day War in order to re-establish the USSR's 'anti-imperialist' reputation in the Third World, there was increasing resentment within Whitehall that the UK was being specifically targeted by Soviet propaganda.

On 22 January 1968 Wilson made his third visit to the USSR, which Foreign Office officials concluded served only a symbolic purpose. Gore-Booth felt that Britain's economic troubles provided 'an unhappy background' to the prime minister's visit, while the ambassador to Moscow reported that the UK had received 'an unrelievedly [sic] bad press' from the Soviet media, with extensive coverage of the devaluation crisis and the withdrawals form East of Suez.[61] Harrison, like other British diplomats, concluded that the

---

[58] B. Burrows (UKDELNATO) to Hood, 8 Mar. 1967; Hood to Hayman, 10 Mar. 1967; Smith note, 13 Mar. 1967, FCO 28/376; Burrows to Hood, 16 Mar. 1967, and FO to UKDELNATO, no. 733, 18 Apr. 1967, FCO 28/377.

[59] Brown–Gromyko conversation, UK embassy, 24 May 1967; 'Visit of the Foreign Secretary to the Soviet Union, 23–26 May 1967', FCO 28/406.

[60] Brown to Harrison, 26 May 1967; Harrison to Brown, 1 June 1967; Smith to Hayman, 2 June 1967; and Hayman to Smith, 6 June 1967, FCO 28/406.

[61] D. Day to Palliser, 21 Nov. 1967, PREM 13/2405; Gore-Booth to Hayman, 8 Jan. 1968, FCO 28/399; Harrison to Smith, 17 Jan. 1968, *DBPO III*, i. 5–8.

Soviets would try to exploit Britain's economic plight by putting pressure on Wilson to loosen ties with the USA. While Foreign Office officials wanted to play down the significance of the visit, the prime minister hoped to follow up the Benn-Kirillin technological agreement with either a long-term Anglo-Soviet trade agreement or a reduction of the COCOM lists.[62] Throughout Wilson's visit his Soviet interlocutors took every opportunity to 'drive wedges' between Britain and its allies. During his talks with the prime minister on 22 January, Kosygin played on British suspicions that other Western powers were bending COCOM's rules, and he suggested that the USSR could increase exports to the UK 'in order to free Britain from dependence on the United States'.[63] Kosygin also stated without subtlety that it was 'a pity ... that [Britain] could not follow the same kind of independent policy as de Gaulle'. The following day Brezhnev treated the prime minister to another lecture on the threat West German 'revanchism' posed to peace in Europe. Wilson's attempts to discuss mutual force reductions were simply ignored.[64]

The course of the visit demonstrated that Kosygin, whom British officials had regarded as a pragmatist comparatively immune (by CPSU standards) to Communist dogma, was now a secondary figure within the Soviet leadership, and Foreign Office analysts recognised that Brezhnev had now effectively assumed Khrushchev's mantle as 'first among equals' in the Kremlin.[65] Wilson's trip also ended with the presentation of the Soviet draft of the 'friendship' treaty, which British officials regarded as completely unacceptable. The Soviet text demanded Britain's endorsement of the USSR's policy on the German question and other European security issues, and was also explicitly aimed against Britain's membership of NATO. Foreign Office officials were concerned that their Soviet counterparts might publish its draft in order to cause Britain further trouble with its allies, and Harrison was instructed to refer Gromyko back to the original draft. However, the latter told the ambassador that a friendship treaty was impossible as long as Britain remained part of NATO; this showed that the Soviet leadership had no interest in pursuing the matter further.[66]

The treaty had been conceived by Wilson and (with markedly less enthusiasm) by the Foreign Office as a means of facilitating enhanced contacts

62 Hood to Dean, 17 Jan. 1968, FCO 28/399; A. Halls (No.10) to B. Meynell (BoT), 8 Jan. 1968, FCO 28/399; Day to Halls, 19 Jan. 1968, CAB 164/406.
63 Kosygin–Wilson conversation, Kremlin, 22 Jan. 1968 (a.m.), and 'Visit of the prime minister to the Soviet Union, 22–24 January 1968', CAB 164/406; Kosygin–Wilson conversation, Kremlin, 23 Jan. 1968 (p.m.), DBPO III, i. 8–13.
64 Kosygin–Wilson conversation, 22 Jan. 1968 (p.m.), and Brezhnev–Wilson conversation, Kremlin, 23 Jan. 1968 (a.m.), PREM 13/2402.
65 Orchard to Palliser, 30 Jan. 1968; Palliser to Orchard, 21 Feb. 1968; and Trend to Palliser, 29 Feb. 1968, PREM 13/2405; Harrison to Brown, 8 Jan. 1968, FCO 28/307
66 Smith to Hayman, 25 Jan. 1968, FCO 28/372; Smith to Hayman, 30 Jan. 1968, and Day to Palliser, 1 Feb. 1968, FCO 28/380.

between the British and Soviet governments and their respective citizens. Its implicit rejection demonstrated that the Soviet leadership was deliberately downgrading relations with the UK. Harrison's dispatch on 6 February described the Soviet leadership's lack of enthusiasm towards Wilson's visit, noting that the final *communiqué* did not even refer to the recently concluded technological treaty. The only positive point that the ambassador could make was that 'contact had been maintained' with the Soviet leadership. However, within the Foreign Office the Kremlin's treatment of Wilson had touched a raw nerve. Four days before the prime minister's arrival in Moscow, Gore-Booth informed William Rodgers (the Parliamentary Under-Secretary of State for Foreign Affairs) that the USSR's pronouncements on 'peaceful coexistence' had been taken at face value by domestic opinion. Gore-Booth also expressed his concerns over Wilson's refusal to confront Kosygin over his public attacks on British foreign policy in February 1967. The Permanent Under-Secretary was worried that Soviet propaganda was having a divisive effect on the Western world as a whole, and that public opinion overlooked the threat that the USSR still posed to Britain's security. Following Wilson's return to London, Gore-Booth concluded that it was time to reappraise the UK's policy towards the Soviet Union.[67]

The Drozdov affair, and evidence of increased KGB activity in the UK, provided an additional impetus for a reassessment of Anglo-Soviet relations, and on 23 February Brown met with Goronwy Roberts (the Foreign Office Minister of State), Greenhill, Smith and Peter Hayman (the Assistant Under-Secretary supervising the Northern Department) for what the latter euphemistically termed a 'most useful and stimulating discussion'. By the end of this meeting, the Foreign Secretary was persuaded that while the UK's essential objective of promoting *détente* should remain unchanged, there should be 'less running after the Russians' and fewer ministerial visits to the USSR. Brown's subordinates concluded that the British government had been 'over-enthusiastic' in pursuing agreements with the USSR, and that Foreign Office propaganda (including the IRD's output) should 'attack the Russians in the area where they are most vulnerable', namely the KGB's suppression of domestic dissent.[68] Harrison's own analysis of Anglo-Soviet relations, sent to London in early March, struck a more cautious note. The ambassador to Moscow drew a distinction between combating Eastern bloc espionage in Britain and criticising the KGB's repressive activities against dissidents. Was the Foreign Office's objective 'retaliation for hurtful attacks by Russian propaganda on our own policies' or was it 'part of the battle for the hearts and minds of the neutral, uncommitted peoples of the world?'. Harrison stated that he was 'not opposed to embarrassing the Russians',

[67] Harrison to Hayman, 6 Feb. 1968, PREM 13/2402; Harrison to Brown, 31 Jan. 1968, FCO 28/402; Gore-Booth to Rodgers, 16 Jan. 1968, Gore-Booth papers, passim.
[68] Hayman to Harrison, 27 Feb. 1968, *DBPO III*, i. 25–8; Maitland note, 23 Feb. 1968, FCO 28/372.

but supported Brown's concerns that there was 'a certain inconsistency' in seeking East-West *rapprochement*, while concurrently attacking the iniquities of the Soviet system.[69]

Harrison was, however, out of step with his colleagues. Brown's discussions with his Foreign Office subordinates on 23 February led to the presentation of a Foreign Office paper, entitled 'Relations with the Soviet Union and Eastern Europe', to the OPD in mid-June. By this time Stewart was again Foreign Secretary. The long-running feud between Wilson and Brown reached its climax in mid-March 1968, and the latter finally resigned from the Cabinet. Brown had reluctantly approved the Foreign Office's interpretation of Soviet policy, but Stewart fully endorsed the conclusions contained in the OPD paper, which presented ministers with an adversarial interpretation of Soviet policy towards Britain. Its Foreign Office drafters reminded Cabinet ministers that the USSR's foreign policy goal of spreading Communism worldwide remained unchanged. The Soviet leadership was prepared to conclude 'specific and limited agreements with the West', such as the LTBT and the NPT, but was also exploiting the rhetoric of 'peaceful coexistence' to 'create friction between the United States and other Western countries and to undermine NATO'. The Soviet government hoped to develop trading links and to establish technological exchange agreements with the West, but its response to the proposed 'friendship treaty' with Britain demonstrated Soviet opposition to any genuine cultural contacts or exchanges of ideas with Western countries. While expressing their concerns over alleged foreign 'subversion', the Soviets were actively involved in espionage operations aimed at undermining the 'imperialists'. The authors of the OPD paper argued that the Soviet government's attitude towards Britain reflected its view that the latter's economic difficulties could be exploited to alter British foreign policy to suit the USSR's interests. Gromyko's blunt statement that a treaty of friendship was incompatible with Britain's NATO membership was interpreted as an affront to British prestige: '[this] sort of language ... has in the past been used by the Russians with Norway and Denmark, but not with us'. The reference to two minor NATO powers was significant, as both countries had a reputation within the Alliance for vulnerability to Soviet diplomatic pressure.[70]

The Foreign Office paper recommended that Britain should continue to encourage the 'evolution' of Eastern European countries through bilateral contacts, without openly seeking to incite the USSR's clients against Moscow. However, its authors also called for a change in tone in Anglo-Soviet relations, recommending that the British government should respond 'clearly, firmly and seriously' whenever its Soviet interlocutor 'addresses itself

69 Harrison to Hayman, 6 Mar. 1968; R. Samuel to Hayman, 22 Mar. 1968; and Smith to Hayman, 1 Apr. 1968, FCO 28/372.
70 Pimlott, *Wilson*, 494–9; OPD(68)45, CAB148/37; J. A. Peduzie (MoD) to R. O'Neill (FO), 6 Sept. 1966, DEFE 13/498.

to us officially in terms which show less than proper respect'. British officials also needed to appraise discreetly public opinion on 'the subversive and repressive aspects of the Soviet regime', in particular the KGB's domestic repression and its espionage activities against the West. The Foreign Office felt, despite Harrison's remarks, that 'a generally false picture of the Soviet Union and its intentions' gave it 'opportunities to attack not only the interests but even the security' of the UK.[71]

The only minister openly to criticise these conclusions was Benn, who was particularly proud of the agreement that he had concluded with Kirillin, and was contemptuous of what he dismissed as the entrenched hostility of the Foreign Office and the intelligence services towards the USSR. Although his diaries give the opposite impression, the Minister of Technology was not alone in supporting bilateral scientific and commercial contacts with the Soviet bloc, but his Pollyanna-esque views on the USSR made him unique among Wilson's ministers. Three days before the technological agreement was signed, Benn unwisely told Kirillin that Britain was 'an isolated country whose relations with the United States were now somewhat strained and who had been locked out of Europe', and that as a consequence 'Soviet friendship was of great importance'. Benn considered 'Relations with the Soviet Union and Eastern Europe' to be 'barely post-Dulles' in its outlook, but his attempts to have its conclusions debated by the whole Cabinet were fruitless. Benn's idiosyncratic views on East-West relations aside, by mid-1968 the majority of British ministers and officials blamed the decline in Anglo-Soviet relations on the USSR's ideological stridency. Roberts epitomised this view when he told the Foreign Secretary that Soviet propaganda attacked the UK and other Western powers because the *Politburo* required 'some cry of external danger' to consolidate both internal opinion and the cohesion of Warsaw Pact. In response, the British government had to 'meet toughness with toughness. Utter clarity, bordering on crudity, pays with the Russians'.[72]

The 'spirit of Kosygin' which Harrison referred to in March 1967 proved to be as ephemeral as the 'spirit of Geneva' had been in the mid-1950s. Anglo-Soviet commercial contacts and the Benn-Kirillin treaty did not contribute to improved political relations between the USSR and UK. Brezhnev and his *Politburo* colleagues were uninterested in concluding a 'friendship treaty' with Britain, while increased KGB and GRU activity in the UK demonstrated both the hostility with which the USSR regarded its 'imperialist' foes, and (as far as officials in Whitehall were concerned) that the Soviet government was exploiting Britain's willingness to develop bilateral contacts in a manner detrimental to the UK's national security. Foreign Office offi-

[71] OPD(68)45, CAB148/37.
[72] Benn, *Office without power*, 21, 74, 77, 84, entries for 19 Jan., 3, 5 June 1968, and note dated 20 June; G. Roberts to Stewart, 13 June 1968, FCO 28/54.

cials had become disillusioned with the meagre results of engagement with the USSR and, as Foreign Secretary, Stewart was less prepared than Brown to 'run after the Russians'. Having begun the decade as one of the most *détente*-minded of NATO powers, during the course of 1968 the UK adopted a less compromising and more adversarial stance towards relations with the USSR.

The British government's lack of progress in developing East-West relations was not unique, and although the Soviet government was quick to blame the UK's policies on Vietnam and Germany, there is little to suggest that a more Gaullist approach would have yielded any better results. Despite the anti-American posturing of the French president, his equivocal policy towards Germany and his own dealings with the Soviet leadership, France gained no practical results from de Gaulle's conduct of *détente*. Brezhnev and Kosygin ignored the French president's proposal for four-power negotiations (involving the superpowers, the UK and France) to diffuse the Arab-Israeli crisis in May 1967, and Gomulka made his disdain for de Gaulle's 'Europe totale' rhetoric evident during the latter's visit to Poland four months later. In the FRG's case, despite Kiesinger's renunciation of the Hallstein doctrine in December 1966, Romania was the only Warsaw Pact state to respond to the FRG's early attempts at *Ostpolitik*.[73]

A more pertinent criticism concerns the fact that until Wilson's January 1968 visit to Moscow Kosygin was the focus of London's efforts to foster Anglo-Soviet goodwill. Wilson placed excessive emphasis on his supposed rapport with the Soviet premier. Foreign Office officials also focused upon Kosygin, overrating his importance in the Kremlin. For British policy-makers, he represented the pragmatic, technocratic class who would promote both the internal reform and 'evolution' of the Soviet system, and would orient the USSR's foreign policy towards *détente*. It was not until early 1968 that British diplomats started to reappraise Kosygin's lack of influence within the *Politburo*.[74] Brezhnev consolidated his position within the Kremlin and had gained the support of the military because of his support for increased defence expenditure. Kosygin, on the other hand, had alienated the CPSU hierarchy with his plans to decentralise the command economy. His reforms were never implemented and by 1970 he had been sidelined. By exaggerating the importance of contacts with Kosygin, Wilson and a number of Foreign Office officials failed to recognise that power within the Soviet system resided in the CPSU, rather than the state structure.[75] Foreign Office officials also overlooked the fact that, as General Secretary of the CPSU, Brezhnev

---

73 Lacouture, *De Gaulle*, 762–9; FO to Washington, no.7030, 23 June 1967, PREM 13/1521; Hanrieder, *Germany, America, Europe*, 182–6.
74 J. A. Dobbs (Moscow) to I. Sutherland (ND), 13 Mar. 1967, FCO 28/314; Harrison to Brown, 8 Jan. 1968, and E. Orchard (FO Research Dept) to E. Bolland (Washington), 9 July 1968, FCO 28/315.
75 Barker, *Divided Europe*, 250–1; Hosking, *Soviet Union*, 365; Service, *Russia*, 379–80.

was strengthening his own position by manipulating the network of patron-client relationships within the party. Within the CPSU independence and initiative on the part of individual apparatchiks was constrained by loyalty to higher-ranking patrons and to the 'party line'. The *Politburo* and the CPSU Central Committee also kept a close eye on lower-level party organisations, enforcing compliance and ensuring that there was no deviation from decisions taken at the centre. As a result, Brezhnev exploited his control over the party apparatus to thwart Kosygin's plans for economic reform and eventually to oust potential rivals from the *Politburo*. The ossification of the party structure, and the Soviet leadership's inherent conservatism, thereby acted as a barrier to internal reform, with consequences evident in the economic stagnation of the USSR in the 1970s and 1980s.[76]

The fundamental problem for the British, French, West German and other NATO governments was that there was an essential incompatibility between Western and Eastern bloc concepts of *détente*. For the latter, *détente* was to be an inter-governmental affair, and while Western trade, credits and technology transfers were welcome, the ruling Communist regimes wanted to control contacts with the capitalist world in order to preserve the ideological *status quo* and their own authority over their subject populations. In contrast, Western concepts such as 'bridge-building', 'evolution', 'Europe totale' or *Neue Ostpolitik* were ultimately intended to transcend the Cold War. Western governments concluded that the only feasible way of ending East-West hostilities was to encourage incremental political and socio-economic reform in the Eastern bloc through greater contacts not just with the ruling regimes, but with their subjects. Yet what would happen if these efforts to encourage 'evolutionary change' were resisted by Warsaw Pact governments (as shown by Andropov's report of May 1968 to Brezhnev)? And what would the implications for East-West relations if internal social pressures for change within Eastern bloc countries acquired an uncontrollable momentum; if evolution became revolution? The problems that the conflict between the irresistible force of popular discontent and the immovable object of Soviet hegemony caused for British and NATO approaches to East-West relations were illustrated by the Czechoslovak crisis of 1968.

---

[76] J. P. Willerton, *Patronage and politics in the USSR*, Cambridge 1992, 1–19; JIC(64)43, CAB 158/53; M. Kramer, 'Ukraine and the Soviet-Czechoslovak crisis of 1968 (part 2): new evidence from the Ukrainian archives', *CWIHP Bulletin* xiv–xv (2004), 274–5.

6

The 'Prague Spring' and its Aftermath, 1968–1970

Five years after the 'white heat' speech at Scarborough, the Labour government had failed to revive the British economy. If its second, and comprehensive, election victory in March 1966 was the high point of the Wilson government's term in office, then the months following the devaluation crisis were arguably its nadir. The pound remained fragile, the economy was in recession and Wilson's tense relationship with his leading ministers deteriorated as a result of his paranoid conviction that his colleagues were plotting to oust him.[1] Other Western states also had their own political crises to resolve. On the continent there was a series of protests and disturbances which were compared to the revolutionary upheavals of 1848. De Gaulle was almost toppled by student riots in Paris in May 1968, while similar outbursts of radical activity fuelled the emergence of far-left terrorism in West Germany and Italy during the subsequent decade.[2] In January 1968 the Johnson administration was shaken by the seizure of an American SIGINT ship, the USS *Pueblo*, by the North Korean navy. The Tet offensive in South Vietnam at the end of the month added further pressure to a beleaguered administration, making a mockery of its claims that the USA was winning in Vietnam. On 31 March Johnson announced that he would not seek re-election. Increased anti-war agitation, widespread racial violence and the assassinations of Martin Luther King and Robert Kennedy contributed to the impression that the USA was in a state of crisis.[3]

The Eastern bloc countries were in no position to gloat over the misfortunes of the capitalist world. In Poland, student riots in Warsaw and Krakow in March 1968 provoked a harsh crackdown by the Gomulka regime, combining police repression with state-supported antisemitism. Prominent Jewish officials like Rapacki were demoted, and thousands of Jews and intellectuals emigrated. Events in Poland were overshadowed by those which followed the overthrow of the First Secretary of the CPCS, Antonin Novotny, on 5 January 1968. The failures of the command economy, student

---

1 Pimlott, *Wilson*, 493–509; Morgan, *People's peace*, 283–4.
2 *Crossman diaries*, iii. 298–9, entries for 24–27 Dec. 1968; Hitchcock, *Europe*, 247–57; J. Suri, *Power and protest: global revolution and the rise of détente*, Cambridge, MA 2003, 181, 186–94.
3 M. Lerner, *The Pueblo incident*, Lawrence, KA 2002; Schulzinger, *Time for war*, 242–4, 259–67; Suri, *Power and protest*, 182–6.

protests, nationalist discontent in Slovakia and Novotny's increasing unpopularity within the CPCS all contributed to his replacement by Alexander Dubcek. At the end of March Novotny was forced to resign the presidency in favour of Ludvik Svoboda. The new leadership – Dubcek, Svoboda and the premier, Oldrich Cernik – introduced an 'action programme' in April, promising economic liberalisation, greater freedom of speech and of travel, and limitations on the powers of the StB.[4] Although Novotny's successors reaffirmed Czechoslovakia's loyalty to the USSR, the Soviets were alarmed by the development of what Dubcek called 'socialism with a human face'. The gradual democratisation of Czechoslovakia provoked widespread concerns in other Warsaw Pact capitals not only over its continued allegiance to the Warsaw Pact, but over the consequences of the 'Prague Spring' for the stability of the Soviet bloc.[5]

On the surface the downfall of Novotny and the 'Action Programme' suggested that the views of British officialdom on the 'evolution' of the Eastern bloc and its gradual political and economic liberalisation had some validity. Following the conference of ambassadors to the Warsaw Pact states in June 1966, Howard Smith wrote that 'objective economic and political realities' would influence the process of long-term reform within Eastern Europe, and that the ruling regimes would be both pragmatic enough to respond to these 'realities' and subtle enough to manage popular pressure for more fundamental internal reforms. In fact, political trends behind the Iron Curtain during the mid-to-late 1960s suggested that the prospects for liberalisation were slim. Kosygin's proposals for economic reform lapsed in the face of entrenched opposition within the CPSU, while Brezhnev reversed both deStalinisation and the limited relaxation of cultural censorship that Khrushchev had initiated. Brezhnev relied far less on overt brutality and state terror than Stalin, but the persecution of dissident intellectuals, as demonstrated by the February 1966 show trial of the writers Yuli Daniel and Andrei Sinyavskii, showed the CPSU's intolerance of any challenge to its authority.[6]

There was a similar reaction on the part of the USSR's client governments in Eastern Europe, which included that of Poland, hitherto associated with the more liberal variant of 'national Communism' practised by

---

[4] Crampton, *Eastern Europe*, 318–19. The 'Action Programme' of April 1968 is in J. Navratil, A. Bencik, V. Kural, M. Michalkova and J. Vondrova (eds), *The Prague Spring, 1968: a national security archive documents reader*, Budapest 1998, 92–5. See also K. Dawisha, *The Kremlin and the Prague Spring*, Berkeley, CA 1984; H. G. Skilling, *Czechoslovakia's interrupted revolution*, Princeton, NJ 1976; and K. D. Williams, 'Political love's labours lost: negotiations between Prague and Moscow in 1968', *Slovo* vii/1 (1994), 72–87.

[5] Hosking, *Soviet Union*, 431–3; W. Loth, 'Moscow, Prague and Warsaw: overcoming the Brezhnev doctrine', *CWH* i/2 (2001), 103–5.

[6] 'Conference of HM representatives', FO 371/188510; Smith, *East-West relations*, 14 June 1966, N1075/66, FO 371/188500; Service, *Russia*, 381.

Gomulka. Even Romania, which had been the most receptive to Western diplomatic overtures and had defied other Warsaw Pact powers by recognising the FRG, combined a more 'independent' policy towards intra-bloc relations with domestic repression and a Stalinist personality cult surrounding its leader, Nicolae Ceausescu. In June 1966 the ambassador to Warsaw, George Clutton, offered a detailed critique of Foreign Office thinking on 'evolution', asserting that in a one-party state 'the free intellect is an illusion, since if the intellect is allowed to be free it destroys the system'. He noted that since 1956 Gomulka had halted the process of internal reform in Poland, and other East European leaders censored any domestic criticism which would undermine their monopoly on power. Clutton predicted that the Eastern bloc regimes would reverse the minimal concessions that they had made towards economic liberalisation and greater freedom of expression, and that the result would be ongoing internal discontent:

> I regard 'national communism', 'liberal communism' and all the other so-called qualified forms of communism as illusions. How long the sort of stagnation that exists in [the Soviet bloc] can in fact endure is hard to say, but my own belief is that the day will come when the whole system will crack and disintegrate, possibly with an explosion, but more probably not.[7]

Clutton's colleagues found this analysis disturbing; any sudden collapse of the Soviet-dominated order in Eastern Europe could destroy *détente* and exacerbate continental tensions. Smith accepted the ambassador to Warsaw's point that Poland had 'stagnated' since the late 1950s, but both he and the majority of Foreign Office officials maintained that '[neither the Polish] example or the logic of the situation should lead us to assume that Czechoslovakia, say, is going to go the same way'. This was an over-optimistic conclusion on Smith's part; the plans which Sik had devised for economic reform within Czechoslovakia were overruled by Novotny prior to his overthrow.[8]

Foreign Office officials displayed an ambivalent attitude towards political transition within the Soviet bloc, reflected both in their concerns at the implications of a violent upheaval in Eastern Europe, and their collective hope that the pace of political change would be dictated by the ruling regimes, rather than by popular protest and insurrection. The assumption that the Communist parties would be pragmatic enough to recognise the need for internal reform reflected the concern that revolutionary outbreaks within the Eastern bloc would, at the very least, undermine progress towards East-West *rapprochement*. British diplomats also underestimated the degree to which a one-party state could stifle dissent without resorting to Stalinist-style

---

7   C. Thompson to J. Whitehead, 20 Oct. 1964, FO 371/177407; G. Clutton (Warsaw) to Smith, 7 Jan., 21 June 1966, N1152/56, N1152/63, FO 371/188510.
8   Smith to Clutton, 23 June 1966, N1152/66; P. Rhodes's (ND) comment on Clutton's letter, 7 June 1966, N1152/62; and A. Morley (Budapest) to Smith, N1152/63, FO 371/188510.

police terror. The *nomenklatura* system within the USSR and East European country made ideological orthodoxy the prerequisite for advancement in the party and government hierarchies, industrial management, the armed forces, academia and throughout 'socialist' society, thereby inhibiting the growth of a more independent-minded, technocratic elite upon which British government officials had placed their hopes for reform within Eastern Europe.[9] Above all, the majority of Foreign Office officials supposed that the Soviet government would acquiesce in 'evolutionary' change in Eastern Europe. The CPSU *Politburo's* response to the events following Novotny's downfall, examined in this chapter, showed how misconceived this assessment was.

The 'Prague Spring' and the UK's reaction, January–August 1968

Czechoslovakia had long been regarded in Western capitals as a servile ally of the USSR. Unlike other Eastern bloc Communist parties, the CPCS had seized power in 1948 and had subsequently eradicated political opposition without much assistance from Stalin.[10] The Czechoslovak regime's reliability was such that, unlike Poland, Hungary or East Germany, there were no Soviet troops permanently stationed in Czechoslovakia, while its army and air force were considered by NATO to be the most combat-effective and reliable of the non-Soviet Warsaw Pact forces.[11] In his annual report for 1967 William Barker described the Novotny regime's record as 'dismal'. Czechoslovakia's foreign policy simply 'parroted' Soviet propaganda, while the party leadership had vetoed Sik's reforms. Following Novotny's resignation from the presidency, Barker reported that the new leadership was unlikely to be any improvement. Such scepticism was understandable. Novotny's enemies included senior conservatives, notably Vasil Bilak, Alois Indra and Drahomir Kolder, as well as the more liberal-minded members of the CPCS Central Committee, and Dubcek was appointed party secretary as a compromise candidate acceptable to would-be reformers and hard-liners alike.[12] Bilak and Kolder's initial support for Dubcek gave way to hostility following the relaxation of state censorship, while the new First Secretary's commitment to

[9] Crampton, *Eastern Europe*, 248–9; N. Davies, *Heart of Europe: a short history of Poland*, Oxford 1986, 47–8; H. Renner, *A history of Czechoslovakia since 1945*, Abingdon 1989, 37–8.

[10] Parrott to Stewart, 2 Apr. 1966, N1075/10, FO 371/188497; M. Myant, *Socialism and democracy in Czechoslovakia, 1945–1948*, Cambridge 1981, 200–8; G. Hughes, 'British policy towards Eastern Europe and the impact of the "Prague Spring", 1964–1968', *CWH* iv/2 (2004), 115–39.

[11] JIC(68)1, 'Periodic intelligence summary for NATO commands', 1 June 1968, and JIC(68)3, 'Soviet bloc war potential, 1968–72', 24 Jan. 1968, CAB158/68.

[12] W. Barker (Prague) to Brown, 9 Jan. 1968, FCO 28/89; Barker to Hayman (ND), 26 Mar. 1968, FCO 28/90; Renner, *Czechoslovakia*, 41–50; Skilling, *Interrupted revolution*, 161–79.

reform was less than whole-hearted. As Zdenek Mlynar (one of the CPCS's leading 'liberals') later noted, the reformist cause was by no means a 'unified, undifferentiated trend' within the party's Central Committee.[13]

To begin with Barker may have discounted the significance of Novotny's overthrow, but Czechoslovakia's neighbours were disturbed by its political transition. The Polish and East German leaders, Gomulka and Ulbricht, were initially even more concerned about the Czechoslovak reform programme than their patrons in the Kremlin. At the Warsaw Pact summit in Dresden on 23 March Brezhnev warned Dubcek and Cernik that the USSR could not 'remain indifferent' to 'counter-revolutionary' activity in Czechoslovakia, and both Gomulka and Ulbricht attacked the new regime's plans for internal liberalisation. The publication of the Action Programme in early April created more alarm within the Warsaw Pact. The relaxation of state censorship and the emergence of independent civil society groups such as KAN (the 'Club for Committed Non-Party Members') and K-231 (a group comprised of former political prisoners) threatened the *status quo* not only in Czechoslovakia, but throughout the Eastern bloc. On 8 May the Soviet, East German, Polish, Hungarian and Bulgarian leaders met in Moscow to decide how to thwart the Czechoslovak 'counter-revolution'. Although Kadar half-heartedly tried to defend Dubcek, the assembled leaders, subsequently dubbed the 'Five', opted to rally the 'healthy forces' (namely Dubcek's opponents) within the CPCS by waging a 'war of nerves' on Prague, combining increasingly shrill propaganda invective with a military build-up near Czechoslovakia's borders.[14]

The American and the West European reaction to this 'war of nerves' was muted. This was due to the West's own internal political and economic crises, and because of NATO's weakened state following the French withdrawal and the offsets crisis. The Harmel report and the Reykjavik declaration were a response to domestic pressure within Western countries for unilateral troop cuts in Central Europe, and it also reflected the Alliance's interest in promoting *détente*. By common consent Western countries opted for a policy of 'collective inaction' over Czechoslovakia in order not to exacerbate East-West tensions; this approach was reflected in the NAC's decision not to raise alert levels for the Alliance's forces in the summer of 1968. NATO was simply too fragile to adopt a proactive common policy in support of reform in Eastern Europe, and member states were unwilling to antagonise the USSR by making gestures of support towards Czechoslovakia.[15]

British diplomats privately feared the consequences of the Czechoslovak

---

13 Williams, 'Love's labours lost', 76–7; Z. Mlynar (trans. P. Wilson), *Night frost in Prague: the end of humane socialism*, London 1980, 76.
14 Transcripts of Dresden and Moscow meetings, 23 Mar., 8 May 1968, in Navratil, Bencik, Kural, Michalkova and Vondrova, *Documents reader*, 64–72, 132–43.
15 J. C. McGinn, 'The politics of collective inaction: NATO's response to the Prague Spring', *JCWS* 1/3 (1999), 112–23; Wiebes and Zeeman, 'Crisis consultation', 102.

government's reform programme continuing to its logical conclusion. Foreign Office officials hoped that Eastern bloc states would assert their independence and loosen their economic and military ties to the USSR, but also wished this process to be a gradual one, controlled by the East European regimes rather than being driven by popular protest. Goronwy Roberts noted in June 1968 that British interests would not be furthered by any revolutionary upheavals, as any uprising similar to that in Hungary in 1956 would undermine the 'evolution of effective co-existence' in Europe. Foreign Office officials concluded that there was 'little the West could say or do to help the liberals in Eastern Europe' and that the British government should avoid any gestures which could worsen Soviet-Czechoslovak tensions.[16] This low-profile approach was reinforced when an arms cache planted by the KGB was 'discovered' in Western Bohemia, providing the pretext for Soviet propaganda accusations of 'imperialist' meddling.[17]

In June and July 1968 the Warsaw Pact 'Five' staged a series of military exercises intended both to force Prague to abandon the Action Programme, and to practise for a possible invasion. The 'Five' also conducted a vitriolic press campaign against the 'counter-revolution' in Czechoslovakia. The publication of the 'Two Thousand Words' manifesto on reform, written by the dissident writer Ludvik Vaculik and endorsed by the majority of the Czech and Slovak intelligentsia, aroused hysterical fury amongst the governing elites in Moscow, Warsaw, East Berlin and Sofia.[18] After a summit meeting in the Polish capital on 14–15 July Czechoslovakia's 'fraternal' allies issued an ultimatum known as the 'Warsaw Letter', demanding the reimposition of censorship, the suppression of independent political groups and the abandonment of the Action Programme. The Warsaw Letter contained the implicit threat of intervention if Prague failed to comply with its demands. Despite the Warsaw Letter's harsh language and the military manoeuvres near Czechoslovakia's border, officials in Whitehall concluded that the 'Five' intended to intimidate the CPCS's reformers into reversing its reforms, and that in the last resort the Warsaw Pact would not intervene in Czechoslovakia's domestic affairs.[19]

The British government and its NATO partners failed to anticipate the Warsaw Pact's invasion of Czechoslovakia in August 1968. In retrospect,

---

[16] Barker to Hayman, 8 Apr. 1968, and Hayman to Barker, 17 Apr. 1968, FCO 28/98; G. Roberts to Stewart, 13 June 1968, FCO 28/90; 'Conference of HM representatives', 9th meeting, 10 May 1968, FCO 28/45.
[17] Andrew and Mitrokhin, *Mitrokhin archive*, i. 7–8, 333; Day (FO) to Palliser (No. 10), 1 June 1968, PREM 13/1993.
[18] The manifesto, dated 27 June 1968, can be found in Navratil, Bencik, Kural, Michalkova and Vondrova, *Documents reader*, 177–81; speech by Petro Shelest to the CPSU Central Committee, 17 July 1968, in Kramer, 'Ukraine (part 2)', 318–20.
[19] Excerpts from the Warsaw meeting and the 'Warsaw letter', 14–15 July 1968, in Navratil, Bencik, Kural, Michalkova and Vondrova, *Documents reader*, 212–38; FO to Washington, no.1948(Saving), 22 July 1968, FCO 28/99.

there were clear indications that a Soviet-led intervention was likely. The exercises staged by the 'Five' during June and July focused upon practising the complex command, movement control and logistical procedures which are essential to the success of any major military operation. The call-up of Soviet reservists and the staging of manoeuvres during a season when Eastern bloc states traditionally used conscripts to gather in the summer harvest were also significant.[20] The American, British and French military missions based in East Berlin also reported on the unusual levels of Soviet and GDR military activity during the summer of 1968. Officers attached to the British mission (BRIXMIS) informed BAOR headquarters of Soviet and East German troop movements towards the Czechoslovak border, tighter travel restrictions imposed on the allied missions, and on the disruption of GSFG's annual training programme. BRIXMIS officers also reported that they had spotted Soviet and East German warplanes with red bands painted on their fuselages, evidently in order to distinguish them from Czechoslovak military aircraft. BRIXMIS veterans subsequently claimed that they had predicted that an invasion of Czechoslovakia was imminent, but that their superiors in the BAOR and the MoD ignored their conclusions.[21]

As far as senior British policy-makers were concerned, the implications of the military build-up were less clear cut. One senior Cabinet Office official observed that '[we] … know how many bullets every [Warsaw Pact] soldier is carrying and what he's eating, but we don't know what orders he'll be given'. The British government had no firm intelligence regarding the intentions, as opposed to the capabilities, of the 'Five'. Within the JIC's Current Intelligence Group the senior DIS representative, a British Army colonel, informed his colleagues that Warsaw Pact intervention was unlikely, while his deputy, a major, vehemently opposed this assessment. In spite of SIS reports indicating that a Soviet-led invasion was a possibility, the JIC's eventual estimate, inspired by the Foreign Office, was that the Warsaw Pact would not risk the international condemnation that would be aroused by the forcible suppression of reform in Czechoslovakia.[22] The Soviet government also repeatedly refuted any intention of intervening in the internal affairs of its 'fraternal ally'. On 20 July the counsellor of the Soviet embassy, V. M. Vasev, accosted Wilson at the Durham Miners' Gala to assure him that the USSR would not use force against the Czechoslovak reformists. Ten days later Stewart warned the Soviet ambassador, Mikhail Smirnovsky, that

20 D. Miller, *The Cold War: a military history*, London 2001, 60; Cradock, *Know your enemy*, 243–4.
21 'British commander's-in-chief mission to the Soviet forces in Germany quarterly report: July-September 1968', 31 Oct. 1968, TNA, WO 208/5256; Tony Geraghty, *BRIXMIS: the untold exploits of Britain's most daring Cold War spy mission*, London 1997, 159–62.
22 Bower, *Perfect English spy*, 362–3; Wilson to Palliser, 20 July 1968, PREM 13/1993; Cradock, *Know your enemy*, 249; S. Dorril, *MI6: fifty years of special operations*, London 2001, 727.

military action against Czechoslovakia would have adverse consequences for *détente*. Despite this, as Crossman noted in his diary, the Labour government had already decided that it would do nothing if the Warsaw Pact decided to crush the Prague Spring.[23]

The USA and other NATO countries likewise did not envisage any intervention in Czechoslovakia, and kept a low profile as tensions intensified. The West German government was particularly careful to avoid providing any excuse for Soviet accusations of 'revanchist' plotting – the Grand Coalition's caution was demonstrated by the decision to move the *Bundeswehr*'s annual exercises away from the Bavarian-Bohemian border. Thanks to NATO's penetration by the East German intelligence service, the HVA, Warsaw Pact governments knew that Western governments were unwilling to intervene in the Czechoslovak crisis, although this had no effect on the USSR's eventual decision to crush the 'counter-revolution' in Prague.[24] What was significant was that the Czechoslovak government never requested any moral or practical support from the West. Although the Dubcek regime declared an interest in improving relations with West European countries, its leadership repeatedly reaffirmed its allegiance to the Warsaw Pact. In late July, Cernik informed his colleagues that the 'capitalist counties' had consigned Czechoslovakia to the 'Soviet "sphere of influence"', adopting 'a cautiously neutral' position as Soviet-Czechoslovak relations deteriorated. The reformers within the CPCS Central Committee knew that they were on their own.[25]

Following the meeting between the Czechoslovak leadership and the 'Five' at Bratislava on 3 August 1968, the British and other Western governments concluded that a compromise had been reached. The Bratislava *communiqué* stressed the need for Warsaw Pact unity, but also acknowledged that the internal policies of 'each fraternal party' would reflect 'specific national features and conditions'. Barker asserted that the Czechoslovak reformers would be able to continue with their policies, and he confidently predicted that Dubcek would defeat his conservative foes at the forthcoming CPCS Congress in September 1968. In contrast, Harrison stated that Brezhnev and the rest of the *Politburo* faced a stark choice. Allowing the Prague Spring to take its course would have cataclysmic consequences for the Communist order in Eastern Europe, while an invasion of Czechoslovakia would provoke worldwide outrage. Although Harrison considered that the Kremlin would prefer a hard-line *coup d'etat* in Prague as an alternative to military interven-

[23] *Crossman diaries*, iii. 142–5, entry for 18 July 1968; FO to Moscow, no. 2026, 30 July 1968, PREM13/1993; Washington to FO, no.100(Saving), 27 July 1968, FCO 28/99.
[24] McGinn, 'Collective inaction', 130–1, 134; D. Laskey (Bonn) to Stewart, 4 May 1968, FCO 28/30; Mastny, '1968', 161–3.
[25] Action programme, and Cernik's comments to CPCS Praesidium, 27 July 1968, in Navratil, Bencik, Kural, Michalkova and Vondrova, *Documents reader*, 92–5, 281–3.

tion, he was one of the few British officials to realise that the Soviet government would not permit the liberalisation of Czechoslovakia to continue.[26]

The CPCS reformers believed that they had negotiated a breathing space to continue with their policies. However, in mid-August relations between Brezhnev and Dubcek deteriorated sharply. In addition, the 'healthy forces' used the Bratislava meeting to pass a 'letter of invitation' to the Soviet leadership requesting military intervention.[27] Brezhnev and his peers decided to launch an invasion, codenamed Operation *Danube*, on 17 August. On the night of the 20–21 August, Soviet paratroopers seized key points in Prague, while an army of twenty-two Soviet divisions, supplemented by East German, Polish, Hungarian and Bulgarian contingents, swiftly established control over the country. The Czechoslovak armed forces offered no resistance to the invaders, and Dubcek, Cernik and other leading reformers were arrested and taken to Moscow. Within the course of day, Czechoslovakia was under complete military occupation.[28]

British and Western responses to the invasion, August–September 1968

Operation *Danube* took Britain and other Western powers by surprise. Wilson and Stewart were both on holiday when Warsaw Pact forces crossed Czechoslovakia's borders, while David Owen, a Parliamentary Under-Secretary of State for Defence at that time, later recalled that on the night of 20 August, 'I was reading highly classified reports which said there would be no invasion. I was then woken up [the following morning] to be told that the Russians were invading'.[29] The Johnson administration was particularly shocked; the day before the invasion Dobrynin told Rusk that the Soviet leadership was ready for strategic arms negotiations and would receive the president for a summit visit in Moscow in early October. As a consequence of *Danube*, the US government postponed the scheduled superpower arms talks. Opinions within Washington on future Soviet intentions were divided. Johnson was disappointed that his plans for both arms talks and a summit in Moscow had

26 The Bratislava declaration, ibid. 3 Aug. 1968, 328–9; Crampton, *Eastern Europe*, 334–6; DP219/68, 'British defence policy: the impact of recent events in Czechoslovakia', 23 Sept. 1968, DEFE 6/106; Barker to Stewart, 12 Aug. 1968, and Harrison to Stewart, 22 Aug. 1968, FCO 28/49.
27 Mlynar, *Night frost*, 157, 173; telephone conversations between Brezhnev and Dubcek, in Navratil, Bencik, Kural, Michalkova and Vondrova, *Documents reader*, 9, 13 Aug. 1968, 336–8, 345–6; 'A letter to Brezhnev: the Czech hard-liners "request" for Soviet intervention, August 1968', trans. M. Kramer, *CWIHP Bulletin* ii (1992), 6.
28 Commentary, in Navratil, Bencik, Kural, Michalkova and Vondrova, *Documents reader*, 312; J. Valenta, 'From Prague to Kabul: the Soviet style of invasion', *IS* v/2 (1980), 133–4.
29 Wilson, *Labour government*, 221–2; Stewart, *Life and Labour*, 551–2; David Owen, *Time to declare*, London 1991, 132.

been dashed. While Rusk envisaged the possibility of either a new Berlin crisis or further Soviet intervention in Eastern Europe, Llewellyn Thompson concluded that the USSR was too cautious to indulge in further military adventures. Dobrynin helped to soothe American concerns by assuring Rusk that the intervention in Czechoslovakia was a one-off.[30]

The British government's immediate response, as decided by Wilson and Stewart following a meeting at 10 Downing Street on 21 August, was to cancel all ministerial visits, to suspend all cultural contacts with the 'aggressor states', and to table a UN Security Council resolution condemning the invasion of Czechoslovakia.[31] Needless to say, that attempt to rally international opinion against the 'Five' was vetoed by the Soviet UN delegation. In Cabinet on 22 August Stewart admitted that the government's position was contradictory. The draft UN resolution was intended 'to obtain world-wide condemnation of the Soviet Union', but Britain did not want to be 'singled out as particularly hostile' by the USSR. The Foreign Secretary's comments reflected the dilemma affecting the Wilson government. Ministers were under pressure from parliament and public opinion to condemn the repression of the Prague Spring, but also hoped to avoid 'petty pinpricks' which would irritate the Warsaw Pact powers and have an adverse effect on Britain's diplomatic and commercial contacts with the Eastern bloc states.[32]

There was no uniform West European response to Operation *Danube*. The French showed the least concern: de Gaulle's Foreign Minister, Michel Debre, cynically described the invasion as a 'traffic accident' ('un accident de parcours') on the road to *détente*. In contrast, the Danish and Norwegian governments were alarmed by Soviet troop and fleet movements in the Baltic and the Kola Peninsula: officials in Oslo wondered if their longstanding fears of a Soviet seizure of Northern Norway were about to be fulfilled.[33] West German politicians were disturbed by the presence of ten more Soviet divisions near the Bavarian frontier, and by NATO's inability to anticipate the Warsaw Pact intervention. The invasion of Czechoslovakia, and the USSR's declarations on its right to defend the 'Socialist Commonwealth', raised the possibility of further Soviet action elsewhere in the continent. Cleveland quoted the reaction of one of his NAC colleagues: '[the] Russians have said they're serious about protecting their harem, but they haven't said how big it is'. Following the NATO Foreign Ministers' meeting at Brussels on 15–16

---

[30] NSC589th, 590th meetings, 20 Aug., 4 Sept. 1968, NSF, LBJLIB, NSC meetings 1–2; Dobrynin, *In confidence*, 180–3.

[31] MISC(219(69)1st meeting, No.10, 21 Aug. 1968, CAB 130/134; FO to UKDEL-NATO, no.991(Saving), 27 Aug. 1968, FCO 28/49; 'Worldwide sense of shock and outrage at Soviet invasion', *The Times*, 22 Aug. 1968.

[32] CC(68)38th Cabinet conclusions, 22 Aug. 1968, CAB 128/43; Skilling, *Interrupted revolution*, 753. 757.

[33] Wolton, *France sous influence*, 446; Wiebes and Zeeman, 'Crisis consultation', 102–3. For Norwegian concerns about the security of the Northern Cape see DI58(N), *NIR*, no.15, Winter 1967, DEFE 63/33.

November 1968, Alliance members explicitly warned the USSR against any further military intervention in Eastern Europe.[34]

Romania and Yugoslavia were of particular concern to NATO officials. Soviet leaders were enraged when Tito and Ceausescu vigorously condemned the invasion of Czechoslovakia, and in late August Yugoslavia mobilised its armed forces. On 27 August the Yugoslav ambassador to London asked Stewart what Britain (and, by implication, the USA) would do if the USSR invaded Romania and Yugoslavia.[35] Foreign Office and MoD officials noted while little could be done to assist the former, a Soviet assault on Yugoslavia – which was not only outside the Warsaw Pact, but also shared borders with Italy and Greece – would directly threaten NATO, and would also signify the adoption of a more aggressive foreign policy by the USSR. Yet an invasion of either, or both, Romania and Yugoslavia would require far more substantial forces than *Danube*, and would also face armed resistance. The British government therefore considered it unlikely that the USSR would try to overthrow Ceausescu or Tito.[36] Wilson, Healey and Stewart met at 10 Downing Street on 5 September to discuss Soviet intentions in the Balkans, but although the Defence Secretary suggested possible contingency measures, including a build-up of NATO forces in the Eastern Mediterranean, consultations with the Johnson administration and military assistance to the Yugoslavs, they did not believe that either Romania or Yugoslavia were directly threatened by Soviet aggression.[37] By early October the issue of assistance to either country became a moot point. Tito's regime was less concerned about a Soviet onslaught against Yugoslavia or its neighbour, and by early 1969 Yugoslav-Soviet relations had significantly improved, with the DIS reporting that the 'close' relationship between the Soviet and Yugoslav armed forces and intelligence services ruled out any Western military assistance to the latter.[38]

Harrison was recalled to London on 20 August, not as a response to *Danube* but because he had been compromised by a sexual liaison with a Russian maid. The affair was a KGB 'honey trap', and Harrison's diplomatic career came to an abrupt end. The Moscow embassy's initial assessments of the invasion of Czechoslovakia were written by the *chargé*, Peter Dalton,

34 H. Cleveland, 'NATO after the invasion', FA xlvii/2 (1969), 257; Heuser, NATO, Britain, France, 7.
35 Note by 'A' Division, Defence Policy Staff, 5 Sept. 1968, DEFE 13/707; D. Deletant and M. Ionescu, 'Romania and the Warsaw Pact, 1955–1989' (CWIHP working paper xliii, 2002), 30; statements by Tito, 21 Aug. 1968, in S. Clissold (ed.), Yugoslavia and the Soviet Union, 1939–1973: a documentary record, London 1975, 297–8.
36 FCO to Washington, no.7055, 2 Oct. 1968, FCO 28/559; K. Nash (AUSPol, MoD) to Healey, 5 Sept. 1968, DEFE 13/707.
37 Maitland to Palliser, 6 Sept. 1968, DEFE 13/707; Dean to Greenhill, 27 Sept. 1968, DEFE 68/25 .
38 T. Garvey (Belgrade) to C. Giffard (EESD), 12 Oct. 1968, FCO 28/525; JIC(A)(69)19(Final), 'The outlook for Yugoslavia', 3 Oct. 1969, CAB 186/2.

who argued that the Kremlin's decision was not 'the action of strong "expansionist" leaders, but of frightened men reacting indecisively to a situation they knew to be dangerous, but which they did not know how to deal [*sic*]'. Dalton told Stewart that the *Politburo* had only decided to intervene on the 17 or 18 August, and that the Soviet leadership feared that Czechoslovakia would either defect to the 'imperialist' camp, or declare neutrality. Brezhnev and his colleagues had demonstrated that they would crack down on any other Eastern bloc state which broke ranks with the 'Socialist Commonwealth', but had no aggressive intentions towards either NATO or Europe's neutral states. He also warned that the invasion of Czechoslovakia did not warrant a strident Western reaction which would jeopardise *détente*.[39] Harrison's successor, Duncan Wilson, reinforced these arguments in his own dispatches, drawing a distinction between the USSR's readiness to employ force against recalcitrant Warsaw Pact states – as expressed in the 'Brezhnev Doctrine' – and its more restrained policies towards the non-Communist world.[40]

Dalton's assessment of the factors behind the Kremlin's decision to invade was fairly accurate. Brezhnev dithered throughout the crisis until the *Politburo* meeting on 17 August, and the decision to intervene was influenced by Andropov, Marshal Andrei Grechko (the Defence Minister), Petro Shelest (the Secretary of the Ukrainian Communist Party), Podgorny (who was, like Shelest, a Ukrainian) and Stepan Chervonenko (the ambassador to Prague). Andropov and Shelest played on the Kremlin's fears that the 'counter-revolution' would 'spill over' and destabilise Eastern Europe, as well as Ukraine, while Chervonenko persuaded the *Politburo* that Bilak and his associates would successfully overthrow Dubcek.[41] Operation *Danube* was supposed to take place concurrently with the seizure of power by the 'healthy forces'. However, the latter failed to oust Dubcek, and the occupying forces faced widespread passive resistance and civil disobedience from Czech and Slovak civilians.[42] Having no alternative leadership to install in Prague, the Soviet leadership forced its Czechoslovak counterparts to sign the Moscow Protocol (26 August). Dubcek was forced to reintroduce censorship, abolish

[39] P. Dalton (Moscow) to Stewart, 29 Sept. 1968, FCO 28/69; Dalton to Stewart, 30 Sept. 1968, *DBPO III*, i. 76–80. See Sir Geoffrey Harrison's obituary in *The Times*, 14 Apr. 1990.

[40] D. Wilson to Stewart, 4 Nov., 9 Dec. 1968, *DBPO III*, i. 100–10; Service, *Russia*, 387–8.

[41] M. Kramer, 'The Prague Spring and the Soviet invasion of Czechoslovakia: new interpretations', *CWIHP Bulletin* iii (Autumn 1993), 2–12, and 'Ukraine and the Soviet-Czechoslovak crisis of 1968 (part 1): new evidence from the diary of Petro Shelest', *CWIHP Bulletin* x (1998), 234–44.

[42] Prague to FO, no. 562, 25 Aug. 1968, PREM 13/1994. The invasion did provoke some violent clashes which led to around 100 civilian deaths: Suri, *Power and protest*, 204–5.

civil society groups, end economic reform and subordinate Czechoslovakia's foreign policy to Soviet interests.[43]

British government assessments of the factors behind the Warsaw Pact's invasion were generally correct, but its views on the consequences of Soviet occupation and the Moscow Protocol were excessively optimistic. The Northern Department and the JIC concluded that despite *Danube* 'some elements of the Dubcek reform programme', particularly its economic policies, 'will continue'. In direct contrast, at the end of August Barker painted a bleaker picture:

> [The] takeover [of Czechoslovakia] has been complete. All the key Ministries will have their quota of supervisory Russians or Soviet stooges; the cherished freedoms of the last seven months or so will be stamped upon; ... co-operation with the West in the fields of trade, technology and culture will be limited; and politically the Czechoslovaks will have to learn again to parrot the Soviet Party and State lines without bothering to consider their own views or their own interests.[44]

Barker's grim predictions were borne out by subsequent events. On 16 October 1968 Brezhnev and Dubcek concluded a treaty authorising the 'temporary' stationing of 75,000 Soviet troops in Czechoslovakia. The following March, after Czechoslovakia beat the USSR in the World Ice Hockey Championships, there were anti-Soviet demonstrations in Prague which, due to the intervention of KGB and StB *agents provocateurs*, led to riots. Using these disturbances as a pretext, the Soviet government forced the CPCS to replace Dubcek with the Slovak hard-liner, Gustav Husak, on 17 April 1969. Under a process dubbed 'normalisation', Husak expelled a third of the CPCS's membership. Howard Smith, Barker's successor, maintained that despite 'normalisation' Czechoslovakia had not 'returned to Stalinism', and the Foreign Office followed Smith's advice by recommending that ministers should avoid 'knocking' Husak.[45] However, his conviction that Husak was a 'centrist' was unwarranted. During the two decades that separated the Prague Spring from the 'Velvet Revolution' of 1989, Czechoslovakia

43 Excerpts from Moscow meeting between Soviet and Czechoslovak leaderships, 23 Aug. 1968, and Moscow Protocol, 26 Aug. 1968, Navratil, Bencik, Kural, Michalkova and Vondrova, *Documents reader*, 465–80; M. Ouimet, *The rise and fall of the Brezhnev doctrine in Soviet foreign policy*, Chapel Hill, NC 2003, 41–8.
44 H. Smith to Hayman, 20 Sept. 1968, FCO 28/69; JIC(68)54(Final), 'The Soviet grip on Eastern Europe', 2 Dec. 1968, CAB 158/71; Barker to Hayman, 30 Aug. 1968, FCO 28/91.
45 Renner, *Czechoslovakia*, 86–101; Soviet-Czechoslovak treaty, 16 Oct. 1968, Navratil, Bencik, Kural, Michalkova and Vondrova, *Documents reader*, 533–6; 'Conference of HM representatives in Eastern Europe 4–8 May 1970', 1st, 2nd, 7th meetings, 4, 7 May 1970, FCO 28/918; Maitland to E. Youde (No.10), 18 Apr. 1969, DEFE 13/741.

remained under the firm grip of an authoritarian, sclerotic and sycophantically pro-Soviet regime.[46]

The impact of the Prague Spring on Anglo-Soviet relations, 1968–70

In late October 1968 Stewart, now in charge of an amalgamated Foreign and Commonwealth Office, informed his subordinates that although the UK would not break off relations with the five countries responsible for the invasion of Czechoslovakia, its relationship with these powers could not operate on a 'business as usual' basis.[47] The Labour government had to respond to public outrage over the Warsaw Pact's intervention in Czechoslovakia's internal affairs, but was also wary of irritating the Soviet leadership. This dilemma was highlighted by a ludicrous quarrel between Wilson and Stewart in Cabinet on 17 December, caused by the prime minister's intention to send Christmas cards to leaders of the 'aggressor countries'. Wilson's willingness to extend the season's greetings to the avowedly atheist rulers of the USSR and their henchmen in Warsaw, Budapest and Sofia raises the question of whether, despite the Foreign Secretary's comments, British policy towards the Eastern bloc after August 1968 was indeed that of 'business as usual'.[48]

As far as trade was concerned, the Cabinet's Commercial Policy Committee reported that if the UK imposed sanctions on the Warsaw Pact 'Five' the only beneficiaries would be Britain's commercial competitors. The invasion of Czechoslovakia did not prevent the conclusion of a new Anglo-Soviet long-term trade agreement in June 1969, or the Labour government's efforts to use the COCOM review to liberalise on trade with the Eastern bloc.[49] Yet after the suppression of the Prague Spring the Johnson administration opposed any attempt to ease the strategic embargo. When COCOM members met in Paris on 14–16 October 1968, the British and French governments were alone in favouring the reduction of the embargo lists. In addition, officials in Washington also blocked ICL's proposals to export computers to the USSR. Despite Benn's assertion that ICL's French competitors would benefit if the computer sales were banned, the Cabinet's Strategic Exports Committee concurred with official recommendations not to challenge the US decision. The British government was, none the less, still interested

---

[46] C. Gati, *The bloc that failed: Soviet-East European relations in transition*, London 1990, 92; M. Glenny, *The rebirth of history*, London 1993, 30–1.

[47] FCO to missions, 29 Oct. 1968, *DBPO III*, i. 85–6. The Foreign and Commonwealth Offices were amalgamated on 14 October 1968.

[48] CC52(68)52nd conclusions, 17 Dec. 1968, CAB 128/43; *Crossman diaries*, iii. 289, entry for 17 Dec. 1968.

[49] Benn, *Office without power*, 99, entry for 5 Sept. 1968; ESC(68)10, 'Invasion of Czechoslovakia: effect on strategic exports policy', 4 Sept. 1968, CAB 134/2796; D. Wilson to Stewart, 10 June 1969, *DPBO III*, i.162.

in ICL's exports to Romania.[50] From 1968 onwards the Romanian regime received preferential trading conditions from Western countries because of Ceausescu's condemnation of Operation *Danube*, and his apparent 'independence' of the Soviet bloc. At the conference of ambassadors to Eastern Europe in May 1968 the ambassador to Bucharest, John Chadwick, praised the Romanian leader for his 'tremendous political ingenuity and toughness', 'personal modesty' and 'humanistic ideals'. In fairness, Chadwick could not have predicted that Romania's leader would preside over a regime which was despotic even by contemporary East European standards. Yet during the 1970s the British and other Western governments courted Romania in spite of Ceausescu's egregious domestic record, even though the Foreign Office concept of 'evolution' ostensibly linked internal liberalisation in the Eastern bloc with the easing of East-West tensions.[51]

Wilson, Benn and Crosland proposed radical changes to the strategic embargo, but when the OPD debated policy towards COCOM in mid-December the FCO, MoD and COS advocated caution. Stewart spoke for these departments, asserting that Anglo-American alliance ties would suffer if Britain continued to advocate greater freedom to export computers to the Eastern bloc. The Johnson administration's hackles had already been raised by the Benn-Kirillin agreement, and the Foreign Secretary warned his colleagues that the Pentagon was restricting defence contacts with the UK. Given the extent of British dependence on intelligence and military collaboration with the USA, Stewart felt that the Labour government's ability to bargain over COCOM was weak.[52] Wilson and his Cabinet were, however, in a stronger position to press their case than they realised. State Department officials feared that the COCOM dispute would do serious damage to the USA's relations with Britain and France, and the State and Commerce Departments were being lobbied by the American business community to reduce restrictions on East-West trade.[53] The US and British governments therefore reached a compromise in January 1969, with the US agreeing to permit the sale of all but the most advanced computers to Soviet bloc states. For their part British officials promised not to allow the export of any computers to China, or to provide more sophisticated information tech-

---

[50] ESC(68)5th meeting, 21 Oct. 1968, CAB 134/2796; ESC(O)(68)12th meeting, 19 Dec. 1968, CAB 134/2800; Barker, *Divided Europe*, 266–7.
[51] 'Ambassadors conference', 1st meeting, FCO 28/45; Deletant and Ionescu, *Romania*, 32; M. Percival, 'Britain's "political romance" with Romania in the 1970s', *CEH* iv/1 (1995), 67–87.
[52] COS60th/68, 17 Dec. 1968, DEFE 4/234; OPD(68)24th meeting, 18 Dec. 1968, CAB148/35.
[53] Memorandum by State Dept, 21 Dec. 1968, *FRUS* ix. 548–50; G. K. Bertch, 'American politics and trade with the USSR', in B. Parrott (ed.), *Trade, technology and Soviet-American relations*, Bloomington, IN 1985, 243–6.

nology to the USSR or Eastern Europe, without the unanimous consent of the USA and other COCOM members.[54]

As far as the strategic implications of *Danube* were concerned, senior commanders in SHAPE were perturbed by the lack of any 'military warning' of the impending invasion. David Miller argues that the Warsaw Pact's intervention against Czechoslovakia demonstrated the theoretical vulnerability of Western Europe to a 'standing start' offensive. One analysis drafted by British military planners in late September 1968 noted that the Warsaw Pact 'Five' had achieved 'tactical surprise' as a consequence of 'the prevailing atmosphere of *détente* in Europe'. Although mobilisation and large troop movements within Eastern Europe would give the Alliance 'political warning' of possible military action, the invasion of Czechoslovakia showed that 'NATO cannot guarantee to predict the enemy's intentions reliably'.[55] Some British military officers and officials within the MoD wondered whether *Danube* undermined Whitehall's assumption that NATO would receive adequate warning time of a Warsaw Pact attack, and also feared that Western restraint over Czechoslovakia could encourage further Soviet military interventions.[56] Similar anxieties were raised in the NAC in November 1968, when Dutch intelligence sources forwarded inaccurate reports of Soviet troop movements against Romania, while the following August an unexplained lull in routine Warsaw Pact air activity caused alarm amongst NATO officials.[57]

None the less, senior military and civilian officials in London were far more sanguine about *Danube*'s strategic implications than their opposite numbers in NATO. The JIC downplayed its failure to anticipate the Warsaw Pact's intervention, arguing that 'while Czechoslovakia was threatened with aggression, NATO was not'. This judgement could conceivably have been based on SIGINT information. The NSA successfully intercepted Soviet military communications during the invasion, and presumably shared its information with GCHQ. The USA, UK and Canada collaborated closely on intelligence-gathering and analysis, but did not distribute particularly sensitive information (such as SIGINT-related material) to other NATO powers. This could explain why the American and British governments were far less concerned about the outcome of the Czechoslovak crisis than their continental allies. The USA and Britain could also rely on information provided by their military missions in East Berlin. In this respect, BRIXMIS

<hr/>

[54] ESC(O)(69)1st meeting, 20 Jan. 1969, and ESC(O)(69)13, 'Outcome of 1968/69 COCOM review', 5 June 1969, CAB 134/2801.

[55] UKDELNATO to FO, no.509, 23 Aug. 1968, FCO 28/100; Miller, *Cold War*, 39, 60–1, 322–3; DP219/68, 'British defence policy: the impact of recent events in Czechoslovakia', 23 Sept. 1968, DEFE 6/106.

[56] Unsigned memorandum, 18 Sept. 1968, and F. Cooper (Asst Under-Secretary, Political Affairs, MoD) note, Sept. 1968, DEFE 24/608.

[57] Wiebes and Zeeman, 'Crisis consultations', 102–3. UKDELNATO to FCO, 20 Nov. 1968, and Air Chief Marshal J. Grandy (acting CDS) to Healey, 8, 12 Aug. 1969, DEFE 13/901.

reported that in the final quarter of 1968 Soviet and East German forces had resumed their normal training cycle, and that the extra divisions sent to the GDR in July-August had returned to the USSR. The fierce clashes on the Sino-Soviet frontier in the spring of 1969, and the ensuing military build-up by both Communist powers in the Far East, also provided an additional disincentive for any adventurism in Europe on the USSR's part.[58]

With reference to the NATO-Warsaw Pact balance, the COS noted on 1 October that although there were now thirty-five Soviet divisions in Eastern Europe (compared to twenty-two before the invasion), the Czechoslovak armed forces could no longer be regarded by Soviet commanders as reliable. The COS therefore concluded that SHAPE exaggerated the threat that the Warsaw Pact posed after *Danube*.[59] Healey concurred with this assessment, expressing confidence in NATO's ability to gain advance warning of any Warsaw Pact aggression, and he informed his OPD colleagues on 25 September that 'the Russians had used force to maintain the *status quo*, not to challenge it'. According to Bruce, the Defence Secretary felt that both the strategic balance in Europe and the assumptions underpinning the NATO strategic review (MC14/3) remained unchanged.[60] On 31 October, the OPD approved Healey and Stewart's recommendations to bolster the Royal Navy's presence in the Mediterranean, and to earmark army units for possible emergency deployment to the Alliance's Northern and Southern flanks. Yet the Wilson government decided not to accelerate the withdrawal of units from East of Suez to reinforce NATO, or to send back to BAOR the infantry brigade redeployed to the UK after the offsets agreement of 1967.[61]

Officials in Whitehall were reassured by the impact of the Czechoslovak crisis on Western political and public opinion. De Gaulle's anti-NATO rhetoric had been discredited, and domestic pressure in the USA and Western European countries for troop reductions in Central Europe had diminished.[62] The JIC was correct in assuming that Soviet objectives were limited to the suppression of the Prague Spring. Recent research on Operation *Danube*

---

58 OPD(68)58, CAB 148/38; Bamford, *Body of secrets*, 153; B. Taylor (MoD) to Healey, 12, 14 Aug. 1969, DEFE 13/901; 'BRIXMIS quarterly report, October-December 1968', 28 Jan. 1969, WO 208/5256.
59 COS50th/68, 1 Oct. 1968, DEFE 4/234; M. Kramer, 'New sources on the 1968 Soviet invasion of Czechoslovakia', *CWIHP Bulletin* ii (1992), 9.
60 OPD(68)17th meeting, 25 Sept. 1968, CAB 148/135; J. K. Mayne (MoD) note, 6 Sept. 1968, DEFE 68/25; London to State Dept., no.12398, 5 Sept. 1968, NSF, LBJLIB, UKCF 211.
61 OPD(68)63, 'NATO and Czechoslovakia', 28 Oct. 1968, CAB 148/38; OPD(68)19th meeting, 31 Oct. 1968, CAB 148/35; FCO to Canberra, no.1677, 8 Nov. 1968, FCO 46/249.
62 OPD(68)17th, CAB 148/135; Burrows (UKDELNATO) to Stewart, 16 Dec. 1968, DEFE 13/741; Heuser, *NATO, Britain, France, FRG*, 108; Kaplan, *NATO*, 54; Hood to Cooper, 11 Sept. 1968, DEFE 68/25.

reveals how fragile, rather than potent, the Warsaw Pact military machine was. Vojtech Mastny argues that morale in the Polish and Hungarian armies was sapped by the intervention, and the invasion of Czechoslovakia revealed logistical deficiencies which would have had graver consequences had Warsaw Pact forces faced armed opposition. None the less, it is possible that the financial considerations surrounding the defence reviews also shaped MoD assessments on Eastern bloc intentions. The prevailing view in London was that the scale of Britain's economic problems made it impossible to increase defence expenditure. During the summer of 1968 the COS concurred that 'no attempt should be made to inflate the Soviet threat lest it should be misconstrued in Whitehall as an attempt to justify greater forces'. Although the service chiefs were specifically referring to emerging Soviet maritime capabilities, a similar attitude evidently underpinned assessments of the impact of *Danube*.[63]

Aside from Czechoslovakia, Anglo-Soviet political relations were strained by Soviet espionage in the UK. On 27 September Stewart wrote to Wilson, arguing that the time had come to challenge the USSR over the rapid expansion of KGB and GRU activities in the UK. The Soviet embassy had grown from sixty-four diplomats in 1964 to eighty in mid-1968, sixty-two of whom were suspected intelligence officers. A further thirty-two out of the ninety-five embassy support staff, in addition to twenty-eight out of 180 officials in the Soviet trade mission, were believed to be involved in espionage. In comparison, the British embassy in Moscow had only forty diplomats (although Stewart did not say how many were actually SIS officers). Unlike the USA, Britain could not insist on parity of representation because of the smaller size of its diplomatic corps, so the Foreign Secretary recommended that the Soviet government should be ordered to limit embassy staff numbers to present levels. The Home Secretary, James Callaghan, supported Stewart's proposals, although MI5 protested that the USSR's trade delegation and consular offices would remain unaffected. Wilson approved Stewart's proposals on 21 October,[64] and on 11 November, Gore-Booth told Smirnovsky that the British government would limit staff at his embassy to eighty diplomats, sixty non-diplomatic staff and eight service personnel. Smirnovksy described this measure as an 'unfriendly gesture', and accused the British government of exploiting events in Czechoslovakia to whip up anti-Soviet sentiment at home and abroad. Having been barred from sending more personnel to

---

[63] JIC(A)(69)26th, 3 July 1969, CAB 185/1; Mastny, '1968', 168; H. Lawrence-Wilson (Cabinet Office) to PM, 24 Sept. 1968, PREM 13/1996; COS29th/68, 21 May 1968, DEFE 4/228.

[64] Bolland (Washington embassy)–M. Toon (State Dept.) conversation, 12 July 1968; NARAII, RG 59, 160, 64–5, 2665; Stewart to Wilson, 27 Sept. 1968, and Palliser to Day, 21 Oct. 1968, PREM 13/2009.

the London embassy, the Soviet Foreign Ministry (and the KGB) simply increased staff levels at the trade mission in Highgate.[65]

Smirnovsky's accusations were taken seriously by Duncan Wilson when he assumed his post as ambassador to Moscow in October 1968. He was concerned by the deterioration in Anglo-Soviet relations after Czechoslovakia, and believed that the UK's criticism of Soviet actions had marked it out for diplomatic reprisals. He commented on Brezhnev's speech in Warsaw in November 1968, in which the CPSU General Secretary had declared that the 'counter-revolution' in Czechoslovakia had threatened the survival of the 'Socialist Commonwealth'. Wilson maintained that the 'Brezhnev Doctrine' was not a 'charter for expansion', and that there was a difference between the USSR's determination to retain its authority over the Eastern bloc, and its 'cautious and pragmatic' policies towards the West and other non-Warsaw Pact countries. He expressed unease at the prospect of Britain waging 'a private Anglo-Soviet cold war', thereby surrendering the benefits of increased trade and technological co-operation to countries that had more cordial relations with Moscow.[66]

Stewart responded to the ambassador's argument that the USSR was genuinely interested in East-West co-operation with ill-disguised scepticism, asserting that the 'Russian humbug about a private British vendetta' was intended to force concessions from the UK, and to foster discord between Britain and its NATO allies. The Foreign Secretary's attitudes towards Anglo-Soviet relations derived from the reassessment of policy towards the USSR that his subordinates had undertaken prior to the Czechoslovak crisis. The prevailing view within the FCO was that the efforts made to develop a working relationship with the Soviet leadership since 1964 had yielded few discernible results.[67] Its sombre prognosis on the future course of East-West relations, which concluded that the prospects for *détente* were 'less hopeful than [was] thought two years ago', was presented to the OPD by Stewart in March 1969. Officials within the East European and Soviet Department (or EESD, as the Northern Department was renamed in October 1968) noted that the Czechoslovak crisis demonstrated the ideological inflexibility of the Soviet government, and its refusal to heed popular demand within the Eastern bloc for internal liberalisation. Stewart also expressed the concern that as a consequence of increased Soviet intervention in Third World conflicts, the USSR might be drawn into regional conflicts, such as the Israeli-Arab struggle, with dangerous consequences. With the exception of superpower discussions on strategic arms control, the FCO believed that

---

65 Stewart to D. Wilson, 11 Nov. 1968, and Giffard (EESD) to D. Bendall (Washington), 8 July 1970, FCO 28/1108.
66 D. Wilson to Stewart, 4 Nov., 9 Dec. 1968, *DBPO III*, i. 87–9, 91–3, 100–10; Roberts, *Soviet Union*, 72.
67 Stewart to D. Wilson, 7 Jan. 1969, *DBPO III*, i.111–15; D. Wilson to Stewart, 28 Jan. 1969, and Palliser to Trend, 28 Jan. 1969, PREM 13/2959.

there was insufficient scope for dialogue with the Soviet government. The invasion of Czechoslovakia had demonstrated that progress towards *détente* depended upon 'changes in the basic attitudes of the Soviet leadership' which were unlikely to occur in the near future. The OPD approved this analysis without comment.[68]

Throughout this paper, and the FCO's thinking on East-West relations, there was an irresolvable contradiction. Despite both widespread discontent in Eastern Europe with socio-economic austerity, and internal pressure for political change, the Soviet bloc regimes would not introduce any reforms which would alleviate this pressure. The logical result would be the 'uncontrollable explosions' of revolutionary upheaval which FCO officials hoped would not occur. As Healey noted in a speech delivered during a visit to West Germany in February 1969, Soviet domination over Eastern Europe had potentially destabilising consequences for continental security:

> The desire for political liberty and national independence is as strong in Eastern Europe as in Africa or Asia. The decay of the Russian empire in Eastern Europe may lead to further explosions like those already seen in East Berlin, Hungary and Czechoslovakia, perhaps in circumstances which pose a more direct threat to the stability of the European military balance.[69]

It was for this reason that British diplomats placed their hopes in the eventual 'evolution' of the Eastern European countries away from Marxist-Leninist dogma and towards a more liberal political and economic order, but there were few signs of such a development taking place after August 1968. The FCO's erroneous conclusions on the impact of 'normalisation' in Czechoslovakia were a product of wishful thinking. The British government's conclusion that the West could do little to help promote reform was realistic, given the USSR's hyper-sensitivity towards 'bridge-building', but ministers and officials alike were unable to explain how leaders like Brezhnev, Ulbricht, Gomulka, Husak or Ceausescu would ever allow 'evolution' to take place.

The prime minister had not, however, given up hopes of a renewal of contacts with the Soviet leadership. In May 1969 Benn visited the USSR for discussions with Kirillin, and although Stewart told him to steer clear of politics, Wilson gave Benn a message to pass to Kosygin. This expressed the prime minister's regret that Anglo-Soviet contacts had stalled because of Czechoslovakia, and suggested a visit to Moscow during which both premiers could discuss 'matters of common interest'. Kosygin responded with alacrity, suggesting that Wilson visit the Soviet capital in June or July. On previous occasions it had been Wilson who had been anxious to pursue bilateral talks, and the Soviet leadership that had been reluctant to receive him.

[68] OPD(69)8, 'The longer term prospects for East-West relations after the Czechoslovak crisis', 18 Feb. 1969, and Stewart cover note, PREM 13/2114; OPD(69)4th meeting, 18 Mar. 1969, CAB 148/91.
[69] Healey speech, Munich, 2 Feb. 1969, PREM 13/2568.

Kosygin's rapid response indicated an intention to salvage the USSR's diplomatic respectability after *Danube*. FCO officials, however, were sceptical of the utility of a visit, and persuaded a reluctant prime minister to delay any Soviet trip until after consultations with Johnson's successor, Richard Nixon, in Washington in January 1970. Stewart reminded Wilson that the NATO powers agreed that bilateral contacts with the 'aggressor states' should be judged not by the level of representation involved, but the prospects for constructive agreement, and he did not consider that Wilson's intended trip to the USSR would serve any practical purpose.[70] The prime minister continued to insist on meeting Kosygin, claiming that during his talks with Nixon at RAF Mildenhall in August 1969 the president stated that a visit by Wilson could be used to sound out Soviet views on strategic arms talks, Vietnam and the Middle East. Stewart was unmoved, and he asserted that unless Nixon specifically requested otherwise Wilson should visit the USA first. The Foreign Secretary asserted that while the British government needed to consult the new Republican administration on a number of issues, it had little to discuss with the leaders of the USSR.[71]

Stewart was as dismissive of Duncan Wilson's opinions on the state of Anglo-Soviet relations. The ambassador reported that British policy on East-West *détente* appeared 'rigid' to friend and foe alike, and that the Warsaw Pact had gained a propaganda coup by calling for a Conference on Security and Co-operation in Europe (CSCE) at their meetings in Budapest and Prague in March and October 1969. However, FCO officials concluded that the USSR was using the CSCE proposal to reinforce its hegemony over Eastern Europe, and they also recalled the *débâcle* surrounding the abortive 'treaty of friendship'. Duncan Wilson did have a case; although Soviet policy objectives behind the CSCE involved reinforcing the continental *status quo*, the Budapest and Prague meetings were also intended to appeal to Western public opinion and to recover some of the propaganda initiative that the Warsaw Pact had ceded after August 1968. It was also significant that the Eastern bloc states had revoked their previous opposition to US participation in the CSCE, making NATO's involvement a more viable option for more *détente*-minded Western politicians.[72]

However, Duncan Wilson's contemporaries concluded that he had gone native, and his differences with his superiors were illustrated at a meeting with Stewart, Greenhill and Brimelow (now Deputy Under-Secretary) at the FCO on 16 January 1970. The Foreign Secretary commented on Brimelow's proposals for a 'more active ... dialogue with the Russians', and rhetori-

---

70 Benn, *Office without power*, 161–73, entries for 12–14 May 1969; Moscow to FCO, no. 464, 14 May 1969, PREM 13/3429; memorandum for Youde, 21 May 1969, and Youde to N. Barrington, 27 May 1969, PREM 13/3429.
71 Nixon and Wilson, Mildenhall, 3 Aug. 1969, PREM 13/3009/1; FCO to Washington, no.1715, 5 Aug. 1969, and Stewart to Wilson, 10 Sept. 1969, PREM 13/3429.
72 Loth, *Détente*, 103; Giffard note, 6 Jan. 1970, *DBPO III*, i. 206–10.

cally asked what the Soviet and British governments 'could profitably talk about?' Stewart, Brimelow and Greenhill believed that discussions with the Soviets were pointless, and that the proposed CSCE would be exploited by the Warsaw Pact powers to manipulate Western public opinion and to weaken NATO. They also opposed the prime minister's plans to visit to the USSR, concluding that Britain had shown too much eagerness to develop Anglo-Soviet goodwill, and that the British government's efforts to promote *détente* had been spurned by the USSR's leaders. Although Wilson did receive another invitation to Moscow on 13 June 1970, Labour's general election defeat five days meant that it was accepted by a new prime minister, Edward Heath.[73]

In his official statement to the Commons on 26 August 1968, Wilson condemned the Warsaw Pact's 'flagrant aggression' against Czechoslovakia, but he also warned against any return to the 'frozen immobilism of the cold war'.[74] This statement reflected both the caution with which the UK and other NATO states approached the Prague Spring and its brutal suppression, and the West's unwillingness to take any action which could damage *détente*; although in this respect, it should be noted that NATO's treaty commitments involved collective defence, rather than any obligation to assist Soviet clients seeking independence from Moscow. The general failure of Western powers to anticipate the Warsaw Pact's intervention should be recognised, although this miscalculation reflected the impossibility of predicting the intentions of the Soviet leadership; the *Politburo* only made the final decision to invade Czechoslovakia three days before Operation *Danube* took place. The Soviet government was confident that the invasion of Czechoslovakia would not increase East-West tensions, and it was ready to risk international protest as the price to be paid for preserving the USSR's hegemony over Eastern Europe.[75] George Brown criticised NATO's response to the Czechoslovak crisis, arguing in November 1968 that the Alliance should have explicitly warned the Soviets against intervention in Czechoslovakia's domestic affairs. However, he did not describe what action the Western allies should have taken if the USSR had called their bluff. From what is known of his attitude towards Anglo-Soviet relations in early 1968, it is also doubtful whether Brown would have adopted such a tough approach had he still been Foreign Secretary.[76] The harsh fact was that throughout the late 1960s Britain and other Western powers were above all concerned that the *status quo* in Europe

[73] Walden, *Lucky George*, 141–3; meeting at FCO, 16 Jan. 1970, PREM 13/3429; memorandum by P. Moon (FCO), 13 June 1970, PREM 13/3495.
[74] Statement by Wilson, 26 Aug. 1968, HC Deb5s, 769 (1968), cols 1273–84; C. Keeble, 'The historical perspective', in Pravda and Duncan, *Soviet-British relations*, 39.
[75] Dawisha, *Prague Spring*, 355–6; Dobrynin, *In confidence*, 186.
[76] 'How we could have stopped the Russians', and 'Alas the brinkmanship was missing', *Evening Standard*, 14–15 Nov. 1968; T. Barker to Hayman, 15 Nov. 1968, FCO 28/69.

should be upheld. NATO members were not prepared to risk either the Alliance's credibility or the intensification of East-West rivalries by making unsolicited pledges to support Czechoslovakia.

More research is needed into Soviet-Romanian and Soviet-Yugoslav relations in the aftermath of Operation *Danube*, particularly as to whether the USSR ever considered military action against Ceausescu or Tito. It is worth noting that when invading Czechoslovakia the Soviets were confident that they would face no armed resistance. The Czechoslovak military hierarchy was generally unsympathetic towards Dubcek, while during *Danube* the StB collaborated with the invaders. The extent of Soviet-Czechoslovak military and security service co-operation was significant not only in ensuring the success of intervention, but in securing the eventual overthrow of Dubcek and the 'normalisation' of Czechoslovakia under Husak. Military intervention in the case of Romania or Yugoslavia case carried with it more risks and, in the aftermath of *Danube*, the USSR sought a *rapprochement* with both countries. Tito's 'non-alignment' did not affect Soviet-Yugoslav military and intelligence co-operation, while Ceausescu's brand of Communism did not pose the same ideological threat to Soviet hegemony in Eastern Europe as that manifested by the Prague Spring. For all his posturing over the USSR's dominance of the Warsaw Pact, the Romanian leader was not actually prepared to undermine the established order in the region, and as such Ceausescu's 'independence' was tolerated by the USSR throughout the remainder of the Cold War.[77]

The long-term impact of the invasion of Czechoslovakia on East-West relations was minimal. After assuming office in January 1969 Nixon pursued an arms control agreement with the Soviets, and also manipulated 'triangular diplomacy' with the USSR and China in an attempt to end the Vietnam War on American terms. Following de Gaulle's resignation in April 1969, Georges Pompidou continued his predecessor's policy on *détente*, albeit with far less emphasis on the overt anti-Americanism that Gaullism traditionally entailed. Six months later Brandt became Chancellor of the FRG, and his conduct of *Ostpolitik* contributed to the non-aggression agreement concluded between the USSR and the FRG in August 1970, the Polish-West German agreement on the Oder-Neisse frontier in December 1970, the quadripartite agreement on Berlin in 3 September 1971 and the reciprocal recognition of the FRG and GDR in 22 December 1972. The spirit of Brandt's *Ostpolitik* was symbolised in December 1970, when the visiting Chancellor knelt in penance in front of the Warsaw ghetto memorial. This act of contrition did much to persuade European opinion, both Eastern and Western, that the FRG was prepared to make amends for its Nazi past. It was under

---

77 Mlynar, *Night frost*, 176–84; Kramer, 'Prague Spring', 6–12; ESC(O)69, 2nd meeting, 26 Feb. 1969, CAB 134/2801; NIE11-4-68, *Main issues in Soviet military policy*, 19 Sept. 1968, LCHMA, MFF 15–431; Mastny, '1968', 169–71.

Brandt that the FRG became the principal player in continental *détente*,[78] and the Wilson government became fervent supporters both of *Ostpolitik* and of a fellow social-democratic ministry in Bonn. Brandt's chancellorship, and his interest in diplomatic engagement with the Eastern bloc, considerably diminished Labour's traditional unease over the future course of West German foreign policy.[79]

Operation *Danube* had no fundamental effect on the essential features of British policy towards the USSR and other Soviet bloc states. The invasion of Czechoslovakia and its aftermath attracted less attention from the Labour government than relations with the EEC, the Nigerian civil war and the outbreak of civil strife in Northern Ireland. As far as East-West relations were concerned, the UK remained committed to *détente*, and was not prepared to sacrifice its commercial relations with the Eastern bloc to protest against the Warsaw Pact intervention. Contrary to Stewart's comments, Britain (like other Western countries) did operate on a 'business as usual basis' after August 1968. Wilson's intention to visit Moscow in May 1969 showed that he regarded the suppression of the Prague Spring as a mere impediment to the development of closer ties with the Soviet leadership, in much the same way that as an opposition backbencher he refused to condemn the USSR's intervention in Hungary in 1956. The strategic consequences of the invasion of Czechoslovakia did not provoke a 'war scare' in London, but both the USA and Britain did attempt to reassure their allies that NATO remained credible, and that the redeployments which followed the 1967 tripartite talks did not affect the Alliance's ability to defend itself. From 1969 onwards the USA annually conducted its *Reforger* exercises, which were intended to demonstrate its ability to reinforce Western Europe in wartime. Britain in turn reinforced its naval presence in the Mediterranean while earmarking the Royal Marines and designated army units to reinforce NATO's Northern and Southern flanks in the event of an East-West crisis or conflict.[80]

The Czechoslovak crisis did have an impact on political and popular perceptions of the USSR. Stewart and FCO officials sought to persuade Cabinet ministers that the Soviets were inflexible both in their dealings with Western governments, and in their response to the need for reform within the Eastern bloc. The Foreign Secretary also blocked Wilson's attempt to meet Kosygin in Moscow, arguing that there was no issue of substance that the two premiers could 'profitably' discuss. According to Ben Pimlott, Stewart

[78] G.-H. Soutou, 'The linkage between European integration and *détente*: the contrasting approaches of de Gaulle and Pompidou, 1965 to 1974', in Ludlow, *Integration*, 12; M. E. Sarotte, *Dealing with the devil: East Germany, détente & Ostpolitik, 1969–1973*, Chapel Hill, NC 2001.
[79] Brown, *My way*, 245–7; Kissinger, Nixon, Wilson and Trend conversation, White House, 27 Jan. 1970, PREM 13/3546; Barker, *Divided Europe*, 260–1.
[80] Morgan, *People's peace*, 290–2; Pimlott, *Wilson*, 491–2, 548–50; *Strategic survey, 1968*, 27; Maloney, 'ACE mobile force', 606–7.

insisted on security of tenure when he was reappointed Foreign Secretary in March 1968, and as Wilson's relationship with his Cabinet colleagues deteriorated, Stewart was one of the few ministers Wilson could confide in and trust. In this respect, it is significant that the Foreign Secretary was able to thwart the prime minister's efforts to undertake a fourth visit to the USSR. Wilson did attempt to out-manoeuvre Stewart by using Benn as a go-between with Kosygin. However, once the Foreign Secretary made his opposition to a visit plain Wilson did not try to overrule him.[81]

While Benn regarded Stewart's thinking on East-West relations as 'barely post-Dulles' in its outlook, the Foreign Secretary did have a point. Khrushchev had dealt mercilessly with the Hungarian rebels in 1956, but had also accepted the development of a more autonomous version of Communism by the Poles. However, Brezhnev and his colleagues had displayed a complete intolerance for any reform whatsoever in Eastern Europe, even if it were undertaken by a 'socialist' regime. It was also significant that Gomulka – the champion of 'national Communism' in 1956 – emerged as one of the more vociferous opponents of the Prague Spring over a decade later. The cynicism that the Warsaw Pact's hard-line leaders had shown in August 1968 discredited the Soviet bloc in Britain and elsewhere. One consequence of the Czechoslovak crisis was that the CPGB – admittedly a marginal force in British politics – was split into two factions: the 'tankies' who supported the invasion, and the 'Euros' who sided with Eurocommunist opposition to Moscow's ideological hegemony. As far as the democratic left was concerned, many would have shared Crossman's feelings, confided to his diary over a fortnight after the invasion of Czechoslovakia: '[Somehow] I had persuaded myself over the past three or four years that a change was setting in and that with the policy of peaceful coexistence, the Russians would grow more civilised. But now they're exactly as bad as they were.'[82]

81 Pimlott, *Wilson*, 502, 546.
82 D. Wilson to Stewart, 28 Jan. 1969, PREM 13/2959; Beckett, *Enemy within*, 164–8; *Crossman diaries*, iii.179, entry for 1 Sept. 1968.

Conclusion

The Conservative government of 1970–4 placed less emphasis on Anglo-Soviet relations than its Labour predecessor. The Foreign Secretary, Douglas-Home, had earlier publicly drawn adverse comparisons between British decolonisation in Africa and Asia and Soviet domination over Eastern Europe, implying that the USSR was a more 'imperialist' power than the UK. Edward Heath was instinctively suspicious of Soviet protestations of goodwill, and was contemptuous of the 'bicycle race' other Western countries undertook to mend fences with the USSR after the Czechoslovak crisis.[1] As prime minister, Heath oversaw the mass expulsion of 105 KGB officers from the Soviet embassy and trade delegation in September 1971, known as Operation *Foot* by the FCO. The pretext for *Foot* was provided by a KGB defector, Oleg Lyalin, who informed his MI5 handlers of the Soviet embassy's preparations for sabotage operations in Britain in the event of a major East-West crisis or war; the expulsions crippled KGB activity in the UK throughout the remainder of the Cold War. A furious Gromyko accused the British government of whipping up an artificial espionage scandal in order to hamper *détente*. While this pronouncement was typical of the USSR's propaganda, the Soviet Foreign Minister's claims contained an element of accuracy. Lyalin's defection provided the catalyst for measures to cut the Soviet diplomatic and KGB presence, a step which the FCO, MI5, Douglas-Home and Heath had long considered overdue. Although Labour opposition condemned *Foot*, claiming that the Conservatives were using the expulsions for party-political reasons, the mass eviction of Soviet 'diplomats' was welcomed by the British media and public.[2]

Foot was also a by-product of the re-assessment of Anglo-Soviet relations which Stewart and his Foreign Office subordinates had overseen in mid-1968. The flagrant breach of diplomatic immunity by Soviet intelligence officers provided a clear example to Whitehall officials of the USSR's disdain for British efforts to foster bilateral goodwill, and the expulsion of many of these KGB operatives provided the British government with an opportunity to 'meet toughness with toughness' (as Roberts put it) when dealing with its Soviet adversary. *Foot* was also a reminder to other NATO powers that *détente* was being exploited by the USSR as a political means of undermining

---

[1] C. Hill and C. Lord, 'The foreign policy of the Heath government', in S. Ball and A. Seldon (eds), *The Heath government, 1970–74: a reappraisal*, London 1996, 309; E. Heath, *The course of my life*, London 1998, 474–6.

[2] G. Hughes, '"Giving the Russians a bloody nose": operation *Foot* and Soviet espionage in the United Kingdom, 1964–1971', *CWH* vi/2 (2006), 229–49.

Western unity and cohesion. British officialdom's interpretation of Soviet objectives was expressed by Douglas-Home's comments to fellow ministers in April 1973, notably in his comments that

> The Russians undoubtedly regarded us as the hardliners among the West Europeans and we had this reputation among the West Europeans themselves. But the present Soviet policy of *détente* was directed to longer term aims hostile to Western interests and it was necessary that we should try to prevent Western opinion from being misled into weakening its political and military defences.

These sentiments were echoed by Duncan Wilson's successor in Moscow, Sir John Killick, who wrote in August 1972 that '"peaceful coexistence" as used by the Russians is a fraud', as it did not preclude political, ideological and subversive efforts to undermine the NATO powers.[3] This attitude shaped the British approach to the CSCE negotiations, as FCO officials feared that the Warsaw Pact powers would exploit talks on European security to exacerbate differences between the USA and its allies, while cementing Soviet dominance over the Eastern half of the continent. Due to the Nixon administration's apathetic attitude towards CSCE, it was the British government and the FCO which took the lead in co-ordinating NATO's position in the preliminary negotiations from 1972 onwards. While the Soviet government intended the CSCE to formalise the continental *status quo*, Britain and its allies forced the Warsaw Pact powers to make concessions on transnational contacts and human rights, which were included in the 'Final Act' signed by all participants in Helsinki (July 1975). Although the FCO had intended to use these 'Basket III' issues as a means of embarrassing the Communist states by highlighting matters, notably human rights abuses in the Eastern bloc, which would undermine Soviet propaganda on *détente*, the 'Final Act' had the unintended consequence of encouraging dissidents behind the Iron Curtain to protest against the ruling regimes. The impact of Helsinki on the internal order in Eastern Europe did not become apparent until the *Solidarity* crisis in Poland in the early 1980s, and subsequently the revolutions of 1989.[4]

Heath's policy towards China was the inverse of Wilson's, although it should be remembered that when Labour held office Mao's regime was virulently anti-Western, and the Cultural Revolution of the late 1960s supported perceptions of the People's Republic as unstable and dangerous. However, the Sino-Soviet border clashes of 1969 and Mao's subsequent reappraisal of relations with the West led both to Nixon's visit to Beijing in February 1972

3 G. Roberts to Stewart, 13 June 1968, FCO 28/54; DOP(73)9th, 6 Apr. 1973, CAB 148/129; Killick to Tickell (Western Organisations Dept, FCO), 4 Aug. 1972, *DBPO III*, i. 497–9.
4 White, *Britain, détente*, 127; Garthoff, *Détente and confrontation*, 531–5; Hughes, '"Prague Spring"', 134.

and to the development of closer Anglo-Chinese relations under Heath. *Rapprochement* with China reflected the fact that British policy-makers were not instinctively hostile to Communist states which did not plan to export their ideology by force or subversion, and the abandonment of China's revolutionary foreign policy by Mao permitted the development of an amicable relationship between the PRC and Britain. In addition, in the same way that the Nixon administration used the 'China card' as a tool of superpower diplomacy, the Conservative government used its growing links with the PRC as a means of placing additional political pressure on the USSR. After 1969 up to a third of Soviet armed forces were deployed in Central Asia and Siberia, and the informal Sino-Western alliance exacerbated the military threat China posed to the USSR. The Heath government's actions therefore complemented the policy of 'triangular' diplomacy practiced by Nixon and his National Security Advisor, Henry Kissinger, during the early 1970s.[5]

Wilson's Sinophobia was comprehensible given the characteristics of Chinese foreign policy during his term in office. Yet his depiction of the USSR as an essentially 'conservative' power (as expressed in talks with Nixon during the latter's brief visit to Britain in August 1969) underestimated the continued influence of Marxism-Leninism on the USSR's leaders. Brezhnev's approach to *détente* did contain elements of pragmatism. Some of the younger challenges to his position (notably Polyanskii, Shelest and Shelepin) whom he expelled from the *Politburo* between 1973 and 1975 opposed any accommodation with the West. As political power within the *Politburo* became concentrated on the CPSU's General Secretary, Brezhnev sought to use *détente* as a means of stabilising the superpower arms race and of confirming the USSR's strategic equality with the USA, while averting the threat of a Sino-American alliance which would threaten Soviet security on two fronts. He also sought international acceptance of the post-1945 order in Europe, as well as increased trade with the Western powers. Yet Brezhnev's tenure of power had two serious consequences for both the USSR and East-West *détente*. First, as Brezhnev consolidated his power base and sidelined Kosygin and other rivals, the *Politburo* became a gerontocracy. Contrary to the assessment of the FCO and JIC in the 1960s the Soviet system was not revitalised by a technocratic class of leaders less supportive of Communist dogma and more inclined towards reform, but became a stagnant, rigid and corrupt order presided over by a leader who, well before his demise in 1982, was a 'helpless geriatric case'.[6] Furthermore, Brezhnev was unable to reconcile the objectives of *détente* with the increasingly ruinous costs of high defence expenditure – caused by the continued pursuit of military parity

[5] K. Hamilton, 'A "week that changed the world": Britain and Nixon's China visit of 21–28 February 1972', *DS* xv/1 (2004), 117–35; Garthoff, *Détente and confrontation*, 228–42, DOP(73)9th, DOP(73)5, 'Anglo-Soviet relations', 18 Jan. 1973, CAB 148/129.
[6] Nixon and Wilson, 3 Aug. 1969, PREM 13/3009/1; Roberts, *Soviet Union*, 66; Service, *Russia*, 391–3, 403–4.

with America – and with what Vladislav Zubok and Constantine Pleshakov called 'the revolutionary-imperial' paradigm, namely the USSR's efforts to support pro-Soviet governments and 'national liberation' movements across the globe. By supporting ideological allies in Africa and Afghanistan during the 1970s, the USSR under Brezhnev paid the price for marginal strategic gains with the collapse of superpower *détente*, and the 'second Cold War' of the 1980s.[7] Contrary to what Wilson supposed, Marxist-Leninist ideology therefore still exerted a powerful influence on the Soviet elite.

Duncan Wilson observed in 1974 that '[the] Soviet Union stands as the Great Power successor to the Tsarist Empire – expansionist and repressive'. The USSR had lost its ideological appeal to left-wing radicals in the West, and the suppression of the Prague Spring had permanently tarred its reputation as a 'progressive' state. Yet Duncan Wilson reiterated his view that the UK could develop closer commercial and cultural contacts with the USSR in the interests of East-West *détente*. In contrast, the majority of FCO officials concluded that the scope for Anglo-Soviet co-operation was limited at best, and that British policy towards East-West relations had to be integrated with multilateral relations with NATO allies, hence the emphasis that the British government placed on achieving a common ground on the CSCE negotiations in the early 1970s.[8] From the FCO's perspective, Britain's efforts to improve relations with the USSR and the Eastern bloc during the 1960s had been a failure. Was this a fair summary of the Labour government's efforts to promote *détente*? In answering this question, the conclusions to this study are best summarised in answers to three further lines of enquiry. To what degree did the Wilson government's approach to East-West relations differ from those of its predecessors? What were the objectives of British policy towards the Eastern bloc from 1964 to 1970? What practical results were achieved during this period, and why were they so limited?

In substantial terms there was little to distinguish Labour's approach to East-West relations from that adopted by the Conservatives between 1951 and 1964. The one exception concerns the decision to end the East of Suez role and to focus British defence policy on the commitment to NATO. The defence decisions of January 1968 had more to do with Britain's economic weakness and, to a lesser degree, with calculations relating to future membership of the EEC than on assessments of the Soviet threat. Although critics argued that the withdrawals from East of Suez left a power vacuum which was filled by an increasingly activist Soviet foreign policy in the 1970s, the decision to pull British forces out of the Middle and Far East did make sense in terms of Cold War strategy. While commitments such as Borneo were

---

7 F. Halliday, *Revolution and world politics*, Basingstoke 1999, 85, 137, 139; Zubok and Pleshakov, *Kremlin*, 282; Westad, *Global Cold War*, 169–70, 202–6; C. Andrew and V. Mitrokhin, *The Mitrokhin archive*, II: *The KGB and the world*, London 2006.
8 Wilson, 'Anglo-Soviet relations', 388–93; Braithwaite interview, DOHP, transcript, 2–3.

hard to shed, particularly at the height of the 'confrontation' with Indonesia, Labour ministers and Foreign Office officials had good grounds for viewing East of Suez deployments as marginal at best to UK security interests and, in some cases, as liabilities. The withdrawal from Aden paradoxically strengthened UK interests in the Middle East, because it removed a source of anti-British nationalism in the region; the Anglo-Egyptian *rapprochement* which took place after 1968 was, for example, assisted by the end of the British military presence in South Arabia.[9]

The decision to seek EEC membership in 1967, although unsuccessful, represented a convergence with Conservative policy. Wilson had been an opponent of the EEC, describing it in 1961 as 'an arid, sterile and tight trading and defensive bloc against the East'. His bid for EEC membership six years later had two political consequences which ran counter to his initial intention to focus on Anglo-Soviet relations. First, British admission to the EEC was unwelcome to the USSR, which opposed European economic integration. Second, it also influenced a change in Labour's approach to Anglo-German relations. Having initially expressed anxiety over a revival of German nationalism, by the end of his premiership Wilson's attitude towards the FRG was positively cordial. The Labour government supported Brandt's *Ostpolitik* not only because of its political affinity with the SPD, but because it helped to defuse the tensions inherent in the German question, and also dispelled the suspicions rife on both sides of the East-West divide concerning the future foreign policy direction of the FRG. The prime minister's enthusiastic support for Brandt, as expressed during his talks with Nixon in Washington in January 1970 was in stark contrast to his earlier indiscreet anti-German declarations during private conversations with Kosygin.[10]

After becoming Labour's leader, Wilson renounced his Bevanite criticisms of American and British foreign policies, and as prime minister he adhered to the essentials of the UK's approach to the Cold War as followed by Attlee, Churchill, Eden, Macmillan and Douglas-Home. He retained the British nuclear deterrent (despite apparent electoral pledges to do otherwise) and placed more symbolic emphasis on the 'special relationship' than Heath. Continuity with established policies was not merely a product of bureaucratic inertia in the civil service (as Crossman claimed), but to the fact that the key portfolios in Wilson's Cabinet – relating to foreign affairs, defence, trade and economic management – were all held by leading figures of the Labour right (Brown, Callaghan, Crosland, Healey, Jay, Jenkins and Stewart), all of whom agreed that the Atlanticist approach to external affairs established under Attlee was essential to Britain's national interests. In contrast, the Labour left was poorly represented. Ministers like Benn, Castle and Crossman

[9] R. McNamara, *Britain, Nasser and the balance of power in the Middle East, 1952–1967*, London 2003, 291–2.

[10] Kissinger, Nixon, Wilson and Trend, 27 Jan. 1970, PREM 13/3546; Wilson and Kosygin, 7 Feb. 1967, PREM 13/1715.

occupied marginal positions within the Wilson government and in consequence had little effect on foreign affairs. For critics within the party, the government's Atlanticism represented at best an outdated dogma based on a clichéd view of the 'red menace', and at worst an unethical betrayal of core Labour principles. Wilson's support for US intervention in Vietnam, the maintenance of defence and diplomatic relations with South Africa and (after 1967) the Greek military *junta*, and the Diego Garcia decision caused particular resentment amongst the Labour left. Yet Wilson's critics within the party were as capable of employing double standards and of neglecting its own strictures against oppressive regimes and in support of human rights. Hard-left Labour MPs failed to condemn Communist atrocities in Vietnam alongside those committed by American and Saigon regime forces, and were also willing to extol the largely illusory virtues of the 'socialist' system in East Germany, and to demand its recognition as a sovereign state.[11]

Wilson and ministers of the Labour right continued to associate British defence policy with a pro-American alignment and membership of NATO, and assumed that both factors enabled the UK and its allies to contain Soviet expansionism without recourse to war. However, the possibility that the US deterrent could become decoupled from the defence of Western Europe was used by both the Wilson government and its predecessors to justify Britain's continued retention of nuclear weapons. Furthermore, as was the case with Conservative administrations, the Labour government's relationship with the USA was more nuanced than its critics argued. The Anglo-American alliance was by no means an equal partnership, but as far as ministers and officials in London were concerned, dependence did not mean submission. The 'special relationship' gave Britain strategic advantages in bilateral military, nuclear and intelligence co-operation which no British policy-maker was willing to jeopardise, but as was the case prior to 1964 there were disputes with the Johnson administration over Vietnam, BAOR and East-West trade which were only resolved through compromise, rather than capitulation by the UK. US official dissatisfaction did not prevent the Wilson government from concluding the Benn-Kirillin agreement on technological co-operation in January 1968, or from pursuing a 'friendship treaty' with the USSR, until it was undermined by the Soviets. Public expressions from London of confidence in US policy also coexisted with concerns within Whitehall – evident in previous Cold War crises – that excessive American belligerence could provoke a major escalation of East-West hostilities. Such sentiments had manifested themselves in the early 1950s over Korea and Indochina and were also present, albeit in a more muted form, throughout the Vietnam War. In addition, the Labour government's refusal to regard political and ideological hostility as a barrier to trade and other transnational

---

11 Ponting, *Breach of promise*, passim; HC Deb.5s, 720 (1965), cols 257–62. See also William Warbey's *apologia* for Vietnamese Communism: *Ho Chi Minh and the struggle for an independent Vietnam*, London 1972.

contacts with the Eastern bloc reflected the policies that the Conservatives had followed in office, while Foreign Office officials had consistently argued that the UK, to use Duncan Wilson's words, 'cannot confine [itself] to dealing with governments whose general policies we approve'.[12]

To use Garthoff's terms of reference, British official views on relations with the USSR and other Communist states combined 'mechanist' with 'interactionist' interpretations, both prior to and during the Labour ministry of 1964–70. Politicians in Westminster and officials in Whitehall generally shied away from the Manichean interpretation of Soviet intentions prevalent within Washington during the early Cold War years, and which re-emerged during the 1980s. During a parliamentary debate in July 1967 Brown poured scorn on a 'goodies and baddies' view of world politics, while officials like Gore-Booth adopted a pragmatic view of the Soviet threat. As Permanent Undersecretary of the Foreign Office, Gore-Booth stressed that the principal problem affecting Britain's relations with Communist states lay not in the latter's internal characteristics (notably their totalitarianism and forcible suppression of political opposition), but in their declared intention to spread their doctrine world-wide. It was feasible for the UK to be on amicable terms with Communist powers (such as Yugoslavia and, after 1972, China) which showed that they were not irreconcilably hostile to the West. Foreign Office officials who suggested propaganda attacks on repression within the USSR from early 1968 onwards did so in order to 'educate' the British public about the nature of the Soviet system, and to respond in kind to press attacks from *Tass*, *Novosti* and other propaganda organs highlighting the UK's domestic difficulties. There was no intention to actively support anti-government dissidents in the USSR and Eastern Europe, or to incite revolts behind the Iron Curtain. As was the case over Hungary and East Berlin, the British government was careful not to openly encourage the Czechoslovak reformists during the spring and summer of 1968, a non-interventionist policy that was mirrored by that of other NATO powers. However, in the aftermath of the Prague Spring there were tensions between an 'interactionist' prime minister and his namesake in the Moscow embassy on the one hand, and the more 'mechanistic' approach followed by Stewart and the majority of FCO officials. While both Harold and Duncan Wilson placed the onus for preserving Anglo-Soviet contacts on the British government, the Foreign Secretary and his subordinates believed that it was the Soviet leadership's responsibility to demonstrate its willingness to compromise in its dealings with the West in the interests of *détente*. Having hitherto been regarded as an uncharismatic dullard, Stewart's influence as Foreign Secretary is worthy of reassessment, as he was able to both promote a harder line on Anglo-Soviet relations from the spring of 1968 onwards, and to thwart Wilson's efforts to meet Kosygin in 1969–70. Stewart helped to shape the reactive

---

[12] Hennessy, *Secret state*, 44–76; Wilson, 'Anglo-Soviet relations', 389–90.

and sceptical approach towards relations with the USSR which Heath and Douglas-Home oversaw in the early 1970s.[13]

The main objectives of the Labour government were essentially embodied in the twin policies of defence and engagement with the Eastern bloc reflected in the Harmel report of 1967. Yet there were differences in the respective approaches followed by the Foreign Office and the prime minister. The former focused on processes (notably trade liberalisation and cultural contacts) which would encourage the incremental liberalisation, or 'evolution', of the East European countries. Wilson's aims were more ambitious: he saw his country as both an interlocutor between the superpowers, and as a pivotal power between the USA and its West European allies. This vision of the UK's international role was shared by Brown during his stint as Foreign Secretary. In the aftermath of France's departure from NATO's military infrastructure in March 1966 Wilson saw an opportunity for the UK to rally other Alliance members behind a collective policy of *détente* with the East. He retained his interest in East-West relations during his second premiership (1974–6) and in his retirement, when he became honorary president of the Great Britain-USSR Association, an FCO-sponsored body established to promote bilateral cultural contacts. However, there is little to suggest that he ever had any firm conception of the nature of *détente*, or of a strategy for involving his country in the alleviation and eventual resolution of East-West rivalries. De Gaulle's concept of 'Europe totale' may have over-estimated both France's influence in continental affairs, and the readiness of 'Russia' to abandon Communist ideology and its sphere of influence in Eastern Europe, but it did represent a conceptual component of his conduct towards East-West relations which the British prime minister lacked. The closest Wilson came to expressing coherent ideas on *détente* or Anglo-Soviet relations occurred the decade before he became prime minister, in his report to Churchill after his May 1953 visit to Moscow. Between 1964 and 1970 only two issues attracted his constant attention, these being Vietnam and trade with the Eastern bloc. In other instances Wilson was a practitioner of 'magpie diplomacy', temporarily seizing on issues only to drop them once they lost their allure. His initial interest in the NPT faded after his visit to the USSR in February 1966, and he devoted a mere six pages of his memoirs to non-proliferation, which the Labour government had initially declared a priority. Wilson also toyed with, and abandoned, NATO-Warsaw Pact mutual force reductions, while his declared intention to rally the Western Alliance after March 1966 was neglected in favour of a fruitless approach to

---

13 Brown's comments are taken from 750 HC Deb5s (1967), col.2489. See also Garthoff, *Détente and confrontation*, 1176–7; SC(67)17, FCO 49/25; OPD(68)24, CAB148/37; and Young, *Labour governments*, 4–7.

force West Germany to offset the foreign exchange costs of BAOR and the RAF component of 2ATAF.[14]

His 'magpie diplomacy' often revealed a superficial understanding of Cold War realities on Wilson's part. Throughout 1965 he persisted in requesting the Soviet government's endorsement of his Vietnam peace initiatives, even though he was aware that it faced accusations of betrayal from the PRC if it collaborated in Western attempts at peacemaking. Furthermore, if Wilson believed that the Soviet leadership genuinely feared a revival of West German militarism, why then did he assume that Brezhnev and his *Politburo* would accept mutual force reductions, which would weaken the USSR's authority over its restive East European satellites and potentially cede continental military preponderance to the FRG? How did Wilson reconcile his confidence that NATO's military strength and political solidarity would prevent Soviet expansionism with measures taken over offsets which would actually weaken NATO, and compound the damage done by de Gaulle in the spring of 1966? There is also little to suggest that Wilson paid any attention to Foreign Office thinking on political developments in the Eastern bloc and, unlike the French president he did not visit any of the East European countries during his term in office (de Gaulle travelled to Poland in 1967 and Romania in 1968). To compound this, the prime minister's nonchalance following the Czechoslovak crisis was evident, as was his view that the forcible suppression of the Prague Spring was a mere impediment to efforts to establish closer ties with the Soviet leadership. Despite his Commons speech condemning the Warsaw Pact's intervention, Wilson's subsequent conduct demonstrated a 'business as usual' approach to contacts with the USSR.[15] While Foreign Office officials had called for a greater focus on relations with Eastern Europe on the eve of Labour's 1964 election victory, Wilson continued the tradition of neglect which inhabitants of 10 Downing Street showed towards this region.

What did the Labour government actually achieve in the field of East-West *détente*? In practical terms, it had little to show for its efforts, aside from the Consular Convention (1965) and the technological exchange agreement (1968). Kosygin's 1967 visit to the UK was a more amicable affair than that of Bulganin and Khrushchev the previous decade, but ultimately it did not fulfil Wilson's expectations. Nor could he claim any successes on the scale of Eden's stewardship of the 1954 Geneva conference, or even Macmillan's role in the 1963 LTBT talks. Furthermore, Wilson showed far more interest in the trappings of Anglo-Soviet concord, as shown by the 'striking

---

14 J. C. Q. Roberts, *Speak clearly into the chandelier: cultural politics between Britain and Russia*, Richmond, UK 2000, 195–204; Wilson to Churchill, 6 June 1953, FO 371/106579; Freeman, *Arms control*, 211.

15 J. Korbel, *Détente in Europe: real or imaginary?*, Princeton, NJ 1972, 61; 769 HC Deb5s, London 1968, cols.1273–420.

initiatives' in trade he hoped for in 1967–8, and his continual preoccupation with meeting the Soviet leadership as often as possible (regardless of the specific agenda), than with the actual results of his efforts. Aside from Phase A/B in February 1967, Wilson could not persuade the Soviets to support his peacemaking initiatives on Vietnam, or to respond to the *Neue Ostpolitik* initiated by Kiesinger. Furthermore, his belief that the UK could act as an intermediary between the superpowers was misconceived. Wilson failed to develop a rapport with Johnson, and for all his claims regarding his relations with Kosygin his contacts with the Soviet leadership yielded little. If Castle accurately recorded Wilson's version of his trip to Moscow in July 1966, then his description as a 'Yorkshire Walter Mitty' has some justification.[16] The harsh fact was that neither the US nor the Soviet governments saw any purpose in involving their British counterpart in their bilateral negotiations, whether on arms control or Vietnam. For all Labour's emphasis on arms control in its 1964 manifesto Brown's attempt to promote preparatory talks on a CTBT in November 1966 was quashed by Gromyko, while the UK's role in the conclusion of the NPT two years later was minimal. In addition, although the Kosygin visit encouraged an ephemeral period of Anglo-Soviet goodwill, by the time that Wilson left office bilateral relations were in a poor state, with the UK being the focus of the officially-sanctioned hostility and invective of the Soviet state media.

The Labour left felt that the lack of progress in Anglo-Soviet relations was due to the UK's dependence on the USA, and it was the rejection of the leadership's Atlanticism which fuelled the party's increasingly radical turn (adopting unilateral disarmament and hostility to NATO) during the 1970s and early 1980s. Yet this was a simplistic view which ignored the problems other Western powers faced in pursuing improved relations with the Eastern bloc states. De Gaulle's own policy of *détente* achieved little, despite his anti-American sentiment and France's withdrawal from NATO's command structure in 1966. The French president's illusion that his country could play a major diplomatic role in a continent unencumbered by ideological and political divisions was shattered by the invasion of Czechoslovakia. West German attempts to improve relations with the Warsaw Pact states also produced scant results (aside from diplomatic ties with Romania) until Brandt became Chancellor. Furthermore, despite Johnson's aim to 'build bridges' between the USA and the Eastern bloc, US-Soviet *détente* was delayed as a consequence of Vietnam and the Sino-Soviet schism. Both the Moscow embassy and the Foreign Office concluded in late 1964 that Khrushchev's successors would be more concerned with their rivalry with Mao for leadership of the Communist world than with improving relations with the capitalist powers. Sino-Soviet rivalry was a constraint on *détente* until 1969, and it is

---

16 FO to Washington, 28 Feb. 1966, PREM 13/805; Colman, '"Summit diplomacy"', 131–51; *Castle diaries*, 151, entry for 21 July 1966.

significant that the USSR was more willing to conclude agreements with the USA and the West Europeans once China emerged as a major military threat. In any case, Britain's status as a propaganda scapegoat for the USSR during the late 1960s and early 1970s reflected its position in Soviet foreign policy. While *détente* with the Nixon administration was too important for Brezhnev and his peers to jeopardise, and Brandt's *Ostpolitik* testified to the FRG's acquiescence in the continental *status quo*, the British government served both as an ideological focus for the CPSU's anti-Western sentiment and as a means of 'wedge-driving' within NATO, with allied powers being encouraged to view the UK as an intransigent power bent on undermining *détente*.[17]

The Sino-Soviet feud, the Vietnam War, the GDR's rigidity on the German question and the relative inexperience in foreign affairs of Khrushchev's successors were all constraints on Soviet policy in the 1960s. Yet the Soviets also squandered opportunities to play on intra-Western differences, particularly those affecting Anglo-American relations during Wilson's term in office. The Johnson administration's impatience with foreign criticism of its policy in South-East Asia soured the USA's relations with allied and neutral powers. The furore surrounding the failure of *Sunflower* in February 1967, and the US government's decision seven months later to develop a 'thin' ABM system, reinforced the impression in London that American policy posed significant obstacles to international agreement, both on arms control and on any resolution of the Vietnam War. The Anglo-Soviet technological agreement of January 1968 aroused American criticism, while in Britain many MPs, businessmen and officials believed that COCOM was in dire need of reform. It should also be noted that in British society itself there was a fracturing of the 'Cold War consensus' similar to that in the USA. A significant section of public opinion remained concerned about the prospects of nuclear war. There were also widespread protests against US intervention in Vietnam – and the British government's support of America's actions – and a growing belief in parliament that *détente* had superseded the rivalries of the Cold War. A more subtle Soviet foreign policy could have exploited such transatlantic tensions over arms control, Indochina and trade, reinforcing the view that the USSR was a respectable, rational power with whom the UK could co-operate not only in commercial but political relations.

The prospects for such an approach to Anglo-Soviet relations prevailing over the UK's established Cold War policies should not be overstated, yet the fact remains that Soviet policy towards Britain during this period, especially in 1967–8, was crude and unsubtle. British officials resented the contemptuous manner with which the USSR treated the UK, in particular

---

[17] Keohane, 'Labour's international policy', 376; Garthoff, *Détente and confrontation*, 135–9, 274–5; Lacouture, *De Gaulle*, 472–4; Sarotte, *Dealing with the devil*, 21–3; Loth, *Détente*, 124; Hamilton, *Last Cold Warriors*, passim.

the Soviet government's off-hand dismissal of the proposed bilateral 'friendship treaty'. The East of Suez withdrawals and the devaluation of the pound had certainly highlighted the decline of British power and influence, but the Foreign Office did not appreciate either Soviet propaganda portrayals of the UK's weaknesses, or Gromyko's statement that a 'friendship treaty' was incompatible with Britain's NATO membership. After this offhand treatment, Operation *Foot* appeared to be an example of paying off old scores. As far as British officials were concerned, the purpose of the 'treaty of friendship' was to establish a framework for increased cultural, scientific and commercial relations. Yet Andropov's report to Brezhnev, cited in chapter 5, showed the Soviet leadership's complete antipathy to freer East-West contacts. 'Bridge-building' was viewed within the Kremlin as a means of subverting Communism, and the Foreign Office's intention of highlighting the KGB's activities within the USSR would have served only to reinforce Andropov's paranoia. The demise of the 'treaty of friendship' in early 1968 showed that due to the Soviet leadership's determination to limit contacts between its subjects and the outside world, it was impossible for the UK and other Western powers to establish a 'normal' relationship with the Soviet bloc states.

The harsh truth was that there was a fundamental distinction between the Eastern bloc's approach to *détente* and that of the West. For the USSR and its East European allies, *détente* was restricted to governmental contacts, and the principal goal was to preserve the division of Europe. The Soviet bloc states also wanted the material benefits of trade with the more prosperous West while isolating their peoples from ideological contamination from the more affluent capitalist world. It was for this reason that cultural contacts intended to promote greater understanding between Communist and Western countries had the opposite effect, hence the complaint made by the head of EESD, Julian Bullard, in July 1971:

> It is not encouraging to know that out of 316 British students sent to Soviet universities during the last 11 years under the Cultural Exchange Programme, at least 70 have been involved in incidents of some kind, apparently provoked by the KGB; or that two Soviet academics admitted to the Public Record Office under the same Programme went straight back to lecture in Moscow on how the British government connived with Hitler in 1939.[18]

Gore-Booth retrospectively commented on the inability of British politicians and diplomats to recognise the role of ideology in international politics; this failing was evident in British thinking on East-West contacts and the Soviet bloc's 'evolution'. The Dubcek regime's introduction of the Action Programme in the spring of 1968 was an example of 'evolution' in practice; the process of change was dictated by reformers within the CPCS, and for all the intellectual ferment and popular debate which characterised the

---

[18] J. Bullard (EESD) to Brimelow, 12 July 1971, FCO 28/1567.

Prague Spring Czechoslovakia did not experience a violent uprising against Communist rule. Yet, as was the case with Hungary in 1956, the USSR eventually resorted to military intervention to suppress 'counter-revolution'. Furthermore, assessments of the Eastern bloc by the Foreign Office and JIC overlooked both the nature of the *nomenklatura* system and the network of patron-client relationships upon which the Communist party bureaucracies were based. Brezhnev exploited his control over the CPSU's patron-client networks to thwart Kosygin's plans for economic reform and to oust potential rivals from the *Politburo*. The ultimate result was the stagnation of the USSR and the Eastern bloc in the 1980s.[19]

The general failure of British and West European policy-makers and diplomats to appreciate the strength of ideology was also demonstrated by one unintended consequence of Western efforts to improve contacts with the Eastern bloc. Contrary to what FCO exponents of 'evolution' argued, the Warsaw Pact regimes intensified repressive measures against their subjects in spite of *détente*. This was evident not only in the content of Andropov's May 1968 report to Brezhnev, but in the steps that the East German leadership took in the early 1970s to strengthen both the MfS (the secret police) and the GDR's border defences.[20] It can also be argued that the Foreign Office's concept of 'evolution' was half-hearted, and that British diplomats placed insufficient emphasis on encouraging grass-roots pressure for political and economic reform in the Eastern bloc. When Gore-Booth proposed in June 1966 that the draft 'declaration of principles' should be addressed to the people as opposed to the governments of the Warsaw Pact states (thereby employing the Soviet tactic of appealing to the subjects of 'imperialism') the head of the Northern Department stated that British policy was intended to avoid drawing 'too sharp a line between the people and the states', or openly encouraging the East European countries to defy the USSR. There were continued concerns within the British policy-making establishment that revolutionary changes to the continental order could only lead to bloody insurrections and possibly an East-West crisis. Such sentiments were evident as late as 1989, when the then Foreign Secretary Douglas Hurd described the post-1945 order as one 'under which we've lived quite happily for forty years' (the 'we' in Hurd's statement referred exclusively to Britons and other West Europeans). Paradoxically enough, the *status quo* in the Eastern bloc was inherently unstable, as it only encouraged nationalist resentment directed

---

[19] Gore-Booth, *With great truth*, 412; Service, *Russia*, 379–80; Willerton, *Patronage and politics*, passim.
[20] Andropov to Brezhnev, in Garthoff and Knight, 'Soviet intelligence', passim; Sarotte, *Dealing with the devil*, 4, 51–4.

against the USSR and increasing popular hostility toward the established regimes in Poland, Czechoslovakia and elsewhere in Eastern Europe.[21]

The official British response to the Prague Spring highlighted the ambivalence with which the Foreign Office regarded political change within Eastern Europe. Essentially, British diplomats placed their hopes in the emergence of a gentler, more enlightened form of authoritarian rule in Eastern Europe, rather than uncontrolled change driven by pressure from below. Having had their hopes in Dubcek dashed by Operation *Danube* in 1968, British diplomats assumed that Husak would govern as a moderate 'centrist'. Yet instead of initiating systematic domestic reforms Husak followed a policy of 'consumer Communism', using Western loans to bribe the populace with an artificially higher standard of living. 'Consumer Communism' became the norm in Eastern Europe. After a series of riots and strikes in Poland's Baltic ports in December 1970, the Warsaw regime resorted to policies similar to those of Husak in an attempt to placate popular opinion. Yet after the 'oil shock' of 1973, and the global recession which followed, the Eastern bloc states suffered economic decline. The failures of 'consumer Communism' fuelled the Polish crisis of 1980–1, and the East European revolutions of 1989.[22]

In conclusion, the course of Britain's interaction with the USSR and the East European states demonstrated how difficult it was for Western democracies to improve diplomatic relations with regimes whose policies were shaped by an ideology based on inimical opposition to 'imperialism', and where *rapprochement* ran the risk of undermining the *raison d'etre* of ruling parties, namely the supremacy of Communist doctrine and its inevitable triumph over 'capitalism'. The limitations of engagement had been outlined by Trevelyan in December 1964, in a dispatch to his superiors outlining the stark dilemmas Khrushchev's successors were obliged to address. Trevelyan reported that the USSR's best hope of overcoming its economic woes was to develop *détente* with the USA and its allies; this would not only ease the military burden on the Soviet economy but would also yield benefits in increased trade and access to Western investment and technology. However, contacts with the West would erode the Communist order, as the peoples of the Soviet bloc would become more aware of the contrast between their poverty and Western prosperity. Khrushchev had been unable to resolve the conflict between Marxist-Leninist ideology and the USSR's diplomatic and economic need for East-West *détente*, and Trevelyan correctly predicted that the same would be true of Brezhnev and his peers. It was not until after Mikhail Gorbachev became CPSU General Secretary in 1985 that the dilemma Trevelyan observed was resolved. By the time Gorbachev discarded the revolutionary-imperial paradigm and the obstacles to reform within the

---

21 Gore-Booth note, 10 June 1966, and Smith, 'East-West relations', N1075/66, FO 371/188500; Garton Ash, *Europe's name*, 377.
22 Hughes, '"Prague Spring"', 134–5; Davies, *Heart of Europe*, 14–16.

Soviet bloc, the irony was that the central planning system that Wilson had referred to in his 'white heat' speech was disintegrating. George Clutton's comment in June 1966 that 'the day will come when the whole system will crack and disintegrate' was justified by events in Eastern Europe in 1989, and by the fall of the USSR in 1991.[23]

[23] Trevelyan to Gordon-Walker, 2 Nov. 1964, FO 371/177671; Clutton to Smith, 7 June 1966, FO 371/188510.

Bibliography

Unpublished primary sources

GREAT BRITAIN
Cambridge, Churchill College Archives
Diplomatic Oral History Programme, transcripts
Patrick Gordon-Walker papers
Michael Stewart papers

London, British Library Newspaper Collection, Colindale
Evening Standard
Express
Guardian
Mirror
Sun
Telegraph
The Times

London, British Library of Political and Economic Science
Alistair Hetherington papers
Labour party, national executive, international subcommittee, correspondence and political records, microfilm 198, reel 6

London, Liddell-Hart Centre for Military Archives, King's College
Lyndon B. Johnson National Security files (microfilm: MF)
373 Eastern Europe and USSR
402–11 Western Europe
790 NSC memoranda
National Security Archives (microfiche: MFF)
'The Soviet estimate: US analyses of the Soviet Union, 1947–1991' (MFF15)
'US nuclear history, 1955–1968' (MFF16).

London, The National Archives, Kew
Air Ministry
AIR 20 Ministry of Defence, air historical branch: miscellaneous files

Board of Trade
BT 11 Commercial Relations and Exports.

Cabinet Office (CAB)
CAB 128 Minutes of Cabinet meetings
CAB 129 Cabinet memoranda
CAB 130 Committee files

CAB 131 Defence Committee: minutes and papers, 1945–63
CAB 133 Commonwealth and international meetings
CAB 134 Subject files
CAB 148 Overseas Policy and Defence Committee (ministerial and official) files
CAB 158 JIC memoranda
CAB 159 JIC minutes.
CAB 163 Central Intelligence Machinery: JIC secretariat
CAB 164 Subject files.
CAB 165 Committee files.
CAB 168 Papers of the chief scientific advisor to the prime minister
CAB 185 JIC(A) minutes, 1969–
CAB 186 JIC(A) memoranda, 1969–

Ministry of Defence
DEFE 4 COS Committee minutes
DEFE 5 COS Committee memoranda
DEFE 6 Joint Planning Staff papers
DEFE 13 Private Office papers
DEFE 24 Defence Secretariat branches
DEFE 31 DIS files
DEFE 63 DIS papers
DEFE 68 Central staff, registered files and branch holders

Foreign and Commonwealth Office
FCO 7 American Department
FCO 15 South-East Asia Department
FCO 17 Eastern Department
FCO 18 Far Eastern Department
FCO 28 Northern Department/East European and Soviet Department
FCO 46 Defence Department
FCO 49 Planning staff

Foreign Office
FO 371 Political series files, 1966–
FO 953 Planning staff papers, 1966–

Prime Minister's Office
PREM 11 papers, 1954–64
PREM 13 papers, 1964–70
PREM 15 Office papers, 1970–

War Office
WO 208 DIS files, 1964–70

Oxford, Bodleian Library
Lord George Brown papers
Paul Gore-Booth papers
Baron Wilson of Rievaulx papers

UNITED STATES
Austin, Texas, Lyndon B. Johnson Presidential Library
Oral history interviews, transcripts
Committee files: Miller Committee papers (boxes16–25)
National Intelligence estimates (boxes 1–5)
National Security Council meetings (boxes 1–2)
National Security files: country files: Eastern Europe (box 162); Czechoslovakia (boxes 179–82); United Kingdom (boxes 206–16); Soviet Union (boxes 217–31)
Walt W. Rostow files (boxes 9–12)

College Park, Maryland, National Archives and Records Administration
RG 59 General records of the State Department
RG 263 Central Intelligence Agency records

Washington, DC, National Security Archives, George Washington University
'Presidential directives on national security from Truman to Clinton' (microfiche)
'Soviet flashpoints documentary collection. Czechoslovakia' (boxes 7–8)

Published primary sources

Official papers
Aldrich, R. J. (ed.), *Espionage security and intelligence in Britain, 1945–1970*, Manchester 1998
Clissold, S. (ed.), *Yugoslavia and the Soviet Union, 1939–1973: a documentary record*, London 1975
Cmnd. 2270, *Statement on defence*, London 1964
Cmnd. 2902, *Statement on defence*, London 1966
Cmnd. 3203, *Statement on defence*, London 1967
Cmnd. 3540. *Statement on defence*, London 1968
Dale, I. (ed.), *Labour Party general election manifestos, 1900–1997*, Abingdon 2000
Documents on British policy overseas, series 3 (1968–1975), I: *Britain and the Soviet Union 1968–1972*, London 1997
—— II: *Conference on Security and Co-operation in Europe*, London 1997
—— III: *Détente in Europe, 1972–76*, London 2001
Foreign Relations of the United States, I: *Vietnam, 1964*, Washington DC 1992
—— II: *Vietnam, 1965*, Washington, DC 1996
—— III: *Vietnam. 1965*, Washington, DC 1996
—— IV: *Vietnam, 1966*, Washington, DC 1998
—— V: *Vietnam, 1967*, Washington, DC 2002
—— VI: *Vietnam, January–August, 1968*, Washington, DC 2002
—— VII: *Vietnam, September 1968–January 1969*, Washington, DC 2003
—— IX: *International development and economic defense policy: commodities*, Washington, DC 1997

—— XI: *Arms control and disarmament*, Washington, DC 1997
—— XII: *Western Europe*, Washington, DC 2001
—— XIII: *Western Europe region, 1964–1968*, Washington, DC 1995
—— XIV: *Soviet Union*, Washington, DC 2001
—— XV: *Germany and Berlin*, Washington, DC 1996
—— XVII: *Eastern Europe, 1964–1968*, Washington, DC 1996
—— XVIII: *Arab-Israeli dispute, 1964–1967*, Washington, DC 2000
—— XIX: *Arab-Israeli crisis and war, 1967*, Washington, DC 2004
—— XX: *Arab-Israeli dispute, 1967–1968*, Washington, DC 2001
—— XXX: *China*, Washington, DC 1998
Hansard 5th ser. Parliamentary Debates: Commons: vols dcci–dccix (Oct. 1964–Apr. 1970)
Herring, G. (ed.), *The secret diplomacy of the Vietnam War: the negotiating volumes of the Pentagon papers*, Austin, Tx 1983
Mastny, V. and M. Byrne (eds), *A cardboard castle? An inside history of the Warsaw Pact, 1955–1991*, Budapest 2005
The military balance, London 1964–70
Navratil, J., A. Bencik, V. Kural, M. Michalkova, and J. Vondrova (eds), *The Prague Spring 1968: a National Security Archive documents reader*, Budapest 1998
Strategic survey, London 1964–70
Vaïsse, M. et al (ed.), *Documents diplomatiques français, 1964*, I: *1 Janvier–30 Juin 1964*, Paris–Brussels 2002
—— *1964*, II: *1 Juillet– 31 Décembre*, Paris–Brussels 2002
—— *1965*, I: *1 Janvier– 30 Juin*, Paris–Brussels 2003
—— *1965*, II: *1 Juillet– 31 Décembre*, Paris–Brussels 2002

Memoirs and diaries etc
'A letter to Brezhnev: the Czech hard-liners "request" for Soviet intervention, August 1968', trans. K. Kramer, *CWIHP Bulletin* ii (1992), 95
Ball, G., *The past has another pattern: memoirs*, New York 1982
Benn, T., *Out of the wilderness: diaries, 1963–1967*, London 1987
—— *Office without power: diaries, 1968–1972*, London 1988
Brown, G., *In my way*, London 1972
Castle, B., *The Castle diaries, 1964–70*, London 1984
—— *The Castle diaries, 1964–1976*, London 1990
Colville, J., *The fringes of power: Downing Street diaries*, II: *October 1941–April 1955*, London 1987
Crossman, R., *The diaries of a Cabinet minister*, I: *Minister of Housing, 1964–1966*, London 1975
—— II: *Lord President of the Council and Leader of the House of Commons, 1966–1968*, London 1976
—— III: *Secretary of State for Social Services, 1968–1970*, London 1977
—— *The backbench diaries of Richard Crossman*, ed. J. Morgan, London 1981
Debre, M., *Trois Républiques pour une France : gouverner autrement: mémoires, 1962–1970*, Paris 1993
Dobrynin, A., *In confidence: Moscow's ambassador to America's six Cold War presidents (1962–1986)*, New York 1995

Gordon-Walker, P., *Patrick Gordon Walker: political diaries. 1932–1971*, ed. R. Pearce, London 1991

Greenhill, D., *More by accident*, York 1993

Healey, D., *The time of my life*, London 1990

Heath, E., *The course of my life*, London 1998

Jenkins, R., *A life at the centre*, Basingstoke 1991

Johnson, L. B., *The vantage point: perspectives of the presidency, 1963–1969*, London 1972

King, C., *The Cecil King diary, 1965–1970*, London 1972

Kissinger, H., *White House years*, London 2000

Macmillan, H., *The Macmillan diaries: the Cabinet years, 1950–1957*, ed. P. Catterall, Basingstoke 2003

McNamara, R. S., *The essence of security: reflections in office*, London 1968

—— *In retrospect: the tragedy and lessons of Vietnam*, New York 1995

Peyrefitte, A., *C'était de Gaulle*, Paris 1994

Roberts, F., *Dealing with dictators: the destruction and revival of Europe, 1930–1970*, London 1991

Rusk, D., *As I saw it: a Secretary of State's memoirs*, London 1990

Shuckburgh, E., *Descent into Suez: diaries, 1951–56*, London 1986

Stewart, M., *Life and Labour: an autobiography*, London 1980

Walden, G., *Lucky George: memoirs of an anti-politician*, London 1999

Williams, M., *Inside Number 10*, London 1972

Wilson, H., *The Labour government, 1964–1970: a personal record*, London 1971

Zuckerman, S., *Monkeys, men and missiles: an autobiography*, London 1986

Secondary sources

Aldrich, R. J., 'British Intelligence and the Anglo-American "special relationship" during the Cold War', *RIS* xxiv/3 (1998), 331–51

—— *The hidden hand: Britain, America and Cold War secret intelligence*, London 2001

Alexander, P., 'A tale of two Smiths: the transformation of Commonwealth policy', *CBH* xx/3 (2006), 303–21

Anderson, D., 'The United States and Vietnam', in Lowe, *Vietnam War*, 95–114

Andrew, C., 'Whitehall, Washington and the intelligence services', *IA* liii/3 (1977), 390–404

—— and O. Gordievsky, *KGB: the inside story of its foreign operations from Lenin to Gorbachev*, London 1990

—— and V. Mitrokhin, *The Mitrokhin archive*, I: *The KGB in Europe and the West*, London 1999

—— *The Mitrokhin archive*, II: *The KGB and the world*, London 2006

Ashton, Nigel, 'Uncertain decade: US-Soviet relations, 1961–68', *DS* xiv/1 (2003), 195–202

Ball, S.. *The Cold War: an international history*, London 1998

——— and A. Seldon (eds), *The Heath government, 1970–74: a reappraisal*, London 1996

Bamford, J., *Body of secrets: how America's NSA and Britain's GCHQ eavesdrop on the world*, London 2001

Bange, O., 'NATO and the Non-Proliferation Treaty', in A. Wenger, C. Nuenlist and A. Locher (eds), *Transforming NATO, beyond deterrence in the 1960s*, Abingdon 2007, 162–80.

Banks, A., 'Britain and the Cambodian crisis of spring 1970', CWH v/1 (2005), 87–106

Bark, D. and D. Gress, *A history of West Germany*, I: *From shadow to substance*, London 1989

——— II: *Democracy and its discontents, 1963–1988*, London 1989

Barker, E., *Britain in a divided Europe, 1945–1970*, London 1971

Bar-Noi, U., 'The Soviet Union and Churchill's appeals for high-level talks, 1953–1954: new evidence from the Russian archives', DS ix/3 (1998), 110–33

Bartlett, C. J., '*The special relationship': a political history of Anglo-American relations since 1945*, London 1992

Baylis, J., *Ambiguity and deterrence: British nuclear strategy, 1945–1964*, Oxford 1995

——— 'British nuclear doctrine: the "Moscow criterion" and the *Polaris* improvement programme', CBH xix/1 (2005), 53–65

——— and A. Macmillan, 'The British global strategy paper of 1952', JSS xvi/2 (1993), 200–26.

——— and K. Stoddart, 'Britain and the Chevaline project: the hidden nuclear programme, 1967–1982', JSS xxvi/4 (2003), 124–55

Beckett, F., *Enemy within: the rise and fall of the British Communist Party*, London 1998

Bertch, G. K., 'American politics and trade with the USSR', in Parrott, *Trade*, 243–82

Bevins, R. and G. Quinn, 'Blowing hot and cold: Anglo-Soviet relations, 1955–1964', in Kaiser and Staerck, *British foreign policy*, 209–38

Blechman, B., *The changing Soviet navy*, Washington DC 1973

Bluth, C., *Britain, Germany and Western nuclear strategy*, Oxford 1995

——— 'Reconciling the irreconcilable: alliance politics and the paradox of extended deterrence in the 1960s', CWH i/2 (2001), 74–93

Bohmer, K., '"We too mean business": Germany and the Second British application to the EEC, 1966–67', in Daddow, *EEC*, 211–26

Borhi, L., '"We Hungarian Communists are realists": Janos Kadar's foreign policy in the light of Hungarian-US relations, 1957–67', CWH iv/2 (2004), 1–32

Bower, T., *The perfect English spy: Sir Dick White and the secret war, 1935–90*, London 1995

Bowker, M. and P. Shearman, 'The Soviet Union and the left in Britain', in Pravda and Duncan, *Soviet-British relations*, 147–67

Bozo, F., *La France et l'OTAN : de la guerre froide au nouvel ordre européen*, Paris 1991

——— 'Détente versus alliance: France, the United States and the politics of the Harmel report (1964–1968)', CEH vii/3 (1998), 343–66

—— *Two strategies for Europe: De Gaulle, the United States and the Atlantic Alliance*, Lanham, MD 2000

—— P. Melandri, and M. Vaisse (eds), *La France et l'OTAN, 1949–1996*, Paris 1996

Brigham, R., *Guerrilla diplomacy: the NLF's foreign relations and the Vietnam War*, Ithaca, NY 1999

Brivati, B. and R. Hefferman (eds), *The Labour Party: a centenary history*, Basingstoke 2000

Brook-Shepherd, G., *The storm birds: Soviet post-war defectors*, London 1988

Buchan, A., 'Britain in the Indian Ocean', IA xlii/2 (1966), 184–93

Bullock, A., *Ernest Bevin: Foreign Secretary, 1945–51*, Oxford 1985

Bundy, W., *A tangled web: the making of foreign policy in the Nixon presidency*, New York 1998

Burr, W., 'Sino-American relations, 1969: the Sino-Soviet border war and steps towards rapprochement', CWH i/3 (2001), 73–105

Busch, P., *All the way with JFK? Britain, the US, and the Vietnam War*, Oxford 2003

Callaghan, J., *The Labour Party and foreign policy: a history*, Abingdon 2007

Campbell, J., *Nye Bevan: a biography*, London 1992

—— *Edward Heath: a biography*, London 1993

Catterall, P., 'Witness seminar: the East of Suez decision', *Contemporary Record* vii/3 (1993), 612–53

—— 'Foreign and Commonwealth policy in opposition: the Labour party', in Kaiser and Staerck, *British foreign policy*, 89–109

Chang, G., *Friends and enemies: the United States, China and the Soviet Union, 1948–1972*, Stanford, CA 1990.

Chichester, M. and J. Wilkinson, *The uncertain ally: British defence policy, 1960–1990*, Aldershot 1982

Clark, I., *Nuclear diplomacy and the special relationship: Britain's deterrent and America, 1957–1962*, Oxford 1994

Cleveland, H., 'NATO after the invasion', FA xlvii/2 (1969), 251–65

Cohen, W. and N. Tucker, *Lyndon Johnson confronts the world: American foreign policy, 1963–1968*, New York 1994

Colman, J., 'Harold Wilson, Lyndon Johnson and Anglo-American "summit diplomacy"', *Journal of Transatlantic Studies* i/2 (2003), 131–51

—— 'The London ambassadorship of David K. E. Bruce during the Wilson-Johnson years, 1964–1968', DS xv/2 (2004), 327–52

—— 'Harold Wilson, Lyndon Johnson and the Vietnam War, 1964–68', *American Studies Online* (Nov. 2005), http://www.americansc.org.uk/Online/Wilsonjohnson.htm.

—— '"Dealing with disillusioned men": the Washington ambassadorship of Sir Patrick Dean, 1965–69', CBH xxi/2 (2007), 247–70

Conquest, R., *Present danger: towards a foreign policy*, London 1979

Cooper, C., *The lost crusade: the full story of US involvement in Vietnam from Roosevelt to Nixon*, London 1971

Coopey, R., S. Fielding and N. Tiratsoo (eds), *The Wilson governments, 1964–1970*, London 1993

Costigliola, F., '"Not a normal French government": la réaction Américaine au retrait de la France de l'OTAN', in Bozo, Mélandri and Vaïsse, *France et l'OTAN*, 403–20

Cradock, P., *Know your enemy: how the Joint Intelligence Committee saw the world*, London 2002

Crampton, R., *Eastern Europe in the twentieth century*, Abingdon 1994

Crockatt, R., *The fifty years war: the United States and the Soviet Union in world politics, 1941–1991*, Abingdon 2000

Curtis, M., *Web of deceit: Britain's real role in the world*, London 2003

Daddow, O. (ed.), *Harold Wilson and European integration: Britain's second application to join the EEC*, Basingstoke 2003

Dallek, R., *Flawed giant: Lyndon Johnson and his times, 1961–1973*, Oxford 1998

Darby, P., *British defence policy East of Suez, 1947–1968*, Oxford 1973

Davies, N., *Heart of Europe: a short history of Poland*, Oxford 1986

Dawisha, K., *The Kremlin and the Prague Spring*, Berkeley CA 1984

Deery, P., '"The secret battalion": Communism in Britain during the Cold War', *CBH* xiii/4 (1999), 1–28

Deighton, A., 'Ostpolitik or Westpolitik? British foreign policy, 1968–75', *IA* lxxiv/4 (1998), 893–901

—— '"A different 1956": British responses to the Polish events, June–November 1956', *CWH* vi/4 (2006), 455–76

Deletant, D., *Ceausescu and the Securitate: coercion and dissent in Romania, 1965–1989*, London 1995

Dickie, J., '"Special" no more: Anglo-American relations: rhetoric and reality*, London 1994

Dockrill, M., *British defence since 1945*, London 1988

—— 'Britain and the first Chinese offshore islands crisis', in Dockrill and Young, *British foreign policy*, 173–98

—— and J. Young (eds), *British foreign policy, 1945–56*, Basingstoke 1989

Dockrill, S., *Britain's policy for West German rearmament, 1951–1955*, Cambridge 1991

—— *Eisenhower's new look national security policy, 1953–61*, Basingstoke 1991

—— 'Britain's motives for troop reductions in Western Germany, 1955–1958', *JSS* xx/3 (1997), 45–65

—— 'Retreat from the continent? Britain's motives for troop reductions in West Germany, 1955–1958', *JSS* xx/3 (1997), 45–65

—— *Britain's retreat from East of Suez: the choice between Europe and the world?*, Basingstoke 2002

—— and G. Bischof (eds), *Cold War respite: the Geneva summit of 1955*, Baton Rouge, LA 2000

—— R. Frank, G.-H. Soutou and A. Varsori (eds), *L'Europe de l'est et de l'ouest dans la Guerre froide, 1948–1953*, Paris 2002

—— and G. A. Hughes (eds), *Advances in Cold War history*, Basingstoke 2006

Dorey, P. (ed.), *The Labour governments, 1964–1970*, Abingdon 2006

Dorril, S., *MI6: fifty years of special operations*, London 2001

—— and R. Ramsay, *Smear! Wilson and the secret state*, London 1992

Duffield, J., 'The Soviet military threat to Western Europe: US estimates in the 1950s and 1960s', *JSS* xv/2 (1992), 208–27

—— *Power rules: the evolution of NATO's conventional force posture*, Stanford, CA 1995

Duiker, W. J., *Sacred war: nationalism and revolution in a divided Vietnam*, Boston MA 1995

—— 'Victory by other means: the foreign policy of the Democratic Republic of Vietnam', in Gilbert, *Vietnam War*, 47–75.

Dujardin, V., 'Go-between: Belgium and *détente*, 1961–73', CWH vii/1 (2007), 95–116

Easter, D., *Britain and the confrontation with Indonesia, 1960–1966*, London 2004

—— '"Keep the Indonesian pot boiling": Western covert intervention in Indonesia, October 1965–March 1966', CWH v/1 (2005), 55–73

Edgerton, D., *Warfare state: Britain, 1920–1970*, Cambridge 2006

Ellis, S., *Britain, America, and the Vietnam War*, Westport, CT 2004

Ellison, J., 'Defeating the General: Anglo-American relations, Europe and the NATO crisis of 1966', CWH vi/1 (2006), 85–111

—— 'Stabilising the West and looking to the East: Anglo-American relations, Europe and *détente*, 1965 to 1967', in Ludlow, *Integration*, 105–27

Folly, M., *Churchill, Whitehall and the Soviet Union, 1940–45*, Basingstoke 2000

Foot, P., *The politics of Harold Wilson*, London 1968

Freedman, L., *US intelligence and the Soviet strategic threat*, Basingstoke 1986

—— *Kennedy's wars: Berlin, Cuba, Laos and Vietnam*, New York 2000.

—— *The evolution of nuclear strategy*, Basingstoke 2003

—— and G. A. Hughes, 'Strategy', in Dockrill and Hughes, *Cold War*, 130–65

Freeman, J. P. G., *Britain's nuclear arms control policy in the context of Anglo-American relations, 1957–68*, New York 1986

Friedman, N., *The fifty-year war: conflict and strategy in the Cold War*, Annapolis, MD 2000

Froland, H. O., 'Distrust, dependency and *détente*: Norway, the two Germanys and "the German question", 1945–1973', CEH xv/4 (2006), 495–517

Fursenko, A. and T. Naftali, *'One hell of a gamble': Khrushchev, Castro, Kennedy, and the Cuban missile crisis, 1958–1964*, London 1997

Gaddis, J. L., *Strategies of containment: a critical appraisal of post-war American national security policy*, New York 1982

—— *We now know: rethinking Cold War history*, Oxford 1998

—— *The Cold War*, London 2007

Gaiduk, I., *The Soviet Union and the Vietnam War*, Chicago 1996

Garthoff, R., *Détente and confrontation: American-Soviet relations from Nixon to Reagan*, Washington, DC 1994

—— *The great transition: Soviet-American relations and the end of the Cold War*, Washington 1994

—— 'Foreign intelligence and the historiography of the Cold War', JCWS vi/2 (2004), 21–56

—— and A. Knight, 'New evidence on Soviet intelligence: the KGB's 1967 annual report', CWIHP Bulletin x (1998), 211–19

Garton Ash, T., *In Europe's name: Germany and the divided continent*, London 1994

Gati, C., *The bloc that failed: Soviet-East European relations in transition*, London 1990

Gavin, F., 'The myth of flexible response: United States strategy in Europe during the 1960s', IHR xxvii/4 (2001), 847–75

Gearson, J., *Harold Macmillan and the Berlin Wall crisis, 1958–1962*, Basingstoke 1998

Geertz, C., *The interpretation of cultures*, New York 1973

Geraghty, T., *BRIXMIS: the untold exploits of Britain's most daring Cold War spy mission*, London 1997

Gilbert, M. (ed.), *Why the North won the Vietnam War*, Basingstoke 2002

Gilpatric, R., 'Our defense needs: the long term view', FA xlii/3 (1964), 366–78

Glees, A., *The Stasi files: East Germany's secret operations against Britain*, London 2003

Glenny, M., *The rebirth of history*, London 1993

Golan, G., *Soviet policies in the Middle East: from World War Two to Gorbachev*, Cambridge 1990

Goodman, A., *The search for a negotiated settlement of the Vietnam War*, Berkeley, CA 1986

Gordon Walker, P., 'The Labor party's defense and foreign policy', FA, xlii/3 (1964), 391–8

—— *The Cabinet*, London 1972

Gore-Booth, P., *With great truth and respect*, London 1974

Goscha, C. and M. Vaïsse (ed.), *La Guerre du Vietnam et l'Europe, 1963–1973*, Brussels 2003

Gray, W. G., *Germany's Cold War: the global campaign to isolate East Germany, 1949–1969*, Chapel Hill, NC 2003

Greenwood, S., *Britain and the Cold War, 1945–1991*, Basingstoke 2000

Grove, E., *Vanguard to Trident: British naval policy since World War Two*, Annapolis, MD 1987

Halliday, F., *Revolution and world politics*, Basingstoke 1999

Hamilton, K., '"A week that changed the world": Britain and Nixon's China visit of 21–28 February 1972', DS xv/1 (2004), 117–35.

Hanrieder, W., *Germany, America, Europe: forty years of German foreign policy*, New Haven, CT 1989

Hanson, P., *Trade and technology in Soviet-Western relations*, Basingstoke 1981

Hennessy, P., *Muddling through: power, politics and the quality of government in postwar Britain*, London 1997

—— *The prime minister*, London 2000

—— *The secret state: Whitehall and the Cold War*, London 2002

Herman, M., *Intelligence power in peace and war*, Cambridge 1996

Herring, G., 'Fighting without allies: the international dimensions of America's defeat in Vietnam', in Gilbert, *Vietnam War*, 77–96

Hershberg, J., 'Peace probes and the bombing pause: Hungarian and Polish diplomacy during the Vietnam War, December 1965–January 1966', JCWS v/2 (2003), 32–67

—— and C. Jian, 'Reading and warning the likely enemy: China's signals to the United States about Vietnam in 1965', IHR xxvii/1 (2005), 47–84

Heuser, B., *Western 'containment' policies in the Cold War: the Yugoslav case, 1948–53*, Basingstoke 1989

—— *NATO, Britain, France and the FRG: nuclear strategy and forces for Europe, 1949–2000*, Basingstoke 1997

—— and C. Buffet, 'Résister à la tempête: les reactions Britanniques au départ de la France de l'intégration militaire de l'OTAN', in Bozo, Mélandri and Vaïsse, *France et l'OTAN*, 427–49

Higham, R. and F. W. Kagan (eds), *The military history of the Soviet Union*, Basingstoke 2002

Hitchcock, W., *France restored: Cold War diplomacy and the quest for leadership in Europe, 1944–1954*, Chapel Hill, NC 1998

—— *The struggle for Europe: the turbulent history of a divided continent*, London 2003

Holloway, D., *Stalin and the bomb*, New Haven, CT 1994

Hopkins, M., '"Worlds apart": the British embassy in Moscow and the search for East-West understanding', CBH xiv/3 (2000), 131–48.

—— 'Herbert Morrison, the Cold War and Anglo-American relations', in Hopkins, Kandiah and Staerck, *Cold War Britain*, 17–29

—— 'Britain's policy to the Soviet Union in the era of *détente*, 1968–76', CBH xviii/1 (2004), 143–52

—— M. Kandiah and G. Staerck (eds), *Cold War Britain, 1945–1964: new perspectives*, Basingstoke 2003

Hosking, G., *A history of the Soviet Union, 1917–1991*, London 1992

Howard, M., 'Britain's strategic problem East of Suez', IA xlii/2 (1966), 179–83

Hudson, G. F., *Fifty years of Communism: theory and practice, 1917–1967*, London 1968

Hughes, G. A., 'A "missed opportunity" for peace? Harold Wilson, British diplomacy, and the *Sunflower* initiative to end the Vietnam War', DS xiv/3 (2003), 106–30

—— 'British policy towards Eastern Europe and the impact of the "Prague Spring", 1964–1968', CWH iv/2 (2004), 115–39

—— '"Giving the Russians a bloody nose": operation *Foot* and Soviet espionage in the United Kingdom, 1964–1971', CWH vi/2 (2006), 229–49

Hughes, R. G., '"We are not seeking strength for its own sake": the British Labour party, West Germany and the Cold War, 1951–64', CWH iii/1 (2002), 67–94

—— *Britain, Germany and the Cold War: the search for a European détente, 1949–1967*, Abingdon 2007.

Ionescu, G., *The break-up of the Soviet empire in Eastern Europe*, London 1965

Jackson, I., *The economic Cold War: America, Britain and East-West trade, 1948–63*, Basingstoke 2001

—— 'Economics', in Dockrill and Hughes, *Cold War*, 166–88

James, S., *British Cabinet government*, Abingdon 1992

Jefferys, K., *Anthony Crosland: a new biography*, London 2000

Jian, C., *Mao's China and the Cold War*, Chapel Hill, NC 2001

—— and Y. Kuisong, 'Chinese politics and the collapse of the Sino-Soviet alliance', in Westad, *Brothers in arms*, 246–94.

Jones, Mark, '"Groping toward coexistence": US-China policy during the Johnson years', DS xii/3 (2001), 175–90

Jones, Matthew, *Conflict and confrontation in South-East Asia, 1961–1965: Britain, the United States and the creation of Malaysia*, Cambridge 2001

Kaiser, D., *American tragedy: Kennedy, Johnson, and the origins of the Vietnam War*, Cambridge, MA 2000

Kaiser, W. and G. Staerck (eds.), *British foreign policy, 1955–64: contracting options*, Basingstoke 2000

Kaplan, L., *NATO divided, NATO united: the evolution of an alliance*, New York 2004

Kaser, M., 'Trade relations', in Pravda and Duncan, *Soviet-British relations*, 193–214

Keeble, C., *Britain and the Soviet Union, 1917–1989*, Basingstoke 1990

—— 'The historical perspective', in Pravda and Duncan, *Soviet-British relations*, 17–46

Kelly, J. A. B., *Arabia, the Gulf and the West*, London 1980

Kennedy, P., *The rise and fall of British naval mastery*, London 1991

Keohane, D., *Labour Party defence policy since 1945*, Leicester 1993

—— 'Labour's international policy: a story of conflict and contention', in Brivati and Hefferman, *Labour party*, 363–82

Kitchen, M., *British policy towards the Soviet Union during the Second World War*, London 1998

Korbel, J., *Détente in Europe: real or imaginary?*, Princeton, NJ 1972

Kramer, M., 'New sources on the 1968 Soviet invasion of Czechoslovakia', *CWIHP Bulletin* ii (1992), 1, 4–13

—— 'The Prague Spring and the Soviet invasion of Czechoslovakia: new interpretations', *CWIHP Bulletin* iii (1993), 2–12

—— 'Ukraine and the Soviet-Czechoslovak crisis of 1968 (part 1): new evidence from the diary of Petro Shelest', *CWIHP Bulletin* x (1998), 234–44

—— 'Ukraine and the Soviet-Czechoslovak crisis of 1968 (part 2): new evidence from the Ukrainian archives', *CWIHP Bulletin* xiv/xv (2004), 273–368

Kronsten, J., 'East-West trade: myth and matter', *IA* xliii/2 (1967), 265–81

Kyle, K., *Suez*, London 1991

Lacouture J. (trans. A. Sheridan), *De Gaulle: the ruler*, London 1991

Lankford, N. (ed.), *The last American aristocrat: the biography of David K. E. Bruce, 1899–1977*, Boston, MA 1996

Lapping, B., *The Labour government, 1964–70*, London 1970

Larres, K., 'Britain, East Germany and *détente*: British policy towards the GDR and West Germany's "policy of movement", 1955–65', in Loth, *Cold War and coexistence*, 111–31

Lebow, R. N. and J. G. Stein, *We all lost the Cold War*, Princeton 1994

Lerner, M., *The Pueblo incident*, Lawrence, KS 2002

Lewis, J. and H. Di, 'China's ballistic missile programs: technologies, strategies, goals', *IS* xvii/2 (1992), 5–40

Logevall, F., *The origins of the Vietnam War*, London 2000

Loory, S. and D. Kraslow, *The diplomacy of chaos: the danger and drama of secret diplomacy*, London 1968

Loth, W., 'Moscow, Prague and Warsaw: overcoming the Brezhnev doctrine', *CWH* i/2 (2001), 103–18

—— *Overcoming the Cold War: a history of détente, 1950–1991*, Basingstoke 2002

—— (ed.), *Europe, Cold War and coexistence, 1953–1965*, London 2004

Lowe, P., *Containing the Cold War in East Asia: British policies toward Japan, China and Korea, 1948–53*, Manchester 1997

—— (ed.), *The Vietnam War*, Basingstoke 1998

Ludlow, N. P. (ed.), *European integration and the Cold War: Ostpolitik-Westpolitik, 1965–1974*, Abingdon 2007

Lunak, P., 'Planning for nuclear war: the Czechoslovak war plan of 1964', *CWIHP Bulletin* xii/xiii (2001), 289–98

McGinn, J. C., 'The politics of collective inaction: NATO's response to the Prague Spring', *JCWS* i/3 (1999), 111–38

McNamara, R., *Britain, Nasser and the balance of power in the Middle East, 1952–1967*, London 2003

Maloney, S., 'Fire brigade or tocsin? NATO's ACE mobile force, flexible response and the Cold War', *JSS* xxvii/4 (2004), 585–613

Martin, G., 'Grandeur et dépendances: the dilemmas of Gaullist foreign policy, 1967–1968', in Ludlow, *Integration*, 36–52.

Mastny, V., '"We are in a bind": Polish and Czechoslovak attempts at reforming the Warsaw Pact', *CWIHP Bulletin* xi (1998), 230–49

—— 'Was 1968 a strategic watershed of the Cold War?', *Diplomatic History* xxix/1 (2005), 149–77

May, A. (ed.), *Britain, the Commonwealth, and Europe*, Basingstoke 2000

Mayhew, C., *Britain's role tomorrow*, London 1967

Mazower, M., *Dark continent: Europe's twentieth century*, London 1999

Middeke, M., 'Britain's global military role, conventional defence and Anglo-American interdependence after Nassau', *JSS* xxiv/1 (2001), 143–64

Miller, D., *The Cold War: a military history*, London 2001

Mlynar, Z. (trans. P. Wilson), *Night frost in Prague: the end of humane socialism*, London 1980

Morgan, A., *Harold Wilson*, London 1992

Morgan, K., *The people's peace: British history, 1945–1990*, Oxford 1992

Myant, M., *Socialism and democracy in Czechoslovakia, 1945–1948*, Cambridge 1981

Narinski, M., 'Les Soviétiques et la décision française', in Bozo, Melandri and Vaisse, *La France et l'OTAN*, 503–16

Nation, R. C., *Black earth, red star*, Ithaca, New York 1992

Newhouse, J., *Cold dawn: the story of SALT*, Toronto 1973

Newman, K., *Macmillan, Khrushchev and the Berlin crisis, 1958–1960*, Abingdon 2007

Nuti, L. and V. Zubok, 'Ideology', in Dockrill and Hughes, *Cold War*, 73–110

O'Hara, G. and H. Parr, 'Introduction: the fall and rise of a reputation', *CBH* xx/3 (2006), 295–7

Odom, General W., *The collapse of the Soviet military*, New Haven, CT 1998

Oren, M., *Six days of war*, Oxford 2002

Ouimet, M. J., *The rise and fall of the Brezhnev doctrine in Soviet foreign policy*, Chapel Hill, NC 2003

Owen, D., *Time to declare*, London 1991

Parker, A., 'International aspects of the Vietnam War', in Lowe, *Vietnam War*, 196–218

Parr, H., 'The Foreign Office and Harold Wilson's policy towards the EEC, 1964–1970', in Daddow, *EEC*, 75–98

—— 'Britain, America, East of Suez and the EEC: finding a role in British foreign policy, 1964–67', *CBH* xx/3 (2006), 403–21

—— and M. Pine, 'Policy towards the European Economic Community', in Dorey, *Labour governments*, 108–29

Parrott, B. (ed.), *Trade, technology and Soviet-American relations*, Bloomington, IN 1985

Percival, M., 'Britain's "political romance" with Romania in the 1970s', *CEH* iv/1 (1995), 67–87

Petersen, T. T., 'Crossing the Rubicon? Britain's withdrawal from the Middle East, 1964–1968: a bibliographical review', *IHR* xxii/2 (2000), 318–40

Pickering, J., *Britain's withdrawal from East of Suez: the politics of retrenchment*, Basingstoke 1998

Pimlott, B., *Harold Wilson*, London 1993

Pipes, R., '*Détente*: Moscow's view', in R. Pipes (ed.), *Soviet strategy in Europe*, London 1976, 3–44

Ponting, C., *Breach of promise: Labour in power, 1964–1970*, London 1989

Prados, J., *The Soviet estimate: US intelligence analysis and Russian military strength*, New York 1982

Pravda, A. and P. Duncan, 'Introduction', in Pravda and Duncan, *Soviet-British relations*, 1–16

—— and P. Duncan (eds), *Soviet-British relations since the 1970s*, Cambridge 1990

Priest, A., 'In American hands: Britain, the United States and the *Polaris* nuclear project, 1962–1968', *CBH* xix/3 (2005), 353–76

—— *Kennedy, Johnson and NATO: Britain, America and the dynamics of alliance, 1962–68*, Abingdon 2006

Qiang, Z., *China and the Vietnam Wars, 1950–1975*, Chapel Hill, NC 2000

Quenoy, P. du, 'The role of foreign affairs in the fall of Nikita Khrushchev in October 1964', *IHR* xxv/2 (2003), 334–56

Ramsay, R., 'Wilson and the security services', in Coopey, Fielding and Tiratsoo, *Wilson governments*, 151–62

Ranft, B. and G. Till, *The sea in Soviet strategy*, Annapolis, MD 1989

Rawnsley, G., 'How special is special? The Anglo-American alliance during the Cuban Missile crisis', *Contemporary Record* ix/3 (1995), 586–601

Reed, B. and G. Williams, *Denis Healey and the politics of power*, London 1971

Renner, H., *A history of Czechoslovakia since 1945*, Abingdon 1989

Roberts, A. and P. Windsor, *Czechoslovakia 1968: reform, repression and resistance*, London 1969

Roberts, G., *The Soviet Union in world politics*, Abingdon 1999

Roberts, J. C. Q., *Speak clearly into the chandelier: cultural politics between Britain and Russia*, Richmond, UK 2000

Sandbrook, D., *White heat: a history of Britain in the swinging sixties*, London 2006

Sarotte, M. E., *Dealing with the devil: East Germany, détente & Ostpolitik, 1969–1973*, Chapel Hill, NC 2001

Schrafstetter, S., 'Preventing the "smiling Buddha": British-Indian nuclear relations and the Commonwealth nuclear force, 1964–68', *JSS* xxv/3 (2002), 87–108

—— and S. Twigge, 'Trick or truth? The British ANF proposal, West Germany and nonproliferation', *DS* xi/2 (2000), 161–79

Schulzinger, R. D., *A time for war: the United States and Vietnam, 1941–1975*, Oxford 1997

Schwartz, T., *Lyndon Johnson and Europe: in the shadow of Vietnam*, Cambridge, MA 2003

Scott, L. V., *Macmillan, Kennedy and the Cuban Missile Crisis*, Basingstoke 1999

—— 'Labour and the bomb: the first 80 years', *IA* lxxxii/4 (2006), 685–700

See, J., 'An uneasy truce: John F. Kennedy and Soviet-American *détente*, 1963', *CWH* ii/2 (2002), 161–94

Service, R., *A history of twentieth century Russia*, London 1998

Shennan, A., *De Gaulle*, London 1993

Sjursen, H., *The United States, Western Europe and the Polish crisis*, London 2003

Skilling, H. G., *Czechoslovakia's interrupted revolution*, Princeton, NJ 1976

Smith, M., *The spying game: the secret history of British espionage*, London 2003

Smith, R. B., *An international history of the Vietnam War*, II: *The Kennedy strategy*, New York 1985

—— III: *The making of a limited war, 1965–1966*, New York 1991

Smith, S. C., 'Power transferred? Britain, the United States, and the Gulf, 1956–71', *CBH* xxi/1 (2007), 1–23

Smolansky, O. and B. Smolansky, *The USSR and Iraq: the Soviet quest for influence*, Durham, NC 1991

Soutou, G.-M., 'France and the Cold War, 1944–63', *DS* xii/4 (2001), 31–49

—— 'De Gaulle's France and the Soviet Union from conflict to *détente*', in Loth, *Cold War and coexistence*, 73–89

—— 'The linkage between European integration and *détente*: the contrasting approaches of de Gaulle and Pompidou, 1965 to 1974', in Ludlow, *Integration*, 11–35

Staerck, G., 'Witness seminar: the role of HM embassy in Moscow', *CBH* xiv/3 (2000), 149–61.

Stocker, J., *The United Kingdom and nuclear deterrence*, Abingdon 2007

Stromseth, J., *The origins of flexible response: NATO's debate over strategy in the 1960s*, Basingstoke 1988

Suri, J., *Power and protest: global revolution and the rise of détente*, Cambridge, MA 2003

Taubman, W., *Khrushchev: the man and his era*, London 2003

Thomas, H., *Armed truce*, London 1986

Thorne, C., *Allies of a kind: the United States, Britain and the war against Japan*, Oxford 1978

Thorpe, A., *A history of the British Labour Party*, Basingstoke 1997

Thorpe, D. R., *Alec Douglas-Home*, London 1997

Trachtenberg, M., *A constructed peace: the making of the European settlement, 1945–1963*, Princeton, NJ 1999

Tucker, S., *Vietnam*, London 1999

Urban, M., *UK eyes alpha: the inside story of British intelligence*, London 1997

Vaïsse, M., 'De Gaulle et la Guerre du Vietnam: de la difficulté d'être Cassandre', in Christopher Goscha and Maurice Vaïsse (eds), *La Guerre du Vietnam et l'Europe, 1963–1973*, Brussels 2003, 169–78

Valenta, J., 'From Prague to Kabul: the Soviet style of invasion', *IS* v/2 (1980), 114–41

Vickers, R., 'Foreign policy beyond Europe', in Dorey, *Labour governments*, 130–46

Warbey, W., *Ho Chi Minh and the struggle for an independent Vietnam*, London 1972

Watt, D. C. (ed.), *Survey of international affairs, 1963*, Oxford 1979

Wenger, A., 'Crisis and opportunity: NATO and the multilateralization of *détente*, 1966–1968', *JCWS* vi/1 (2004), 22–74

——, C. Nuenlist and A. Locher (eds), *Transforming NATO in the Cold War: challenges beyond deterrence in the 1960s*, Abingdon 2007

Westad, O. A., *The global Cold War: Third World interventions and the making of our times*, Cambridge 2005

—— (ed.), *Brothers in arms: the rise and fall of the Sino-Soviet alliance, 1945–1963*, Washington, DC 2000

White, B., *Britain, détente and changing East-West relations*, Abingdon 1992

Wiebes, C. and B. Zeeman, '"I don't need your handkerchiefs": Holland's experience of crisis consultation in NATO', *IA* lxvi/1 (1990), 91–113

Wilford, H., *The CIA, the British left and the Cold War, 1945–1960: calling the tune?*, London 2003

Willens, A., 'New *Ostpolitik* and European integration: concepts and policies in the Brandt era', in Ludlow, *Integration*, 71

Willerton, J. P., *Patronage and politics in the USSR*, Cambridge 1992

Williams, K. D., 'Political love's labours lost: negotiations between Prague and Moscow in 1968', *Slovo* vii/1 (1994), 72–87

Williams, Phil, *The senate and US troops in Europe*, Basingstoke 1985

Williams, Philip, *Hugh Gaitskell: a political biography*, London 1979

Wilson, D., 'Anglo-Soviet relations: the effect of ideas on reality', *IA* l/3 (1974), 380–93

Wilson, H., *In place of dollars*, London 1952

—— *The new Britain: Labour's plan: outlined by Harold Wilson*, London 1964

Wolfe, T. W., *Soviet power and Europe, 1945–1970*, Baltimore, MD 1970

Wolton, T., *La France sous influence: Paris–Moscou: 30 ans de relations secrets*, Paris 1997

Wrigley, C., 'Now you see it, now you don't: Harold Wilson and Labour's foreign policy, 1964–1970', in Coopey, Fielding and Tiratsoo, *Wilson governments*, 123–35

Yang, K., 'The Sino-Soviet border clash of 1969: from Zhenbao Island to Sino-American *rapprochement*', *CWH* i/1 (2000), 21–49

Young, J., *Cold War Europe, 1945–89: a political history*, London 1991

—— *Winston Churchill's last campaign*, Oxford 1996

—— 'George Wigg, the Wilson government and the 1966 report into security in the diplomatic service and GCHQ', *Intelligence and National Security* xiv/3 (1998), 198–208

—— 'The Wilson government and the Davies peace mission to North Vietnam, July 1965', *RIS* xxiv (1998), 545–62

—— 'Britain and "LBJ's war", 1964–68', *CWH* ii/3 (2002), 63–92

—— 'Killing the MLF? The Wilson government and nuclear sharing in Europe, 1964–66', *DS* xiv/2 (2003), 295–324

—— *The Labour governments, 1964–1970, II: International policy*, Manchester 2003

Zagoria, D., *The Sino-Soviet conflict, 1956–61*, Princeton, NJ 1967

Zaloga, S., 'Nuclear forces', in Higham and Kagan, *Military history*, 199–220.

Ziegler, P., *Wilson*, London 1993

Zimmerman, H., 'The sour fruits of victory: Sterling and security in Anglo-German relations during the 1950s and 1960s', *CEH* ix/2 (2000), 225–34

Zubok, V. and C. Pleshakov, *Inside the Kremlin's Cold War: from Stalin to Khrushchev*, Cambridge, MA 1996

Unpublished dissertations and papers

Bar-Noi, U., 'The Soviet Union and the Six Day War', CWIHP e-dossier no. viii, http://wwics.si.edu/ downloaded 23 Jan. 2007

Bekes, C., 'The 1956 Hungarian revolution and world politics' (CWIHP working paper xvi, 1996)

Clearwater, J., 'The birth of strategic arms control during the Johnson administration, 1964–1969', PhD diss. King's College London 1996

Deletant, D. and M. Ionescu, 'Romania and the Warsaw Pact, 1955–1989' (CWIHP working paper xliii, 2002)

Evangelista, M., '"Why keep such an army?" Khrushchev's troop reductions' (CWIHP working paper xix, 1997)

Hamilton, K., 'The last Cold Warriors: Britain, *détente* and the CSCE, 1972–1975', St Anthony's College, Oxford, European Interdependence Research Unit, EIRU/991, July 1999

Hershberg, J., 'Who murdered "*Marigold*"? New evidence on the mysterious failure of Poland's secret initiative to start US–North Vietnamese peace talks, 1966' (CWIHP working paper xxvii, 2000)

Hughes, G. A., 'Harold Wilson, the USSR and British foreign and defence policy in the context of East-West *détente*, 1964–1968', PhD diss. King's College London 2002

Mastny, V., 'NATO in the beholder's eye: Soviet perceptions and policies, 1949–56' (CWIHP working paper xxxv, 2002)

Qiang, Z., 'Beijing and the Vietnam peace talks, 1965–1968: new evidence from Chinese sources' (CWIHP working paper xviii, 1997)

Radchenko, S., 'The China puzzle: Soviet policy towards the People's Republic of China, 1962–1967', diss. LSE 2005

Rainer, J., 'The new course in Hungary in 1953' (CWIHP working paper xxxviii, 2002)

Selvage, D., 'The Warsaw Pact and nuclear nonproliferation, 1963–1965' (CWIHP working paper xxxii, 2001)

Tismaneanu, V., 'Gheorghiu-Dej and the Romanian Workers party: from de-Sovietization to the emergence of national Communism' (CWHIP working paper xxxvii, 2002)

Yang, K., 'Changes in Mao Zedong's attitude toward the Indochina War, 1949–1973' (CWIHP working paper xxxiv, 2002)

Young, J., 'The British Foreign Office and Cold War fighting in the early 1950s: PUSC(51)16 and the 1952 "sore spots" memorandum' (Leicester University discussion papers in politics, P95/2, 1995)

Internet sites

Cold War International History Project: http://cwihp.si.edu/
Foreign Relations of the United States: http://www.state.gov/r/pa/ho/frus/
Lyndon B. Johnson Presidential Library: http://www.lbjlib.utexas.edu/
The National Archives (Kew, London): http://www.pro.gov.uk/
National Security Archive: http://www.gwu/edu/~nsarchiv/
Parallel History Project on Cooperative Security: http://www.php.isn.ethz.ch/

Index

154; foundation, 23; military planning, 39, 103, 144

West Germany, *see* Federal Republic of Germany

Western European Union (WEU), 17, 23, 26, 99

Wilson, Duncan, 37, 44, 150, 157, 159, 170

Wilson, Harold: domestic criticism of, 2, 59; early political career, 19, 35, 47, 49, 57; extra-parliamentary career, 46, 48; Labour Party and, 1, 35, 46, 62, 80, 139, 168–9; opinions on East-West relations, 7, 34, 49, 56, 59–60, 63, 71; policy on East-West trade, 47; Vietnam and efforts to mediate, 59, 62–3, 65, 71, 74–8, 81, 169, 172; visits to USSR, 48–9, 51, 54, 59, 67–9, 79, 101, 128, 132–3, 171

Wright, Oliver, 116

Yugoslavia, 40, 149, 170

Zuckerman, Sir Solly, 97